Medusa

KING ZAIDE

Medusa

Narrative of a Voyage to Senegal in 1816
J. B. Henry Savigny & Alexander Correard

•

The Sufferings of the Picard Family
After the Shipwreck of the Medusa
Charlotte-Adélaïde Dard [née Picard]
Translated by Patrick Maxwell

Medusa
Narrative of a Voyage to Senegal in 1816
by J. B. Henry Savigny & Alexander Correard

The Sufferings of the Picard Family After the Shipwreck of the Medusa
by Charlotte-Adélaïde Dard [née Picard]
Translated by Patrick Maxwell

Narrative of a Voyage to Senegal in 1816
originally published under the title:
Narrative of a Voyage to Senegal in 1816 Undertaken by Order of the French Government, Comprising an Account of the Shipwreck of the Medusa, the Sufferings of the Crew, and the Various Occurrences on Board the Raft, in the Desert of Zaara, at St. Louis, and at the Camp of Daccard. To Which Are Subjoined Observations Respecting the Agriculture of the Western Coast of Africa, from Cape Blanco to the Mouth of the Gambia
by Pierre Raymond de Brisson & Jean Godin

The Sufferings of the Picard Family After the Shipwreck of the Medusa
originally published in the book *Perils & Captivity* under the title
The Sufferings and Misfortunes of the Picard Family After the Shipwreck of the Medusa on the Western Coast of Africa in 1816

Leonaur is an imprint of Oakpast Ltd

Text in this form and material original to this edition
copyright © 2008 Oakpast Ltd

ISBN: 978-1-84677-552-9 (hardcover)
ISBN: 978-1-84677-551-2 (softcover)

http://www.leonaur.com

Publisher's Notes

The opinions expressed in this book are those of the author
and are not necessarily those of the publisher.

Contents

Narrative of a Voyage to Senegal in 1816   7

The Sufferings of the Picard Family After the
    Shipwreck of the *Medusa*   201

Narrative of a Voyage to Senegal in 1816

J. B. Henry Savigny &
Alexander Correard

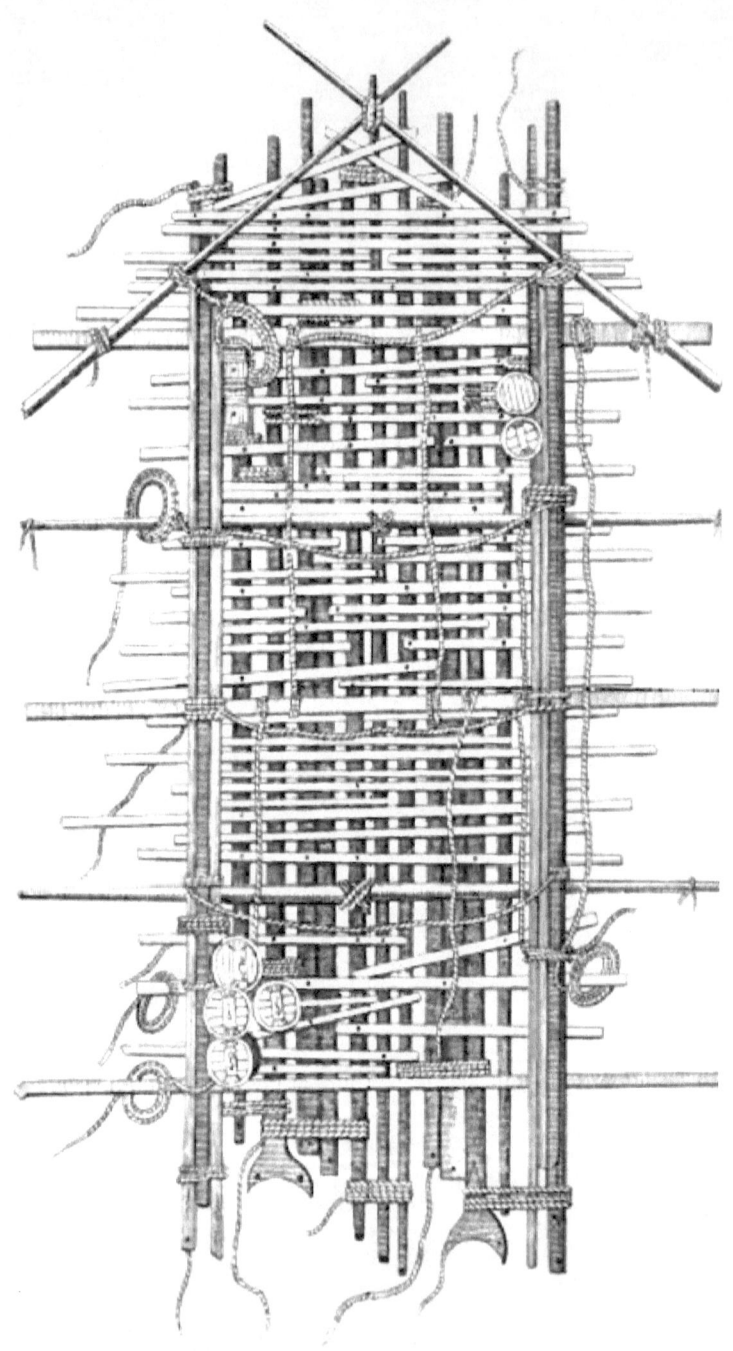

A Plan of the raft of the *Medusa*

Preface

The annals of the marine, record no example of a shipwreck so terrible as that of the *Medusa* frigate. Two of the unfortunate crew, who have miraculously escaped from the catastrophe, impose upon themselves the painful and delicate task, of describing all the circumstances which attended it.

It was in the midst of the most cruel sufferings that we took the solemn resolution, to make known, to the civilized world, all the details of our unhappy adventure, if heaven permitted us again to see our dear country. We should believe that we failed in our duty to ourselves, and to our fellow citizens, if we left buried in oblivion facts which the public must be desirous to know. All the details of the events at which we were not present, have been communicated to us by respectable persons, who have warranted their authenticity. We shall, besides, advance nothing which cannot be proved.

Here, we hear some voices ask, what right we have to make known to the government, men who are, perhaps, guilty, but whom their places, and their rank, entitle to more respect. They are ready to make it a crime in us, that we have dared to say, that officers of the marine had abandoned us. But what interest, we ask, in our turn, should cause a fatal indulgence to be claimed for those, who have failed in their duties; while the destruction of a hundred and fifty wretches, left to the most cruel fate, scarcely excited a murmur of disapprobation? Are we still in those times, when men and things were sacrificed to the caprices of favour?

Are the resources and the dignities of the State, still the exclusive patrimony of a privileged class? and are there other titles to places and honours, besides merit and talents?

Let us venture to advance another truth, a truth useful to the Minister himself. There exists among the officers of the Marine, an intractable *esprit de corps*, a pretended point of honour, equally false and arrogant, which leads them to consider as an insult to the whole navy, the discovery of one guilty individual. This inadmissible principle, which is useful only to insignificance, to intrigue, to people the least worthy to call on the name of honour, has the most ruinous consequences for the State, and the public service. By this, incapacity and baseness are always covered with a guilty veil, which they dare to attempt to render sacred; by this, the favours of government are bestowed at random, upon persons, who impose upon it the strange obligation of being perpetually in the dark respecting them. Under the protection of this obligation of officious silence, hitherto seconded by the slavery of the press, men without talents survive every revolution, exhibit in every antechamber their privileged incapacity, and braving public opinion, even that of their comrades, who are the first victims of a foolish and arrogant prejudice, which deceives them, show themselves more eager to monopolise favours and honours, in proportion as they are less able to render themselves worthy of them.

We shall believe that we have deserved well of our government, if our faithful narrative can make it sensible how much its confidence is abused. Just, besides, and not animated by passion, it is with real pleasure that we shall make those known, who, by their conduct in our shipwreck, have acquired a right to general esteem. Others will doubtless complain of the severity of our accusing language; but honest men will grant us their approbation. If we hear it said, that our frankness may have been useful to our country, this success will be, at once, our justification and our recompense.

We have questioned, concerning the nautical details, several gentlemen of the navy who were on board; we confess, however, that on comparing their accounts, we have observed that they did not always entirely agree; but we have taken those facts which had the most witnesses in their favour. We shall be sometimes obliged to record cruel truths; they will, however, be directed only to those, whose unskilfulness, or pusillanimity have caused these dreadful events. We venture to affirm, that the numerous observations, which we have collected, will give to our work all the accuracy rigorously required in so interesting a narrative.

We must observe to our readers that it has been impossible for us to avoid the use of naval terms, which will, perhaps, give a great degree of roughness to our narrative, but we hope that the public who are always indulgent, will be so on this occasion, to two unfortunate men, who pretend only to make them acquainted with the truth, and not to give them a superior work. Besides, as we in a manner, submit these events, to the judgment of the gentlemen of the French Navy, it was necessary to make use of the technical terms, that they might be able to understand us.

This second edition is enriched with notes, which will give the reader interesting details on many points, which in the former we could only slightly touch upon. He will have nothing more to desire, particularly respecting the march in the desert after the stranding of the long-boat.

These notes begin with the moment that the frigate stranded, and terminate with the arrival at St. Louis.

They were communicated to us by Mr. Landry, an officer of the Royal University, Professor Emeritus of the Academy of Paris, and at present at the head of a school or Academy, in the Rue Cerisaye, No. 2, quarter of the Arsenal, at Paris. He has had the kindness to extract them for us from a narrative, written by his nephew, Mr. Bredif, Engineer of Mines, belonging to the expedition to Senegal.

The narrator sent this account to his family above a year ago, addressing it to his sister. The reader will, therefore, not be surprised at the tone of simplicity which prevails in this recital. Mr. Landry would not take away any part for fear of injuring the truth of the circumstances, by meddling with it. If Mr. Bredif, is always placed in the fore-ground, that is not surprising; in a sister, a brother is the principal object which she cannot lose sight of for a moment.

He who loves to observe men, in all the circumstances, in which they may be placed, will easily judge, after what Mr. Bredif did or felt, what may have been done or felt by the sharers in the same misfortunes, who are, besides, never forgotten.

Mr. Bredif is now in the interior of Africa, employed upon the Mission which the government has entrusted to him; the last accounts from him are of the 14th of October, 1817. The manner in which he knows how to give an account of the facts which he has observed, and still more the courage, the prudence, and humanity, which he displayed in the disaster of the *Medusa*, and in all that followed it, give reason to hope, and this hope cannot be deceived, that he will duly execute his Mission, and render himself worthy of his Majesty's favours.

Introduction

The French settlements, situated on the western coast of Africa, from Cape Blanco to the mouth of the river Gambia, have been alternately possessed by France and England, and have remained definitively in the hands of the French, whose ancestors laid the foundations of them previously to the fourteenth century, when they discovered this country.

The English made themselves masters in 1758 of the Isle of St Louis, the seat of the general government of all the settlements which the French have on that part of the coast; we recovered it twenty years after, in 1779 and our possessions were again confirmed to us by the treaty of peace between France and England, concluded on the 3rd of September, 1783. In 1808, our possessions fell again into the power of the English, less by the superiority of their arms, than by the treachery of some individuals unworthy of bearing the name of Frenchmen. They were finally restored to us by the treaties of peace of 1814, and 1815, which confirmed that of 1783 in its whole extent.

The stipulations of this treaty regulate the respective rights of the two nations on the western coast of Africa; they fix the possessions of France as follows:—from Cape Blanco situated in longitude 19 deg. 30', and latitude 20 deg. 55' 30", to the mouth of the river Gambia in longitude 19 deg. 9', and latitude 13 deg.; they guarantee this property exclusively to our country, and only permit the English to trade together with the French, for gum, from the river St. John to Fort Portendick inclusive, on condition, that they shall not form establishments of any kind whatsoever in this river, or upon any point of this coast. Only it is said, that the possession of the factory of Albreda, situated at the month of the river Gambia, and that of fort James, are confirmed to England.

The rights of the two nations being thus regulated, France thought of resuming her possessions and the enjoyment of her rights. The minister of the marine after having long meditated, and taken two years to prepare an expedition of four vessels, at last gave orders that it should sail for Senegal. The following is a list of the persons who composed the expedition.

A Colonel, to command in chief for the king on the whole coast from Cape Blanco to the mouth of the river Gambia, and charged with the superior direction of the administration	1
A Lieutenant-Colonel, (*chef de bataillon*) commandant of Goree	1
A Lieutenant-Colonel commanding the African battalion, composed of three companies of 84 men each	253
A Lieutenant of Artillery, inspector of the powder magazines and batteries, and commanding ten workmen of his arm	11
A Commissary, inspector of the marine, chief of the administration	1
Four Store-keepers	4
Six Clerks	6
Four Scouts (*guetteurs*)	4
Two Cures	2
Two Schoolmasters (*instituteurs*)	2
Two Writers (*greffiers*, they supply the place of the notaries and even of the mayors)	2
Two Hospital Directors	2
Two Apothecaries	2
Five Surgeons	5
Two Port Captains	2
Three Pilots	3
A Gardener	1
Eighteen Women	18
Eight Children	8
Four Bakers	4

Farther for an intended expedition into the country of Galam

An Engineer of mines	1
A Geographical Engineer	1
A Naturalist (*cultivateur naturaliste*)	1

Farther for an expedition which was to seek upon Cape Verde, or in its neighbourhood for a spot proper for the foundation of a colony

A Physician	1
An Agriculturist for European productions	1
An Agriculturist for colonial productions	1
Two Geographical Engineers	2
A Naturalist	1
An officer of the marine	1
Twenty workmen	20
Three Women	3
Total	365

This expedition consisted therefore of 365 persons, of whom about 240 were embarked on board the *Medusa* frigate

CHAPTER 1

On the Way to Senegal

On the 17th of June, 1816, at seven in the morning, the expedition for Senegal sailed from the roads of the Island of Aix, under the command of Captain Chaumareys; the vessels composing it were the *Medusa* frigate of 44 guns, Captain Chaumareys; the *Echo* corvette, Captain Cornet de Venancourt; the flute *La Loire*, commanded by Lieutenant Giquel Destouches; and the *Argus* brig, commanded by Lieutenant Parnajon. The wind was northerly, blowing a fresh breeze; we carried all our sails; but had hardly cleared the port when the wind scanted a little, and we tacked to double the Tower of Chassiron, which is placed at the extremity of the Isle of Oleron. After having plied to windward the whole day, in the evening about five o'clock, the *Loire* being unable to stem the currents which were at that time contrary, and hindered her from entering the passes, desired leave to cast anchor; M. de Chaumareys granted it, and ordered the whole squadron to anchor. We were then half a league from the Isle of Rhe, within what is called the Pertuis d'Antioche. We cast anchor the first, and all the other vessels came and placed themselves near us. The *Loire* being a dull sailer, was the last which came to an anchor. The weather was fine: the wind N.W. and consequently too near to allow us to double Chassiron, with a contrary current. At seven in the evening, at the beginning of the ebb, we weighed anchor, and hoisted our sails; all the other vessels did the same: the signal to get under way had been given them a few minutes before. At night we found ourselves between the lights of Chassiron and

La Baleine. A few moments sufficed to double them; we were scarcely clear, when the wind became almost calm; the vessels no longer obeyed the helm, the sky grew dark, the sea was very hollow, in short everything announced a storm; the wind threatened to blow from the west, and consequently to become contrary; it was variable and squally; towards ten o'clock it was perceived that we were running directly upon a danger, called Les Roches Bonnes. We tacked to escape certain destruction; between eleven and twelve at night, a storm arose in the north, and brought on wind from that quarter; we were then able to advance; the clouds dispersed, and the next day the weather was very fine, with a breeze from the N.E. but very faint; for some days we made but very little progress.

On the 21st or 22nd we doubled Cape Finisterre; beyond this point which bounds the Gulph of Gascony, the *Loire* and the *Argus* parted company; these vessels sailing very ill, it was impossible for them to keep up with the frigate, which to enable them to do so, would have been obliged to take in her top-gallant sails and studding sails.

The *Echo* alone was in sight, but at a great distance, and carrying a press of sail not to lose sight of us. The frigate was so much a better sailer than the corvette, that with a small quantity of sail, she not only kept up with her, but even got a-head of her in a surprising manner; the wind had freshened and we were going at the rate of nine knots.

An unfortunate accident disturbed the pleasure we felt at being so favoured by the wind; a sailor lad 15 years of age, fell into the sea, through one of the fore port-holes, on the larboard side; a great many persons were at the time, on the poop and the breast work, looking at the gambols of the porpoises. The exclamations of pleasure at beholding the sports of these animals, were succeeded by cries of pity; for some moments the unfortunate youth held by the end of a rope, which he caught hold of in his fall; but the rapidity with which the frigate sailed, soon forced him to let go; a signal was made to acquaint the *Echo* with this accident; that vessel was at a considerable distance, and we were going to fire a gun to second the signal, but there was not one loaded, however we threw out the life buoy. The sails were clewed up, and the ship hove to. This manoeuvre was long; we should have come to the wind, as soon as they cried, "a man overboard," it is true that somebody cried aloud from the poop, that he was saved; and a sailor had indeed caught him by the arm, but he had been obliged to let him go, because he would have been pulled overboard himself: a boat was however let down; it was a six-oared barge in which there were only three men: it was all in vain; and after having looked for some time, the boat came on board again without having found even the buoy. If the unfortunate youth, who seemed to swim pretty well, had strength to reach it, he doubtless perished on it, after having experienced the most cruel sufferings. The ship was trimmed, and we resumed our course.

The *Echo* rejoined us, and for some time she kept within hail; but we soon lost her. On the 26th, we plied to windward during the night, fearing lest we should strike on the eight rocks, which are situated the most northerly, in 34 deg. 45', Latitude, and the most southerly in latitude, 34 deg. 30', so that the extent of this danger is about five leagues from north to south and about four leagues from east to west: the most southerly rock is distant about forty leagues to the north, 5 deg. east, from the east point of Madeira.

On the 27th, in the morning we expected to see the island of Madeira, we however proceeded to no purpose till noon, at which hour we made an observation to ascertain our situation. The solar observation made us east, and west of Porto Santo; we continued on the same tack, and in the evening at sunset, the man at the mast head discovered, land. This error in the arrival, was at least thirty leagues in the east. It was attributed to the currents of the straits of Gibraltar; if this error really arises from the currents of the strait, it merits the attention of vessels which frequent these seas. The whole night we proceeded with few sails up; at midnight we tacked, in order not to approach too near to the land.

The next morning at day break we saw very distinctly the islands of Madeira Porto Santo; on the larboard, were those called Desert; Madeira was at least twelve leagues off: sailing before the wind we made nine knots, and in a few hours we were very near it. For a considerable time we ran along the coast of the island at a small distance from shore: we passed before the principal towns, Funchal and Do Sob.

Madeira appears like an amphitheatre; the country houses which cover it seem to be in a very good taste, and give it a charming appearance. All these delightful habitations are surrounded by fine gardens, and fields covered with orange and lemon trees, which when the wind blows from the shore, diffuse for full half a league in the open sea, the most agreeable perfume. The hills are covered with vineyards, bordered with banyan trees: in short everything is combined to render Madeira one of the most beautiful islands of Africa. Its soil is only a vegetable sand, mixed with an ash, which gives it astonishing fertility; it shows every where nothing but the remains of a volcanised earth, the colour of which is that of the element, by which it was long consumed. Funchal, the capital town of the islands is situated in long. 19 deg.. 20'. 30." in lat. 32 deg. 37'. 40". This town is far from handsome, the streets are narrow and the houses in general ill built: the highest part of the island is the Pic de Ruvio, which rises about two hundred metres above the level of the sea. The population of Madeira is from 85,000 to 90,000, inhabitants as we are assured by a person worthy of credit, who has resided for some time in that fine colony.

We sailed in this manner along the coast of Madeira, because the intention of the commander was to send a boat on shore for refreshments; but being surprised by a calm under the land, we were afraid of approaching too near, lest we should not be able to stem the strong currents which set towards it. A gentle breeze arising, enabled us to get out to sea, where the wind became favourable, and pretty brisk; it was resolved that the boat should not go on shore: and we resumed our course going at eight knots. We had remained three hours opposite Funchal bay.

At nightfall Madeira was in full sight: the next morning at sunrise we saw the islands called Salvages, and in the evening we descried the Pico of Tenerife, on the island of that name. This lofty mountain, behind which the sun had just set, presented a sight truly magnificent; its summit seemed to be crowned with fire: its elevation above the level of the sea, is 3711 metres; it is situated in lat. 28 deg. 17' and in long. 19 deg.. Several persons on board affirmed that they saw the Pico at eight o'clock in the morning; and yet we were at least thirty leagues distant from it; the sky it is true, was extremely clear.

The commander resolved to send a boat to St. Croix, one of the principal towns in the island, to fetch fruits, and some filtering stones, which are made in that town; they are only a kind of mortar, made of the volcanic stone of the country. In consequence, during the whole night we made short tacks; the next morning we coasted the island, at the distance of two musket shot, and passed under the guns of a little fort, called Fort Francais. One of our companions leaped for joy, at the sight of this little fort, which was raised in haste by a few Frenchmen, when the English, under Admiral Nelson, attempted to take possession of the Colony. It was there, said he, that a numerous fleet, commanded by one of the bravest Admirals of the English navy, failed before a handful of French, who covered themselves with glory and saved Tenerife; the Admiral was obliged to take flight, after having lost an arm in the contest, which was long and obstinate.

Having doubled a point which extends into the sea, we entered the bay, at the bottom of which is the town of St. Croix. The appearance of Tenerife is majestic: the whole island is composed of mountains, which are extremely high, and crowned with rocks terrifying from their size, which on the north side, seem to rise perpendicularly above the surface of the ocean, and to threaten every moment to crush by their fall, the vessels which pass near their base. Above them all rises the Pico, the summit of which is lost in the clouds. We did not perceive that the Pic was constantly covered with snow as some voyagers affirm, nor that it vomits forth lava of melted metal; for when we observed it, its summit seemed entirely destitute of snow and of volcanic eruptions. At the foot of the mountain, and up to a certain elevation excavations filled with sulphur are observed; and in its neighbourhood several of the sepulchral caverns of the Guanches, the ancient inhabitants of the island.

Towards noon the *Echo* corvette, which had parted company, rejoined us, and passed under the stern of the frigate: she was ordered to imitate our manoeuvres, which she instantly did; she did not send any boat on shore. Thus united, we lay to together in the bay of St. Croix. About four o'clock in the afternoon, the boat having returned on board we directed our course for Senegal. They had bought in the town some earthen jars of a large size, precious wines, oranges, lemons, banyan figs, and vegetables of all kinds.

Several unfortunate Frenchmen were on the island who had been long prisoners of war; they lived upon what the Spaniards chose to give them. They had been restored to liberty on the conclusion of peace, and waited only for a favourable opportunity to return to France. Their entreaties to the officer who commanded the boat were useless; he had the cruelty to refuse to restore them to their country and their families. In this boat there was another officer M. Laperere, who strongly insisted on bringing away these unfortunate persons; his entreaties could not move him who commanded the boat.

The depravity of morals at St. Croix is extreme; so much so that when the women heard that some Frenchmen were arrived in the town, they placed themselves at their doors, and when they passed, urged them to enter. All this is usually done in the presence of the husbands, who have no right to oppose it, because the Holy Inquisition will have it so, and because the monks who are very numerous in the island take care that this custom is observed. They possess the art of blinding the husbands, by means of the *prestiges* of religion, which they abuse in the highest degree; they cure them of their jealousy, to which they are much inclined, by assuring them that their passion, which they call ridiculous, or conjugal mania, is nothing but the persecution of Satan which torments them, and from which they alone are able to deliver them, by inspiring their dear consorts with some religious sentiments. These abuses are almost inevitable in a burning climate, where the passion of love is often stronger than reason, and sometimes breaks through the barriers which religion attempts to oppose to it: this depravity of morals must therefore be attributed to inflamed passions, and not to abuses facilitated by a religion so sublime as ours.

The Island of Tenerife is not equal to that of Madeira: one cannot even compare their agricultural productions, on account of the great difference of their soils: but in a commercial view, Tenerife has the advantage of Madeira. Its geographical position in the middle of the Canaries, enables it to carry on an extensive trade, while Madeira is confined to the sale and exchange of its wines for articles of European manufacture.

The soil of Tenerife is much drier; a great part of it is too volcanic to be used for agriculture: every part of it however, which is capable of producing anything is very well cultivated, which should seem to prove, that the Spaniards of this country are naturally much less indolent than they have been represented.

When we were in the open sea we had favourable winds from the N.N.E.

CHAPTER 2

We Run Aground

In the night of the 29th of June the frigate caught fire between decks, by the negligence of the master baker; but being discovered in time, the fire was extinguished. In the following night the same accident was repeated; but this time it was necessary, in order to stop the progress of the fire, to pull down the oven which was rebuilt the next day.

On the 1st of July we descried Cape Bayados, situated in latitude 26 deg. 12' 30", and in longitude 16 deg. 47'. We then saw the skirts of the immense desert of Zaara, and we thought we perceived the mouth of the river St. John , which is very little known. We passed the tropic at ten o'clock in the morning; the usual ceremony was there performed with a certain pomp; the jokes of the sailors amused us for some moments; we were far from thinking of the cruel event which was soon to deprive of their lives a third of the persons who were on board the frigate. This custom of tropical baptism is strange enough; the chief object of it, is, to procure the sailors some money.

From St. Croix, we had constantly steered to the S.S.W. During the ceremony at the tropic we doubled Cape Barbas, situated in lat. 22 deg. 6', and long. 19 deg. 8': two officers suddenly had the course changed, without informing the captain; this led to a pretty warm dispute, which however had no serious consequences. These two officers affirmed that we were running upon a group of rocks, and that we were already very near to the breakers. We had sailed the whole morning in the Gulf of St. Cyprian, the bottom of which is strewed with rocks, so that at low water, brigantines cannot frequent these seas, as we were told at Senegal by M. Valentin, senior, who is perfectly acquainted with this whole coast, and could not conceive how the frigate could have passed amidst all these reefs without striking. The shore was within half a cannon shot, and we clearly saw enormous rocks over which the sea broke violently. If it had fallen calm, there is no doubt but the strong currents which set, in-shore, would have infallibly carried us into danger.

In the evening we thought we descried Cape Blanco, and according to the instructions given by the Navy Office, we steered W.S.W. During a part of the night the *Echo*, with which we had constantly kept company since we left Madeira, burnt several charges of powder and hung a lanthorn at the mizzen-mast; her signals were not answered in the same manner; only a lanthorn was hung for a few moments to the fore-mast; it went out soon after, and was not replaced by another light. M. Savigny was on deck where he remained a part of the night: he had full opportunity to perceive the negligence of the officer of the watch, who did not even deign to answer the signals made by the *Echo*. Why, in the neighbourhood of so formidable a danger, not compare the points of the two ships, as is usual when vessels sail in company? The captain of the frigate was not even informed of the signals of the corvette. At eleven o'clock, she bore off the larboard bow; and soon after he perceived that the direction of her course made a pretty large angle with ours, and that it tended to cross us passing a-head; he soon perceived her on the starboard: it is affirmed that her journal states that she sailed the whole night W.S.W. ours does the same. We must necessarily have hauled to the larboard, or she to the starboard, since at day-break the corvette was no longer in sight.

At sea a vessel may easily be perceived at the distance of six leagues. From midnight till six in the morning, she must have gained above six leagues of us, which is not to be imagined, for she sailed much slower than we and stopped every two hours to take soundings. To explain this separation we must necessarily admit either that the frigate steered more south, or the corvette more west, if the two vessels had run on the same tack it would be impossible to explain it.

Every two hours the frigate brought-to, to sound; every half hour the lead was cast without lowering the sails; we were always upon shallows, and stood out to sea, to find a greater quantity of water: at length about six o'clock in the morning we had above a hundred fathoms; we then stood-to the S.S.E.; this course made almost a right angle with that which we had followed in the night: it bore directly in-shore, the approach to which, in this place, is rendered terrible by a very long reef, called Arguin, which according to instructions we had on board extends above thirty leagues in breadth. According to the instructions given by the Minister of the Marine, this danger is avoided by running only twenty-two leagues in the open sea; it is true they recommend not to approach the shore but with the greatest precaution, and with the sounding line in the hand: the other ships of the expedition which sailed according to those instructions all arrived at St. Louis without any accident, which is a certain proof of their exactness. Besides it is said, that one must make W.S.W., when one has discerned Cape Blanco; and it is probable we had not got sight of it in the evening, as was supposed. We therefore had an uncertain point of departure; hence the error which was so fatal to us.

According to my Comrade Correard, we cannot pass over in silence, a scene which took place in the morning. The Captain was deceived in the most singular manner; about five or six o'clock he was called up; some persons who were on deck persuaded him that a great cloud which was in the direction of Cape Blanco and in truth very near it, was that Cape itself. My companion in misfortune, who sees clearly, and who knows how to distinguish between a rock and a cloud, because he has seen enough of them in the Alps, where he was born, told those gentlemen that it was only a cape of vapour; he was answered that the instructions which the minister had given to the captain prescribed to him to make this cape; but that we had passed it above ten leagues; that at this moment the question was, to make the captain believe that the instructions of the minister had been punctually followed, and that they desired to persuade him, which was not difficult, that this cloud was the Cape. Many have deposed, as we have been told, that Cape Blanco, had been seen in the evening of the 1st of July: we venture to affirm that that rock was not seen at all.

After this pretended reconnaissance of the 2nd July, if we were persuaded that we had seen that Cape, we should have steered west, to double the bank of Arguin; the danger once passed, the course should have been again directed to the south which is the route to Senegal; but he who for some days past had guided the course of the ship, thought proper to persuade the captain, to take immediately the southerly course, and to steer for Portendic. We are ignorant of the reasons which induced the commander of the frigate to give his confidence to a man who did not belong to the staff. He was an ex-officer of the marine, who had just left an English prison, where he had been for ten years; he certainly had not acquired there knowledge superior to that of the officers on board, whom this mark of deference could not but offend. M. de Chaumareys, while we were doubling Cape Barbas, presided at the farce performed in passing the Tropic, while he who had gained his confidence, was walking up and down the deck of the frigate, coolly observing the numerous dangers, spread along the coast. Several persons remonstrated against this management of the vessel, particularly Mr. Picard the *greffier* of Senegal, who had struck upon the bank of Arguin eight years before; this enlightened man declared at that time that we were running into danger.

As soon as the sun's altitude was observed to ascertain our position, we saw, on the quarter deck, Mr. Maudet, ensign of the watch, working the day's work, (making out the reckoning) upon a chicken coop; this officer who knows all the duties of his profession, affirmed that we were on the edge of the reef; he communicated this to the person who for some days past had given his counsel to the commander respecting the course to be steered; he received for answer; never mind, we are in eighty fathoms.

If our course during the night had partly averted all our dangers, that which was taken in the morning led us into them again. Mr. Maudet, convinced that we were upon the reef, took upon him, to have soundings taken; the colour of the water was entirely changed, which was observed even by those who were the least used to recognise the depth of the sea, by the appearance of the water; we even thought that we saw sand roll amid the little waves that rose; numerous sea weeds were seen by the ship's side, and a great many fish were caught. All these facts proved indubitably that we were on shallow water: in fact the lead announced only eighteen fathoms; the officer of the watch immediately informed the captain, who gave orders to come a little more to the wind; we were going before the wind the studding sails on the larboard; these sails were immediately lowered; the lead was again cast, and showed six fathoms; the captain gave orders to haul the wind as close as possible, but unhappily it was too late.

The frigate luffing, almost immediately gave a heel; it proceeded a moment longer; gave a second and then a third; it stopped at a place where the sounding line showed only a depth of five metres sixty centimetres, and it was the time of high water.

Unhappily we were in the season of the high tides, which was the most unfavourable time for us because they were going to decline, and we ran aground just when the water was at the highest; for the rest, the tides do not much differ in these seas; at the time of full moon they do not rise more than fifty centimetres more than usual; in the spring tides the water does not rise above one hundred and twenty centimetres on the reef. We have already said that when we grounded, the sounding line marked only five metres, and sixty centimetres; and at low water it marked, four metres sixty centimetres, the frigate therefore saved by a metre: however, as soon as we had stranded, the boats which went out to sound, met with places deeper than that, where we struck, and many others not so deep; which made us suppose that the reef is very uneven and covered with little elevations. All the different manoeuvres which had been performed since the moment when we found ourselves in eighteen fathoms, to that in which we struck, succeeded each other with extraordinary rapidity: not above ten minutes passed. Several persons have assured us that, if the ship had come entirely to the wind, when we were in eighteen fathoms, the frigate might perhaps have got clean, for she did not run wholly aground till she got to the west part of the reef, and upon its edge.

We stranded on the 2nd of July, at a quarter after three p.m. in 19 deg. 36' north latitude, and 19 deg. 45' west longitude. This event spread the most profound consternation; if in the midst of this disorder, there were any men who remained collected enough to make observations, they must have been struck with the extraordinary changes impressed on every countenance; some persons were not to be recognised. Here you might see features become shrunk and hideous; there a countenance which had assumed a yellow and even a greenish hue, some men seemed thunderstruck and chained down to their places, without strength to move. When they had recovered from the stupefaction, with which they were at first seized, numbers gave themselves up to excess of despair; while others uttered imprecations upon those whose ignorance had been so fatal to us. An officer going upon deck, immediately after the accident, spoke with energy to him, who, as we have already said, had directed for some days the course of the ship, and said to him, "See, Sir, to what your obstinacy has brought us; I had warned you of it."

Two women alone seemed insensible to this disaster; they were the wife and daughter of the governor. What a shocking contrast! men who for twenty or twenty-five years, had been exposed to a thousand dangers, were, profoundly affected, while Madame and Mademoiselle Chemals, appeared insensible, and as if unconcerned in these events.

As soon as the frigate stranded, the sails were hastily lowered, the top gallant masts got down, the top masts lowered, and everything necessary arranged to get her off the reef. After numerous efforts, night being come, they were suspended to give some repose to the crew, who had displayed extreme activity. The next day, the third, the top masts were got down, the yards lowered, and they heaved at the capstan upon an anchor which had been fixed the evening before, at a cable's length a-stern of the frigate. This operation was fruitless; for the anchor, which was too weak, could not make sufficient resistance and gave way: a bower anchor was then used, which, after infinite pains, was carried out to a considerable distance, to a place where there was only a depth of five metres sixty centimetres; in order to carry it so far, it was fixed behind a boat, under which was placed a number of empty barrels fastened together because the boat was not able to carry so considerable a weight. The sea ran very high, and the current was extremely strong.

This boat, when it reached the spot where it was to cast the anchor, could not place it in the proper position to make the flukes fix in the sand, for one of the extremities already touched the bottom, while the other was still put of the water: being thus ill fixed, it could not answer the purpose intended; when they began to heave upon it, it made very little resistance, and would have been dragged on board again if they had continued to work at the capstan. In the course of the day, we staved several water butts which were in the hold, and pumped immediately, the top masts, except the small one which could not be got down, were thrown into the sea; the yards, the boom, and all the pieces of wood which afterwards composed.

If the loss of the vessel was certain, it was proper to secure the escape of the crew: a council was called, at which the governor of Senegal gave the plan of a raft, capable, it was said, of carrying two hundred men, with provisions. It was necessary to have recourse to an expedient of this nature, because our six boats were judged to be incapable of taking on board four hundred men, which was our number. The provisions were to be deposited on the raft, and at the hours of meals, the crews of the boats would have come to receive their rations: we were to reach all together the sandy coast of the desert, and there furnished with arms and ammunition, which were to be taken in by the boats before we left the frigate, we were to form a caravan, and proceed to the Island of St. Louis.

The events which happened in the sequel, proved that this plan was perfectly well laid, and that it might have been crowned with success: unhappily these decisions were traced upon a loose sand, which was dispersed by the breath of egotism.

In the evening another anchor was cast, at a pretty considerable distance from the frigate: just before high water, we began to work at the capstan, but in vain. The work was put off till the next morning's tide; during all this time, the operations were performed with the greatest difficulty; the sea was hollow, the winds strong, the boats which had to go to a distance either to sound or fix: anchors, could not attain their object, without the greatest efforts; rapid currents, added to the difficulties. If the weather had not been so extremely unfavourable to us, perhaps the frigate might have been got afloat the next day, for it had been resolved to carry out very long warps, but the violence of the wind, and the sea, baffled these arrangements which nothing but a calm could favour. The weather was bad during the whole night; about four or five o'clock, at the morning tide, all our efforts to raise her were still fruitless; we began to despair of even being able to save her from this danger; the boats were repaired, and the construction of the raft diligently prosecuted: during the day of the 4th. several barrels of flour were thrown into the sea, some water casks staved; some barrels of powder, intended as articles to trade with Senegal, were also got overboard.

In the evening, a few minutes before high water, the labours at the capstan recommenced; this time the anchors did not deceive our expectations; for, after a few moments labour, the frigate moved on the larboard; this motion was effected by means of an anchor fixed on the north west; the stream cable which was bent to its ring, came by the head of the ship and tended to make it swing; while another much stronger one, the cable of which passed through one of the stern ports, tended to prevent it from running a-head, by supporting its quarters the motions of which were commanded by means of this force. This first success gave us great hopes; we worked with ardour.

After some further efforts, the *Medusa* began to swing sensibly; we redoubled our efforts, she swung entirely and then had her head turned, to the open sea. She was almost afloat, only her stern touched a little; the work could not be continued, because the anchor was too near, and it would have been hove up. If a warp had been carried out in the open sea, by continuing to haul upon it, the frigate would have been got wholly afloat that evening. All the things which had been thrown overboard had lightened her, by twenty or thirty centimetres at the most, her draught of water might certainly have been lessened still more; but it was not done because the Governor of Senegal objected to throwing the barrels of flour into the sea, alleging that the greatest scarcity prevailed in the European factories. These considerations, however, should not have caused it to be overlooked that we had on board fourteen twenty-four pounders, and that it would have been easy to throw them overboard, and send them even to a considerable distance from the frigate, by means of the yard tackle; besides, the flour barrels might have been carefully fastened together, and when we were once out of danger, it would have been easy for us to remove them. This plan might have been executed without any fear of doing much damage to the flour, which when it is plunged in the water forms round the inside of the barrel a pretty thick crust, in consequence of the moisture, so that the interior is preserved from injury: this method was indeed attempted, but it was given up, because the means employed were insufficient. More care should have been used, and all the difficulties would have been conquered; only half measures were adopted, and in all the manoeuvres great want of decision prevailed.

If the frigate had been lightened as soon as we struck, perhaps she might have been saved. The weather, however, as we have already said, was almost always unfavourable, and often hindered the operations.

Some persons expected to see the frigate got afloat the next day, and their joy showed that they were fully persuaded of it: there were indeed some probabilities, but they were very slight; for the vessel had been merely got out of its bed. We had hardly succeeded in changing its place to a distance of about two hundred metres, when the sea began to ebb: the frigate rested on the sand, which obliged us to suspend for ever our last operations. If it had been possible to hold her this night to two or three cables more in the open sea, still lightening her, perhaps, we repeat it, she might have been placed out of danger.

At night the sky became cloudy, the winds came from the sea, and blew violently. The sea ran high, and the frigate began to heel with more and more violence, every moment we expected to see her bulge; consternation again spread, and we soon felt the cruel certainty that she was irrecoverably lost. She bulged in the middle of the night, the keel broke in two, the helm was unshipped, and held to the stern only by the chains, which caused it to do dreadful damage; it produced the effect of a strong horizontal ram, which violently impelled by the waves, continually struck the poop of the ship; the whole back part of the captain's cabin was beat in, the water entered in an alarming manner. About eleven o'clock there was a kind of mutiny, which was afterwards checked by the presence of the governor and the officers; it was excited by some soldiers, who persuaded their comrades that it was intended to abandon them on board the frigate, while the crew escaped in the boats; these alarms were excited by the imprudence of a young man; some soldiers had already taken their arms, and had ranged themselves on the deck, all the avenues to which they occupied.

The raft, impelled by the strength of the current and of the sea, broke the cable which fastened it to the frigate and began to drive; those who beheld this accident announced it by their cries, and a boat was immediately sent after it, which brought it back. This was a distressing night for us all; agitated by the idea that our frigate was totally lost, and alarmed by the violent shocks which it received from the waves, we were unable to take a moment's repose.

At day-break, on the 5th, there were two metres seventy centimetres water in the hold, and the pumps could no longer work with effect: it was decided we ought to quit the vessel as soon as possible. The frigate, it was said, threatened to upset; a childish fear, doubtless; but, what particularly made it absolutely necessary to abandon her, was, that the water had already penetrated between decks. A quantity of biscuit was hastily taken from the store-room; wine and fresh water were also got out; these provisions were intended to be placed in the boats and on the raft. To preserve the biscuit from the salt water it was put into strong iron hooped barrels, which were perfectly fit for the purpose. We are ignorant why these provisions, so carefully prepared were not embarked either on the raft or in the boats; the precipitation with which we embarked was the cause of this negligence, so that some boats did not save above twenty-four pounds of biscuit, a small cask of water and very little wine: the rest was abandoned on the deck of the frigate or thrown into the sea during the tumult of the evacuation. The raft alone had a pretty large quantity of wine, but not a single barrel of biscuit, and if any was put upon it, it was thrown off by the soldiers when they placed themselves upon it. To avoid confusion, there was made, the day before, a list of the persons who were to embark, assigning to everyone the post he was to occupy; but no attention was paid to this wise arrangement; every one took the means which he thought the most favourable to reach the shore; those who executed the orders which they had received to place themselves on the raft, had certainly reason to repent it. Mr. Savigny was unfortunately of this number; he might have stopped on board a boat, but an invincible attachment to his duty made him forget the danger of the part which was allotted him.

CHAPTER 3

"Abandon Ship!"

At length, the moment when we were to abandon the frigate arrived. First, the soldiers were embarked, who were almost all placed upon the raft: they wanted to take their muskets and some cartridges: this was formally opposed. They left them on the deck, and preserved only their sabres: some few, however, saved their carbines, and, almost all the officers, their fowling pieces and pistols. In all, we were about one hundred and forty-seven or one hundred and fifty; such is pretty nearly the account of the persons who embarked on this fatal machine, one hundred and twenty soldiers, including the officers of the army, twenty-nine men, sailors and passengers, and one woman. The barge, commanded by a lieutenant, on board of which were the governor and his family, took in thirty-five persons in all: this large fourteen-oared vessel, could certainly have carried a larger number: besides the people, there were three trunks; another fourteen-oared boat took in forty-two persons; the captain's barge took twenty-eight; the long boat, though in a very bad condition, destitute of oars, took in, however, eighty-eight; an eight-oared boat which was to be left at Senegal, for the service of the port, took twenty-five sailors; the smallest of the boats had fifteen persons on board; among whom were the interesting family of Mr. Picard, of whom we have spoken above: it was composed of three young ladies, his wife, and four young children. All these numbers added together, form a total of three hundred and ninety-seven persons; there were on board the frigate, near four hundred sailors and soldiers: thus it appears that several poor wretches were abandoned; when the *Medusa* was again found, fifty-two days after, it was ascertained that the number of those, who had been abandoned, was seventeen; which proves to us, that there were more than one hundred and forty seven of us on the raft, and that it is more correct to fix the number of the men at a hundred and fifty. It is said, that when the last boat, which was the long boat, left the frigate, several men refused to embark in her; the others were too much intoxicated to think of their safety. A man of the name of Dales, one of the seventeen who remained on board the frigate, deposed in the council, that fourteen men had left the long boat, because they did not think it capable of carrying so many, and that he, with two others hid themselves, that they might not be compelled to go on board. We are ignorant of the depositions of his two companions.

What a sight was it to behold a multitude of wretches, who all wanted to escape death, and all sought to save themselves, either in the boats or upon the rafts! The frigate's ladder was insufficient for so many: some threw themselves from the vessels, trusting to the end of a rope, which was scarcely able to bear a man's weight; some fell into the sea, and were recovered; what is surprising is, that amidst all this confusion, there was not a single serious accident.

Though in so terrible a situation, on our fatal raft, we cast our eyes upon the frigate, and deeply regretted this fine vessel, which, a few days before, seemed to command the waves, which it cut through with astonishing rapidity. The masts, which had supported immense sails, no longer existed, the barricade was entirely destroyed: the vessel itself was cast on the larboard quarter.

All the boats, after they had sheared off, proceeded in different manners, as we shall afterwards relate; but the men on board, when they reached the shore, had to contend with a thousand causes of destruction. We will first exactly relate all the operations that were executed till the moment when the raft was abandoned.

About seven o'clock, the signal for departure was given; four of the boats stood out to sea, the raft was still along side of the frigate, where it was moored: the captain's barge was under the bowsprit and the barge near our machine, on which it had just embarked some men. At length we were ordered to depart; but whether from a presentiment of what was to happen to us, or whether Mr. Correard entertained just fears, which the event proved to be but too well founded, he would not depart, till he had convinced himself that our raft was provided with all the necessary instruments and charts, to navigate with some degree of safety in case bad weather should oblige the boats to separate from us. As it was impossible to move upon the raft, because we were so crowded together he thought it the easiest to call to Mr. —— who immediately answered to his call. Coming to the larboard, he asked what we wanted? The following questions were then put to him: "Are we in a condition to depart? Have we instruments and charts?" "Yes, yes, replied he, "I have provided you with everything that can be necessary for you." He was then asked, what naval officer was to come and command us? he answered: "It is I; in a moment I shall be with you." After saying this he disappeared, and went on board one of the boats.

How is it possible that a French sea officer should be guilty of such bad faith to his unhappy countrymen, who placed all their confidence in him?

At last, the barge came to the head of the frigate, and the governor caused himself to be let down in an arm chair; it then threw a tow rope to our raft, and we stood off with this one boat; the second boat then gave a tow line to the first; the Senegal boat came afterwards, and did the same; there remained three boats, the captain's, which was still at the head of the frigate, on board of which last there were above eighty men, who uttered cries of despair, when they saw the boats and the raft stand off. The three boats which towed us, soon brought us to a distance from the vessel; they had a good wind, and the sailors rowed like men who were resolved to save themselves from the imminent danger which threatened us. The long-boat, and the pinnace were at some distance, and attempted to return on board; lastly, M. De Chaumareys embarked in his barge, by one of the ropes a-head: some sailors threw themselves into it, and loosened the ropes, by which it was lashed to the frigate. Immediately the cries of the people who remained on board redoubled, and an officer of the troops even took up a carbine to fire at the captain: but was prevented. We soon saw that this man was not equal to his duty; from the manner in which he abandoned his people. We regretted that the arm of the officer had been withheld when he wished to prevent the captain's design; but, our regret was unavailing; the mischief was done; it was irreparable; he had no idea of repairing it, and he could not return on board, for he was sure to meet there with that death, which he sought to avoid, at the expense of honour.

M. de Chaumareys, however, went on board the long-boat, and gave order that it should take in the men who remained on board the frigate. Some persons belonging to this boat have informed us, that they were told there were, at the most, about twenty who could not embark; but, the long-boat, destitute of oars, attempted, to no purpose, to get back to the frigate; a boat tried, without success, to tow it; it could not attain the object, till it sent the pinnace to fetch some long ropes, one end of which was lashed to the frigate, and the other brought on board the long-boat, which was thus towed to the larboard side of the ship. Lieutenant Espiau, who commanded this large boat, was surprised at finding above sixty soldiers and sailors, instead of twenty. This officer went on board with Mr. Bredif, engineer of mines, who tried to recall to their reason, those whose intellectual faculties had been impaired by the presence of danger. Mr. Espiau, embarked with proper order, the men who were on the deck; seventeen only as we have said, refused; some fearing that the boat would founder before she could reach the raft, and the other boats, which left it more and more behind; some others, because they were too much intoxicated as we have stated, to think of their safety. The fears of the former, (and they are probably those who, according to the deposition of Dales, returned on board the frigate) were founded on the bad condition of the long-boat, which let in the water on every side. After promising the men who persisted in remaining, that assistance should be sent them, as soon as the others arrived at Senegal, the long-boat stood off to join the little division. Before he left the frigate, Mr. Espiau had the grand national flag hoisted.

When this boat left the frigate to join us, we were, at least, a league and a half distant; the captain's barge had come some time before to take the towrope, and was at the head of the line; the smallest of the boats (the pinnace) did not take the towline; it preceded the little division, probably to take soundings.

As soon as all the boats had taken their post, cries of *"Vive le Roi!"* were a thousand times repeated by the men upon the raft, and a little white flag was hoisted at the top of a musket. Such was the order of the boats and the raft. The chiefs of the little division which was to conduct us to the land, had sworn not to abandon us: we are far from accusing all those gentlemen of having violated the laws of honour; but a series of circumstances obliged them to renounce the generous plan which they had formed to save us, or to perish with us. These circumstances deserve to be scrupulously examined; but our pen, guided by truth, must not fear to record facts which truth itself dictates. It is true they are of so strange a nature, that it is unpleasant to make them known. It is painful to us, to have to recount such events: we have to show to what a degree the imagination of man is susceptible of being struck by the presence of danger, so as to make him even forget the duties which honour imposes on him. We, doubtless, admit that in forsaking the raft, the minds of those who did so, were greatly agitated, and that the desire of withdrawing themselves from danger, made them forget that a hundred and fifty unfortunate men were going to be abandoned to the most cruel sufferings. We shall relate the facts as we observed them, and as they have been communicated to us, by some of our companions in misfortune.

Before we proceed, we will describe the construction of this raft, to which a hundred and fifty persons were entrusted.

It was composed of the top-masts of the frigate, yards, fishes, boom, &c. These different pieces joined together by very strong ropes, were perfectly solid; the two principal pieces were two top-masts, which were placed at the extremity of the two sides; four other masts, two of which were of the same length and strength as the first, joined two by two, at the centre of the machine, added to its solidity. The other pieces were placed within these four first but were not equal to them in length. Boards were nailed on this first foundation, and formed a kind of parapet, which would have been of great service to us if it had been higher. To render our raft still more solid, long pieces of wood had been placed across, which projected at least three metres: on the sides, there was a kind of railing, but it was not above forty centimetres in height: it would have been easy to add some crotches to it, which would have formed a breast-work of sufficient height; but it was not done, probably because those who had the machine built, were not to be exposed upon it. To the ends of the top-masts, two top-gallant yards were lashed, the farther ends of which were bound by a very strong cord, and thus formed the front part of the raft. The angular space, formed by the two yards, was filled with pieces of wood laid across, and planks ill adjusted. This fore part, which was at least two metres in length, had very little solidity, and was continually submerged. The hinder part did not terminate in a point like the fore part, but a considerable length of this part was not more solid, so that in fact, there was only the centre which was really to be depended upon: an example will enable the reader to judge of its dimensions. When we were no more than fifteen in it, we had not space enough to lie down, and yet we were extremely close together. The raft, from one extremity, to the other was at least twenty metres in length, and about seven in breadth; this length might induce one to think, at the first sight, that it was able to carry two hundred men, but we soon had cruel proofs of its weakness. It was without sails or mast. As we left the frigate they threw us the fore-top-gallant and the main-top-gallant sails; but they did it with such precipitation, that, some persons who were at their post, were in danger of being wounded by the fall of these sails, which were bent to the yards. They did not give us any ropes to set up our mast.

There was on board the raft a great quantity of barrels of flour, which had been deposited there the preceding day, not to serve for provisions during the passage, from the frigate to the coast, but because the raft, formed of the barrels, not having succeeded, they were deposited on the machine, that they might not be carried away by the sea, there were also six barrels of wine and two small casks of water, which had been put there for the use of the people.

Scarcely fifty men had got upon the raft, when it sunk at least seventy centimetres under water; so that to facilitate the embarkation of the other soldiers it was necessary to throw into the sea all the flour barrels, which lifted by the waves, began to float and were violently driven against the men who were at their post; if they had been fixed, perhaps some of them might have been saved: as it was, we saved only the wine and the water, because several persons united to preserve them, and had much difficulty to hinder them from being thrown into the sea like the flour barrels. The raft, lightened by throwing away these barrels, was able to receive more men; we were at length a hundred and fifty. The machine was submerged at least a metre: we were so crowded together that it was impossible to take a single step; at the back and the front, we were in water up to the middle. At the moment that we were; putting off, from the frigate, a bag with twenty-five pounds of biscuit was thrown us, which fell into the sea; we got it up with difficulty; it was converted into a paste, but we preserved it in that condition. Several considerate persons fastened the casks of wine and water to the cross pieces of the raft, and we kept a strict watch over them. Thus we have faithfully described the nature of our situation when we put off from the vessel.

The Commander of the raft was named Coudin who was, what is called in the French marine an Aspirant of the first class. Some days before our departure from the roads of the Isle of Aix, he had received a severe contusion on the fore part of the right leg, which was not approaching to its cure, when we stranded and wholly incapacitated him from moving. One of his comrades, moved by his situation, offered to take his place, but Mr. Coudin, though wounded, preferred repairing to the dangerous post which was assigned him, because he was the oldest officer of his class on board. He was hardly on board the raft, when the sea water so increased the pain in his leg, that he nearly fainted; we gave notice of his situation to the nearest boat, we were answered that a boat would come and fetch this officer. I do not know whether the order was given, but it is certain that Mr. Coudin was obliged to remain on the fatal raft.

The long-boat, which we have been forced to lose sight of for a moment, in order to give these necessary details, at length rallied; it was, as we have stated, the last that left the frigate. The lieutenant who commanded her, justly fearing that he should not be able to keep the sea, in a crazy boat destitute of oars, badly rigged, and making much water, ran along-side of the first boat, begging it to take in some men; they refused. This long boat was to leave us some ropes to fix our mast; which an instant before had been hauled to us, by the first boat, which we had before us: we do not know what reason hindered it from leaving us these ropes, but it passed on, and ran along-side the second boat, which equally refused to take any body on board. The officer, who commanded the long-boat, seeing that they refused to take any of his men, and falling more and more under the wind, because his sails were badly trimmed, and the currents drove him, made up to the third-boat, commanded by a sub-lieutenant named Maudet; this officer, commanding a slight boat which the day before had a plank beat in, by one of the cross pieces of the raft, (an accident which had been remedied by covering the hole with a large piece of lead,) and being besides heavily laden, in order to avoid the shock of the long-boat, which might have been fatal to him, was forced to let loose the tow-rope, which held him to the barge, and thus broke in two the line formed by the boats before the craft, by separating himself from it with the captains boat which was at the head: when the captain and Mr. Maudet had disengaged themselves they hauled the wind, and then put about to come and take their post; Mr. Maudet even hailed M. de Chaumareys, "Captain take your towrope again," he received for answer, "Yes my friend." Two boats were still at their post, but before the other two were able to rejoin them, the barge separated itself; the officer who commanded it, expressed himself as follows respecting his thus abandoning us. "The towrope was not let go from my boat, but from that behind me." This second desertion was the forerunner of another still more cruel; for the officer who commanded the last boat in which was the governor, after having towed us alone, for a moment, caused the rope to be loosened which held it to the raft. When the towropes were let go, we were two leagues from the frigate; the breeze came from the sea, which was as favourable as could be desired. This last tow-rope did not break, as the governor has tried to persuade the minister of the marine, and several persons who escaped from the raft. Walking on the terrace of a French merchant at Senegal, in the presence of Messrs. Savigny and Coudin, the governor explained the affair as follows: "Some men were on the front of the raft, at the place where the tow-rope was fixed; which they pulled so as to draw the boat nearer to them; they had already pulled several fathoms of it to them, but a wave coming, gave a violent shock; these men were obliged to let go; the boats then proceeded more rapidly, till the rope was stretched; at the moment when the boats effected this tension the effort was such, that the rope broke." This manner of explaining this last desertion is very adroit, and might easily deceive those who were not on the spot, but it is not possible for us to accede to it, since we could even name the person who loosened it.

Some persons belonging to the other boats have assured us, that all the boats were coming to resume their post, when a cry of "we forsake them," was heard: we have this fact from many of our companions in misfortune. The whole line was thrown into disorder, and no measures were taken to remedy it: it is probable, that if one of the first officers had set the example, order would have been restored; but everyone was left to himself; hence there was no concert in the little division; everyone thought of escaping from personal danger.

Let us here do justice to the courage of Mr. Clanet, pay-master of the frigate, who was on board the governor's boat; if he had been listened to, this tow-rope would not have been let go; every moment an officer who was in the governor's boat cried out aloud, "shall I let go?" Mr. Clanet opposed it, answering with firmness, "No no!" Some persons joined him, but could obtain nothing, the tow-rope was let go: we considered it as certain, that the commander of the other boats, on seeing the chief of the expedition courageously devote himself, would have come and resumed their posts: but it may be said that each individual boat was abandoned by all the others: there was wanting, on this occasion, a man of great coolness: and ought not this man to have been found among the chief officers? How shall their conduct be justified? There are, certainly, some reasons to be alleged. Impartial judges of events, we will describe them, not as unhappy victims of the consequences of this desertion, but as men free from all personal resentment, and who listen only to the voice of truth.

The raft, drawn by all the boats united, dragged them a little back; it is true that we just had the ebb, and the currents set from shore. To be in the open sea with undecked vessels, might well inspire some apprehensions: but, in a few hours, the currents would change and favour us; we ought to have waited for this moment, which would have infallibly demonstrated the possibility of drawing us to the coast, which was not above twelve or fifteen leagues distant: this is so true that the boats discovered the coast, the same evening, before sunset. Perhaps they would have been forced to forsake us the second night after our departure, if indeed more than thirty-six hours had been required to tow us to land; for the weather was very bad; but we should then have been very near to the coast, and it would have been very easy to save us: at least we should have had only the elements to accuse!—We are persuaded that a short time would have sufficed to tow us within sight of land, for, the evening of our being deserted, the raft was precisely in the direction which the boats had followed between the frigates and the coast, and, at least, five leagues from the former. The next morning, at daybreak, we could no longer see the *Medusa*.

At the first moment we did not really believe that we had been so cruelly abandoned. We imagined that the boats had let loose, because they had perceived a vessel, and hastened towards it to ask assistance. The long-boat was pretty near us to leeward on the starboard. She lowered her foresail half way down: her manoeuvre made us think that she was going to take the first tow-rope: she remained so a moment, lowered her foresail entirely, setup her main-mast, hoisted her sails, and followed the rest of the division. Some men in this boat, seeing that the others deserted us, threatened to fire upon them, but were stopped by Lieutenant Espiau. Many persons have assured us that it was the intention of this officer to come and take the tow-rope; but his crew opposed it; had he done so, he would certainly have acted with great imprudence. His efforts would have been of little use to us, and his devotedness would but have increased the number of victims. As soon as this boat was gone, we had no doubt but that we were abandoned; yet we were not fully convinced of it till the boats had disappeared.

It was now that we had need of all our courage, which, however, forsook us more than once: we really believed that we were sacrificed, and with one accord, we cried that this desertion was premeditated. We all swore to revenge ourselves if we had the good fortune to reach the shore, and there is no doubt but that, if we could have overtaken, the next day, those who had fled in the boats, an obstinate combat would have taken place between, them and us.

It was then that some persons who had been marked out for the boats, deeply regretted that they had preferred the raft, because duty and honour had pointed out this post to them. We could mention some persons: for example, Mr. Correard, among others, was to go in one of the boats; but twelve of the workmen, whom we commanded, had been set down for the raft; he thought that in his quality of commander of engineers, it was his duty not to separate from the majority of those who had been confided to him, and who had promised to follow him wherever the exigencies of the service might require; from that moment his fate became inseparable from theirs, and he exerted himself to the utmost to obtain the governor's permission to have his men embarked in the same boat as himself; but seeing that he could obtain nothing to ameliorate the fate of these brave men, he told the governor that he was incapable of committing an act of baseness: that since he would not put his workmen in the same boat with him, he begged him to allow him to go on the raft with them, which was granted.

Several military officers imitated their example; only two of those who were to command the troops did not think fit to place themselves upon the raft, the equipment of which, in truth, could not inspire much confidence.

One of them, Captain Beiniere, placed himself in the longboat with 36 of his soldiers. We had been told that these troops had been charged to superintend the proceedings of the other boats, and to fire upon those who should attempt to abandon the raft. It is true, as we have seen above, that some brave soldiers listening, perhaps, more to the voice of humanity and French honour, than to the strict maxims of discipline, were desirous of employing their arms against those who basely abandoned us, but, that their will and their actions were paralyzed by the passive obedience which they owed to their officers, who opposed this resolution.

The other, Mr. Danglas, a lieutenant, who had lately left the *gardes-du-corps*, had at first embarked with us upon the raft, where his post was assigned him, but when he saw the danger which he incurred on this unstable machine, he made haste to quit it, on the pretext that he had forgotten something on board the frigate, and did not return. It was he whom we saw, armed with a carbine, threaten to fire on the barge of the governor, when it began to move from the frigate. This movement, and some other actions which were taken for madness, nearly cost him his life; for while he was thus giving himself up to a kind of extravagance, the captain took flight, and abandoned him on board the frigate with the sixty-three men whom he left there. When M. Danglas saw himself treated in this manner, he gave marks of the most furious despair. They were obliged to hinder him from attempting his own life. With loud cries he invoked death, which he believed inevitable in the midst of perils so imminent. It is certain that if Mr. Espiau, who had his long-boat already full, had not returned to take from on board the frigate, the forty-six men, among whom, was Mr. Danglas, he and all his companions would not, perhaps, have experienced a better fate than the seventeen who were finally left on board the *Medusa*.

CHAPTER 4

Terror on the High Seas

After the disappearance of the boats, the consternation was extreme: all the terrors of thirst and famine arose before our imaginations, and we had besides to contend with a perfidious element, which already covered the half of our bodies: when recovered from their stupefaction, the sailors and soldiers gave themselves up to despair; all saw inevitable destruction before them, and gave vent in lamentations to the gloomy thoughts which agitated them. All we said did not at first avail to calm their fears, in which we however participated, but which a greater degree of strength of mind enabled us to dissemble. At last, a firm countenance and consoling words succeeded in calming them by degrees, but could not wholly dispel the terror with which they were struck; for according to the judicious reflection, made after reading our deplorable story, by Mr. Jay, whose authority we quote with pleasure, "To support extreme misfortunes, and what is worthy of remark, to bear great fatigues, moral energy is much more necessary than corporeal strength, nay, than the habit of privations and hard labour. On this narrow theatre where so many sufferings are united, where the most cruel extremes of hunger and thirst are experienced, strong and indefatigable men who have been brought up to the most laborious professions, sink in succession under the weight of the common destiny, while men of a weak constitution, and not inured to fatigue, find in their minds the strength which their bodies want, endure with courage unheard-of trials, and issue victorious from their struggle with the most horrible afflictions. It is to the education they have received, to the exercise of their intellectual faculties, that they owe this astonishing superiority and their deliverance," When tranquillity was a little restored, we began to look upon the raft for the charts, the compass and the anchor, which we presumed had been placed there, from what had been said to us at the time we quitted the frigate. These highly necessary articles had not been put upon our machine. The want of a compass in particular, greatly alarmed us, and we uttered cries of rage and vengeance. Mr. Correard then recollected, that he had seen one in the hands of one of the chief workmen under his command, and enquired of this man about it: "Yes, yes," said he, "I have it with me." This news transported us with joy, and we thought that our safety depended on this feeble resource. This little compass was about the size of a crown-piece, and far from correct. He who has not been exposed to events, in which his existence was in imminent peril, can form but a faint idea of the value which one then sets upon the most common and simple objects, with what avidity one seizes the slightest means, that are capable of softening the rigour of the fate with which one has to contend. This compass was given to the commander of the raft; but an accident deprived us of it forever: it fell, and was lost between the pieces of wood which composed our machine: we had kept it only for a few hours; after this loss, we had nothing to guide us but the rising and setting of the sun.

We had all left the frigate without taking any food: hunger began to be severely felt; we mixed our biscuit-paste (which had fallen into the sea) with a little wine, and we distributed it thus prepared: such was our first meal, and the best we had the whole time we were on the raft.

An order, according to numbers, was fixed for the distribution of our miserable provisions. The ration of wine was fixed at three quarters a day: we shall say no more of the biscuit: the first distribution consumed it entirely. The day passed over pretty quietly: we conversed on the means which we should employ to save ourselves; we spoke of it as a certainty, which animated our courage: and we kept up that of the soldiers, by cherishing the hope of being soon able to revenge ourselves upon those who had so basely abandoned us. This hope of vengeance inspired us all equally, and we uttered a thousand imprecations against those who had left us a prey to so many misfortunes and dangers. The officer who commanded, the raft being unable to move, Mr. Savigny took on himself the care of setting up the mast; he caused the pole of one of the frigate's masts to be cut in two; we employed the main-top-gallant sail; the mast was kept up by the rope which had served to tow us, of which we made shrouds and stays: it was fixed on the anterior third of the raft. The sail trimmed very well, but the effect of it was of very little use to us; it served only when the wind came from behind, and to make the raft preserve this direction it was necessary to trim the sail, as if the wind came athwart. We think that the cross position which our raft always retained, may be attributed to the too great length of the pieces of wood which projected on each side.

In the evening, our hearts and our prayers, with the impulse natural to the unfortunate, were directed towards heaven; we invoked it with fervour, and we derived from our prayers the advantage of hoping in our safety: one must have experienced cruel situations, to imagine what a soothing charm, in the midst of misfortune, is afforded by the sublime idea of a God, the protector of the unfortunate. One consoling idea still pleased our imaginations; we presumed that the little division had sailed for the Isle of Arguin, and that after having landed there a part of its people, would return to our assistance: this idea, which we tried to inspire into our soldiers and sailors, checked their clamours. The night came, and our hopes were not yet fulfilled: the wind freshened, the sea rose considerably. What a dreadful night! Nothing but the idea of seeing the boats the next day, gave some consolation to our people; who being most of them unused to the motion of a vessel, at every shock of the sea, fell upon each other. Mr. Savigny, assisted by some persons, who, in the midst of this disorder, still retained their presence of mind, fastened some ropes to the pieces of the raft: the men took hold of them, and by means of this support, were better able to resist the force of the waves: some were obliged to fasten themselves. In the middle of the night the weather was very bad; very heavy waves rolled upon us, and often threw us down with great violence; the cries of the people were mingled with the roaring of the billows; a dreadful sea lifted us every moment from the raft, and threatened to carry us away. This scene was rendered still more awful by the horrors of a very dark night; for some moments we thought that we saw fires at a distance. We had taken the precaution to hang, at the top of the mast, some gun-powder and pistols, with which we had provided ourselves on board the frigate: we made signals by burning a great many charges of powder; we even fired some pistol-shot, but it seems that these fires were only an illusion of the eyesight, or perhaps they were nothing but the dashing of the breakers.

This whole night we contended against death, holding fast by the ropes which were strongly fastened. Rolled by the waves from the back to the front, and from the front to the back, and sometimes precipitated into the sea, suspended between life and death, lamenting our misfortune, certain to perish, yet still struggling for a fragment of existence with the cruel element which threatened to swallow us up. Such was our situation till day-break; every moment were heard the lamentable cries of the soldiers and sailors; they prepared themselves for death; they bid farewell to each other, imploring the protection of Heaven, and addressing fervent prayers to God: all made vows to him, notwithstanding the certainty that they should never be able to fulfil them. Dreadful situation! How is it possible to form an idea of it, which is not below the truth!

About seven o'clock, in the morning, the sea fell a little, the wind blew with less fury; but what a sight presented itself to our view! Ten or twelve unhappy wretches, having their lower extremities entangled in the openings between the pieces of the raft, had not been able to disengage themselves, and had lost their lives; several others had been carried off by the violence of the sea. At the hour of repast we took fresh numbers, in order to leave no break in the series: we missed twenty men: we will not affirm that this number is very exact, for we found that some soldiers, in order to have more than their ration, took two, and even three numbers. We were so many persons crowded together, that it was absolutely impossible to prevent these abuses.

Amidst these horrors, an affecting scene of filial piety forced us to shed tears: two young men raised and recognised, for their father, an unfortunate man who was stretched senseless under the feet of the people; at first, they thought he was dead, and their despair expressed itself by the most affecting lamentations; it was perceived, however, that this almost inanimate body still had breath; we lavished on him all the assistance in our power; he recovered by degrees, and was restored to life and to the prayers of his sons, who held him fast embraced in their arms. While the rights of nature resumed their empire in this affecting episode of our sad adventures, we had soon the afflicting sight of a melancholy contrast. Two young lads, and a baker, did not fear to seek death, by throwing themselves into the sea, after having taken leave of their companions in misfortune. Already the faculties of our men were singularly impaired; some fancied they saw the land; others, vessels which were coming to save us; all announced to us by their cries these fallacious visions.

We deplored the loss of our unhappy companions; we did not presage, at this moment, the still more terrible scene which was to take place the following night; far from that, we enjoyed a degree of satisfaction, so fully were we persuaded that the boats would come to our relief. The day was fine, and the most perfect tranquillity prevailed on our raft. The evening came, and the boats did not appear. Despondency began again to seize all our people, and a mutinous spirit manifested itself by cries of fury; the voice of the officers was wholly disregarded. When the night came, the sky was covered with thick clouds; the wind, which during the day had been rather high, now became furious, and agitated the sea, which, in an instant, grew very rough.

If the preceding night had been terrible, this was still more horrible. Mountains of water covered us every moment, and broke, with violence, in the midst of us; very happily we had the wind behind us, and the fury of the waves was a little checked by the rapidity of our progress; we drove towards the land. From the violence of the sea, the men passed rapidly from the back to the front of the raft, we were obliged to keep in the centre, the most solid part of the raft; those who could not get there, almost all perished. Before and behind the waves dashed with fury, and carried off the men in spite of all their resistance. At the centre, the crowd was such that some poor men were stifled by the weight of their comrades, who fell upon them every moment; the officers kept themselves at the foot of the little mast, obliged, every instant, to avoid the waves, to call to those who surrounded them to go on the one or the other side, for the waves which came upon us, nearly athwart, gave our raft a position almost perpendicular, so that, in order to counterbalance it, we were obliged to run to that side which was raised up by the sea.

The soldiers and sailors, terrified by the presence of an almost inevitable danger, gave themselves up for lost. Firmly believing that they were going to be swallowed up, they resolved to soothe their last moments by drinking till they lost the use of their reason; we had not strength to oppose this disorder; they fell upon a cask which was at the middle of the raft, made a large hole at one end, and with little tin cups which they had brought from on board the frigate, they each took a pretty large quantity, but they were soon obliged to desist, because the sea water entered by the hole which they had made.

The fumes of the wine soon disordered their brains, already affected by the presence of danger and want of food. Thus inflamed, these men, become deaf to the voice of reason, desired to implicate, in one common destruction, their companions in misfortune; they openly expressed their intention to rid themselves of the officers, who they said, wished to oppose their design, and then to destroy the raft by cutting the ropes which united the different parts that composed it. A moment after, they were proceeding to put this plan in execution. One of them advanced to the edge of the raft with a boarding-axe, and began to strike the cords: this was the signal for revolt: we advanced in order to stop these madmen: he who was armed with the axe, with which he even threatened an officer, was the first victim: a blow with a sabre put an end to his existence. This man was an Asiatic, and soldier in a colonial regiment: a colossal stature, short curled hair, an extremely large nose, an enormous mouth, a sallow complexion, gave him a hideous air. He had placed himself, at first, in the middle of the raft, and at every blow of his fist he overthrew those who stood in his way; he inspired the greatest terror, and nobody dared to approach him. If there had been half-a-dozen like him, our destruction would have been inevitable.

Some persons, desirous of prolonging their existence, joined those who wished to preserve the raft, and armed themselves: of this number were some subaltern officers and many passengers. The mutineers drew their sabres, and those who had none, armed themselves with knives: they advanced resolutely against us; we put ourselves on our defence: the attack was going to begin. Animated by despair, one of the mutineers lifted his sabre against an officer; he immediately fell, pierced with wounds. This firmness awed them a moment; but did not at all diminish their rage. They ceased to threaten us, and presenting a front bristling with sabres and bayonets, they retired to the back part, to execute their plan. One of them pretended to rest himself on the little railing which formed the sides of the raft, and with a knife began to cut the cords. Being informed by a servant, we rushed upon him—a soldier attempted to defend him—threatened an officer with his knife, and in attempting to strike him, only pierced his coat—the officer turned round—overpowered his adversary, and threw both him and his comrade into the sea!

After this there were no more partial affairs: the combat became general. Some cried lower the sail; a crowd of madmen instantly threw themselves on the yards and the shrouds, and cut the stays, and let the mast fall, and nearly broke the thigh of a captain of foot, who fell senseless. He was seized by the soldiers, who threw him into the sea: we perceived it—saved him, and placed him on a barrel, from which he was taken by the seditious; who were going to cut out his eyes with a penknife. Exasperated by so many cruelties, we no longer kept any measures, and charged them furiously. With our sabres drawn we traversed the lines which the soldiers formed, and many atoned with their lives for a moment of delusion. Several passengers displayed much courage and coolness in these cruel moments.

Mr. Correard was fallen into a kind of trance, but hearing every moment cries of "To arms! To us, comrades! We are undone!" joined to the cries and imprecations of the wounded and the dying, he was soon roused from his lethargy. The increasing confusion made him sensible that it was necessary to be upon his guard. Armed with his sabre, he assembled some of his workmen on the front of the raft, and forbid them to hurt anyone unless they were attacked. He remained almost always with them, and they had several times to defend themselves against the attacks of the mutineers; who falling into the sea, returned by the front of the raft; which placed Mr. Correard and his little troop between two dangers, and rendered their position very difficult to be defended. Every moment men presented themselves, armed with knives, sabres and bayonets; many had carbines, which they used as clubs. The workmen did their utmost to stop them, by presenting the point of their sabres; and, notwithstanding the repugnance they felt to combat their unhappy countrymen, they were however obliged to use their arms without reserve; because many of the mutineers attacked them with fury, it was necessary to repulse them in the same manner. In this action some of the workmen received large wounds; he who commanded them reckons a great number, which he received in the various combats they had to maintain. At last their united efforts succeeded in dispersing the masses that advanced furiously against them.

During this combat, Mr. Correard was informed, by one of his workmen who remained faithful, that one of their comrades, named Dominique, had taken part with the mutineers, and that he had just been thrown into the sea. Immediately forgetting the fault and the treachery of this man, he threw himself in after him, at the place where the voice of the wretch had just been heard calling for assistance; he seized him by the hair, and had the good fortune to get him on board. Dominique had received, in a charge, several sabre wounds, one of which had laid open his head. Notwithstanding the darkness we found the wound, which appeared to us to be very considerable. One of the workmen gave his handkerchief to bind it up and stanch the blood. Our care revived this wretch; but as soon as he recovered his strength, the ungrateful Dominique, again forgetting his duty and the signal service that he had just received from us, went to rejoin the mutineers. So much baseness and fury did not go unpunished; and soon afterwards, while combating us anew, he met with his death, from which he, in fact, did not merit to be rescued, but which he would probably have avoided, if faithful to honour and to gratitude, he had remained among us.

Just when we had almost finished applying a kind of dressing to the wounds of Dominique, another voice was heard; it was that of the unfortunate woman who was on the raft with us, and whom the madmen had thrown into the sea, as well as her husband, who defended her with courage. Mr. Correard, in despair at seeing two poor wretches perish, whose lamentable cries, especially those of the woman, pierced his heart, seized a large rope which was on the front of the raft, which he fastened round the middle of his body, and threw himself, a second time, into the sea, whence he was so happy as to rescue the woman, who invoked, with all her might, the aid of Our Lady of Laux, while her husband was likewise saved by the chief workman, Lavillette. We seated these two poor people upon dead bodies, with their backs leaning against a barrel. In a few minutes they had recovered their senses. The first thought of the woman was to enquire the name of him who had saved her, and to testify to him the warmest gratitude. Thinking, doubtless, that her words did not sufficiently express her sentiments, she recollected that she had, in her pocket, a little snuff, and immediately offered it to him—it was all she possessed. Touched by this present, but not making use of this *antiscorbutic*, Mr. Correard, in turn, made a present of it to a poor sailor, who used it three or four days. But a more affecting scene, which it is impossible for us to describe, is the joy which this unfortunate couple displayed when they had sufficiently recovered their senses to see that they were saved.

The mutineers being repulsed, as we have said above, left us at this moment a little repose. The moon with her sad beams, illumined this fatal raft, this narrow space, in which were united so many heart-rending afflictions, so many cruel distresses, a fury so insensate, a courage so heroic, the most pleasing and generous sentiments of nature and humanity.

The man and his wife, who just before had seen themselves attacked with sabres and bayonets, and thrown at the same moment into the waves of a stormy sea, could hardly believe their senses when they found themselves in each other's arms. They felt, they expressed, so fervently, the happiness which they were alas, to enjoy for so short a time, that this affecting sight might have drawn tears from the most insensible heart; but in this terrible moment, when we were but just breathing after the most furious attack, when we were forced to be constantly on our guard, not only against the attacks of the men, but also against the fury of the waves: few of us had time, if we may say so, to suffer ourselves to be moved by this scene of conjugal friendship.

Mr. Correard, one of those whom it had most agreeably affected, hearing the woman still recommend herself, as she had done when in the sea, to our Lady of Laux, exclaiming every instant, "our good Lady of Laux do not forsake us," recollected that there was, in fact, in the Department of the Upper Alps, a place of devotion so called, and asked her if she came from that country. She replied in the affirmative, and said she had quitted it 24 years before, and that since that time she had been in the Campaigns in Italy, &c. as a sutler; that she had never quitted our armies. "Therefore," said she, "preserve my life, you see that I am a useful woman." "Oh! if you knew how often I also have braved death on the field of battle, to carry assistance to our brave men." Then she amused herself with giving some account of her campaigns. She mentioned those she had assisted, the provisions which she had provided them, the brandy with which she had treated them. "Whether they had money or not," said she, "I always let them have my goods. Sometimes a battle made me lose some of my poor debtors; but then, after the victory, others paid me double or triple the value of the provisions which they had consumed before the battle. Thus I had a share in their victory." The idea of owing her life to Frenchmen, at this moment, seemed still to add to her happiness. Unfortunate woman! she did not foresee the dreadful fate that awaited her among us! Let us return to our raft.

After this second check, the fury of the soldiers suddenly abated, and gave place to extreme cowardice: many of them fell at our feet and asked pardon, which was instantly granted them. It is here, the place to observe and to proclaim aloud for the honour of the French army, which has shown itself as great, as courageous, under reverses, as formidable in battle, that most of these wretches were not worthy to wear its uniform. They were the scum of all countries, the refuse of the prisons, where they had been collected to make up the force charged with the defence and the protection of the colony. When, for the sake of health, they were made to bathe in the sea, a ceremony from which some of them had the modesty to endeavour to excuse themselves, the whole crew had ocular demonstration that it was not upon the breast that these heroes wore the insignia of the exploits, which had led them to serve the state in the Ports of Toulon, Brest or Rochefort.

This is not the moment, and perhaps we are not competent to examine whether the penalty of branding, as it is re-established in our present code, is compatible with the true object of all good legislation, that of correcting while punishing, of striking only as far as is necessary to prevent and preserve; in short, of producing the greatest good to all with the least possible evil to individuals. Reason at least seems to demonstrate, and what has passed before our own eyes authorises us to believe that it is as dangerous, as inconsistent, to entrust arms for the protection of society, to the hands of those whom society has itself rejected from its bosom; that it implies a contradiction to require courage, generosity, and that devotedness which commands a noble heart to sacrifice itself for its country and fellow creatures, from wretches branded, degraded by corruption, in whom every moral energy is destroyed, or eternally compressed by the weight of the indelible opprobrium which renders them aliens to their country, which separates them forever from the rest of mankind.

We soon had on board our raft a fresh proof of the impossibility of depending on the permanence of any honourable sentiment in the hearts of beings of this description.

Thinking that order was restored, we had returned to our post at the centre of the raft, only we took the precaution to retain our arms. It was nearly midnight: after an hour's apparent tranquillity, the soldiers rose again: their senses were entirely deranged; they rushed upon us like madmen, with their knives or sabres in their hands. As they were in full possession of their bodily strength, and were also armed, we were forced again to put ourselves on our defence. Their revolt was the more dangerous, as in their delirium they were entirely deaf to the cries of reason. They attacked us; we charged them in our turn, and soon the raft was covered with their dead bodies. Those among our adversaries who had no arms, attempted to tear us with their teeth; several of us were cruelly bitten; Mr. Savigny was himself bitten in the legs and the shoulder; he received also a wound with a knife in his right arm which deprived him, for a long time, of the use of the fourth and little fingers of that hand; many others were wounded; our clothes were pierced in many places by knives and sabres. One of our workmen was also seized by four of the mutineers, who were going to throw him into the sea. One of them had seized him by the right leg, and was biting him cruelly in the sinew above the heel. The others were beating him severely with their sabres and the butt end of their carbines; his cries made us fly to his aid. On this occasion, the brave Lavillette, ex-sergeant of the artillery on foot, of the old guard, behaved with courage worthy of the highest praise:

we rushed on these desperadoes, after the example of Mr. Correard, and soon rescued the workman from the danger which threatened him. A few moments after, the mutineers, in another charge, seized on the Sub-Lieutenant Lozach, whom they took, in their delirium, for Lieutenant Danglas, of whom we have spoken above, and who had abandoned the raft when we were on the point of putting off from the frigate. The soldiers, in general, bore much ill will to this officer, who had seen little service, and whom they reproached with having treated them harshly while they were in garrison in the Isle of Rhe. It would have been a favourable opportunity for them to satiate their rage upon him, and the thirst of vengeance and destruction which animated them to fancy that they had found him in the person of Mr. Lozach, they were going to throw him into the sea. In truth, the soldiers almost equally disliked the latter, who had served only in the Vendean bands of Saint Pol de Leon. We believed this officer lost, when his voice being heard, informed us that it was still possible to save him. Immediately Messrs. Clairet, Savigny, l'Heureux, Lavillette, Coudin, Correard, and some workmen, having formed themselves into little parties, fell upon the insurgents with so much impetuosity that they overthrew all who opposed them, recovered Mr. Lozach, and brought him back to the centre of the raft.

The preservation of this officer cost us infinite trouble. Every moment the soldiers demanded that he should be given up to them, always calling him by the name of Danglas. It was in vain we attempted to make them sensible of their mistake, and to recall to their memory, that he, whom they demanded, had returned on board the frigate, as they had themselves seen; their cries drowned the voice of reason; everything was in their eyes Danglas; they saw him everywhere, they furiously and unceasingly demanded his head, and it was only by force of arms, that we succeeded in repressing their rage, and in silencing their frightful cries.

On this occasion we had also reason to be alarmed for the safety of Mr. Coudin. Wounded and fatigued by the attacks which we had sustained with the disaffected, and in which he had displayed the most dauntless courage, he was reposing on a barrel, holding in his arms a sailor boy, of twelve years of age, to whom he had attached himself. The mutineers seized him with his barrel, and threw him into the sea with the boy, whom he still held fast; notwithstanding this burden, he had the presence of mind to catch hold of the raft, and to save himself from this extreme danger. Dreadful night! thy gloomy veil covered these cruel combats, instigated by the most terrible despair.

CHAPTER 5

Mutiny & Cannibalism

We cannot conceive how a handful of individuals could resist such a considerable number of madmen. There were, certainly, not more than twenty of us to resist all these furious wretches. Let it, however, not be imagined, that we preserved our reason unimpaired amidst all this disorder; terror, alarm, the most cruel privations had greatly affected our intellectual faculties; but being a little less deranged than the unfortunate soldiers, we energetically opposed their determination to cut the cords of the raft. Let us be allowed to make some reflections on the various sensations with which we were affected.

The very first day, Mr. Griffon lost his senses so entirely, that he threw himself into the sea, intending to drown himself. Mr. Savigny saved him with his own hand. His discourse was vague and unconnected. He threw himself into the water a second time, but by a kind of instinct he kept hold of one of the cross pieces of the raft: and was again rescued.

The following is an account of what Mr. Savigny experienced in the beginning of the night. His eyes closed in spite of himself, and he felt a general lethargy; in this situation the most agreeable images played before his fancy; he saw around him, a country covered with fine plantations, and he found himself in the presence of objects which delighted all his senses; yet he reasoned on his situation, and felt that courage alone would recover him from this species of trance; he asked the master gunner of the frigate for some wine: who procured him a little; and he recovered in a degree from this state of torpor. If the unfortunate men, when they were attacked by these first symptoms, had not had resolution to struggle against them, their death was certain. Some became furious; others threw themselves into the sea, taking leave of their comrades with great coolness; some said "Fear nothing, I am going to fetch you assistance: in a short time you will see me again." In the midst of this general madness, some unfortunate wretches were seen to rush upon their comrades with their sabres drawn, demanding the wing of a chicken, or bread to appease the hunger which devoured them; others called for their hammocks, "to go," they said, "between the decks of the frigate and take some moments' repose." Many fancied themselves still on board the *Medusa*, surrounded with the same objects which they saw there every day. Some saw ships, and called them to their assistance, or a harbour, in the back ground of which there was a magnificent city.

Mr. Correard fancied he was travelling through the fine plains of Italy; one of the officers said to him, gravely, "I remember that we have been deserted by the boats; but fear nothing; I have just written to the governor, and in a few hours we shall be saved."

Mr. Correard replied in the same tone, and as if he had been in an ordinary situation, "Have you a pigeon to carry your orders with as much celerity?"

The cries and the tumult soon roused us from the state in which we were plunged; but scarcely was tranquillity restored, when we sunk back into the same species of trance: so that the next day we seemed to awake from a painful dream, and asked our companions if, during their sleep, they had seen combats and heard cries of despair. Some of them replied that they had been continually disturbed by the same visions, and that they were exhausted with fatigue: all thought themselves deceived by the illusions of a frightful dream.

When we recall to our minds those terrible scenes, they present themselves to our imagination like those frightful dreams which sometimes make a profound impression on us; so that, when we awake, we remember the different circumstances which rendered our sleep so agitated. All these horrible events, from which we have escaped by a miracle, appear to us like a point in our existence: we compare them with the fits of a burning fever, which has been accompanied by a delirium: a thousand objects appear before the imagination of the patient: when restored to health, he sometimes recollects the visions that have tormented him during the fever which consumed him, and exalted his imagination. We were really seized with a fever on the brain, the consequence of a mental exaltation carried to the extreme. As soon as daylight beamed upon us, we were much more calm: darkness brought with it a renewal of the disorder in our weakened intellects. We observed in ourselves that the natural terror, inspired by the cruel situation in which we were, greatly increased in the silence of the night: then all objects seemed to us much more terrible.

After these different combats, worn out with fatigue, want of food and of sleep, we endeavoured to take a few moments' repose, at length daylight came, and disclosed all the horrors of the scene. A great number had, in their delirium, thrown themselves into the sea: we found that between sixty and sixty-five men had perished during the night; we calculated that, at least, a fourth part had drowned themselves in despair. We had lost only two on our side, neither of whom was an officer. The deepest despondency was painted on every face; every one, now that he was come to himself, was sensible of his situation; some of us, shedding tears of despair, bitterly deplored the rigour of our fate.

We soon discovered a new misfortune; the rebels, during the tumult, had thrown into the sea two barrels of wine, and the only two casks of water that we had on the raft. As soon as Mr. Correard perceived that they were going to throw the wine into the sea, and that the barrels were almost entirely made loose, he resolved to place himself on one of them; where he was continually thrown to and fro by the impulse of the waves; but he did not let go his hold. His example was followed by some others, who seized the second cask, and remained some hours at that dangerous post. After much trouble they had succeeded in saving these two casks; which being every moment violently driven against their legs had bruised them severely. Being unable to hold out any longer, they made some representations to those who, with Mr. Savigny, employed all their efforts to maintain order and preserve the raft. One of them took his (Mr. Correard) place; others relieved the rest: but finding this service too difficult, and being assaulted by the mutineers, they forsook this post. Then the barrels were thrown into the sea.

Two casks of wine had been consumed the preceding day; we had only one left, and we were above sixty in number; so that it was necessary to put ourselves on half allowance.

At daybreak the sea grew calm, which enabled us to put up our mast again; we then did our utmost to direct our course towards the coast. Whether it were an illusion or reality we thought we saw it, and that we distinguished the burning air of the Zaara Desert. It is, in fact, very probable that we were not very distant from it, for we had had winds from the sea which had blown violently. In the sequel we spread the sail indifferently to every wind that blew, so that one day we approached the coast, on the next ran into the open sea.

As soon as our mast was replaced, we made a distribution of wine; the unhappy soldiers murmured and accused us for privations, which we bore as well as they: they fell down with fatigue. For forty-eight hours we had taken nothing, and had been obliged to struggle incessantly against a stormy sea; like them we could hardly support ourselves; courage alone still made us act. We resolved to employ all possible means to procure fish. We collected all the tags from the soldiers, and made little hooks of them; we bent a bayonet to catch sharks: all this availed us nothing; the currents carried our hooks under the raft, where they got entangled. A shark bit at the bayonet, and straightened it. We gave up our project. But an extreme resource was necessary to preserve our wretched existence. We tremble with horror at being obliged to mention that which we made use of! we feel our pen drop from our hand; a deathlike chill pervades all our limbs; our hair stands erect on our heads!—Reader, we beseech you, do not feel indignation towards men who are already too unfortunate; but have compassion on them, and shed some tears of pity on their unhappy fate.

Those whom death had spared in the disastrous night which we have just described, fell upon the dead bodies with which the raft was covered, and cut off pieces, which some instantly devoured. Many did not touch them; almost all the officers were of this number. Seeing that this horrid nourishment had given strength to those who had made use of it, it was proposed to dry it, in order to render it a little less disgusting. Those who had firmness enough to abstain from it took a larger quantity of wine. We tried to eat sword-belts and cartouche-boxes. We succeeded in swallowing some little morsels. Some eat linen. Others pieces of leather from the hats, on which there was a little grease, or rather dirt. We were obliged to give up these last means. A sailor attempted to eat excrements, but he could not succeed.

The day was calm and fine: a ray of hope allayed our uneasiness for a moment. We still expected to see the boats or some vessels; we addressed our prayers to the Eternal, and placed our confidence in him. The half of our men were very weak, and bore on all their features the stamp of approaching dissolution. The evening passed over, and no assistance came. The darkness of this third night increased our alarm; but the wind was slight, and the sea less agitated. We took some moment's repose: a repose which was still more terrible than our situation the preceding day; cruel dreams added to the horrors of our situation. Tormented by hunger and thirst, our plaintive cries sometimes awakened from his sleep, the wretch who was reposing close to us. We were even now up to our knees in the water, so that we could only repose standing, pressed against each other to form a solid mass. The fourth morning's sun, after our departure, at length rose on our disaster, and showed us ten or twelve of our companions extended lifeless on the rail. This sight affected us the more as it announced to us that our bodies, deprived of existence, would soon be stretched on the same place. We gave their bodies to the sea for a grave; reserving only one, destined to feed those who, the day before, had clasped his trembling hands, vowing him an eternal friendship. This day was fine; our minds, longing for more agreeable sensations, were harmonized by the soothing aspect of nature, and admitted a ray of hope. About four in the afternoon a circumstance occurred which afforded us some consolation: a shoal of flying fish passed under the raft, and as the extremities left an infinite number of vacancies between the pieces which composed it, the fish got entangled in great numbers. We threw ourselves upon them, and caught a considerable quantity: we took near two hundred and put them in an empty cask; as we caught them we opened them to take out what is called the milt. This food seemed delicious to us; but one man would have wanted a thousand. Our first impulse was to address new thanksgivings to God for this unexpected benefit.

An ounce of gunpowder had been found in the morning, and dried in the sun, during the day, which was very fine; a steel, some gun-flints and tinder were also found in the same parcel. After infinite trouble we succeeded in setting fire to some pieces of dry linen. We made a large hole in one side of an empty cask, and placed at the bottom of it several things which we wetted, and on this kind of scaffolding we made our fire: we placed it on a barrel that the seawater might not put out our fire. We dressed some fish, which we devoured with extreme avidity; but our hunger was so great and our portion of fish so small, that we added to it some human flesh, which dressing rendered less disgusting; it was this which the officers touched, for the first time. From this day we continued to use it; but we could not dress it any more, as we were entirely deprived of the means; our barrel catching fire we extinguished it without being able to save anything whereby to light it again next day. The powder and the tinder were entirely consumed. This repast gave us all fresh strength to bear new fatigues. The night was tolerable, and would have appeared happy had it not been signalised by a new massacre.

Some Spaniards, Italians, and Negroes, who had remained neuter in the first mutiny, and some of whom had even ranged themselves on our side, formed a plot to throw us all into the sea, hoping to execute their design by falling on us by surprise. These wretches suffered themselves to be persuaded by the negroes, who assured them that the coast was extremely near, and promised, that when they were once on shore, they would enable them to traverse Africa without danger. The desire of saving themselves, or perhaps the wish to seize on the money and valuables, which had been put into a bag, hung to the mast, had inflamed the imagination of these unfortunate wretches. We were obliged to take our arms again; but how were we to discover the guilty? they were pointed out to us, by our sailors, who remained faithful, and ranged themselves near us; one of them had refused to engage in the plot. The first signal, for combat, was given by a Spaniard, who, placing himself behind the mast, laid fast hold of it, made the sign of the Cross with one hand, invoking the name of God, and held a knife in the other: the sailors seized him, and threw him into the sea. The servant of an officer of the troops on board was in the plot. He was an Italian from the light artillery of the Ex-King of his country. When he perceived that the plot was discovered, he armed himself with the last boarding-axe that there was on the raft, wrapped himself in a piece of drapery, which he wore folded over his breast, and, of his own accord, threw himself into the sea. The mutineers rushed forward to avenge their comrades, a terrible combat again ensued, and both sides fought with desperate fury. Soon the fatal raft was covered with dead bodies, and flowing with blood which, ought to have been shed in another cause, and by other hands. In this tumult cries, with which we were familiar, were renewed, and we heard the imprecations of the horrid rage which demanded the head of Lieutenant Danglas! Our readers know that we could not satisfy this mad rage, because the victim, demanded, had fled the dangers to which we were exposed; but even if this officer had remained among us, we should most certainly have defended his life at the expense of our own, as we did that of Lieutenant Lozach. But it was not for him that we were reduced to exert, against these madmen, all the courage we possessed.

We again replied to the cries of the assailants, that he whom they demanded was not with us; but we had no more success in persuading them; nothing could make them recollect themselves; we were obliged to continue to combat them, and to oppose force to those over whom reason had lost all its influence. In this confusion the unfortunate woman was, a second time, thrown into the sea. We perceived it, and Mr. Coudin, assisted by some workmen, took her up again, to prolong, for a few moments, her torments and her existence.

In this horrible night, Lavillette gave further proofs of the rarest intrepidity. It was to him, and to some of those who have escaped the consequences of our misfortunes, that we are indebted for our safety. At length, after unheard-of efforts, the mutineers were again repulsed, and tranquillity restored. After we had escaped this new danger, we endeavoured to take some moment's repose. The day at length rose on us for the fifth time. We were now only thirty left; we had lost four or five of our faithful sailors; those who survived were in the most deplorable state; the sea-water had almost entirely excoriated our lower extremities; we were covered with contusions or wounds, which, irritated by the salt-water, made us utter every moment piercing cries; so that there were not above twenty of us who were able to stand upright or walk. Almost our whole stock was exhausted; we had no more wine than was sufficient for four days, and we had not above a dozen fish left. In four days, said we, we shall be in want of everything, and death will be unavoidable. Thus arrived the seventh day since we had been abandoned; we calculated that, in case the boats had not stranded on the coast, they would want, at least, three or four times twenty-four hours to reach St. Louis. Time was further required to equip ships, and for these ships to find us; we resolved to hold out as long as possible. In the course of the day, two soldiers slipped behind the only barrel of wine we had left; they had bored a hole in it, and were drinking by means of a reed; we had all sworn, that he who should employ such means should be punished with death. This law was instantly put in execution, and the two trespassers were thrown into the sea.

This same day terminated the existence of a child, twelve years of age, named Leon; he died away like a lamp which ceases to burn for want of aliment. Everything spoke in favour of this amiable young creature, who merited a better fate. His angelic countenance, his melodious voice, the interest inspired by his youth, which was increased by the courage he had shown, and the services he had performed, for he had already made, in the preceding year, a campaign in the east Indies, all this filled us with the tenderest interest for this young victim, devoted to a death so dreadful and premature. Our old soldiers, and our people in general, bestowed upon him all the care which they thought calculated to prolong his existence. It was in vain; his strength, at last, forsook him. Neither the wine, which we gave him without regret, nor all the means which could be employed, could rescue him from his sad fate; he expired in the arms of Mr. Coudin, who had not ceased to show him the kindest attention. As long as the strength of this young marine had allowed him to move, he ran continually from one side to the other, calling, with loud cries, for his unhappy mother, water, and food. He walked, without discrimination, over the feet and legs of his companions in misfortune, who, in their turn, uttered cries of anguish, which were every moment repeated. But their complaints were very seldom accompanied by menaces; they pardoned everything in the poor youth, who had caused them. Besides, he was, in fact, in a state of mental derangement, and in his uninterrupted alienation he could not be expected to behave, as if he had still retained some use of reason.

We were now only twenty-seven remaining; of this number but fifteen seemed likely to live some days: all the rest, covered with large wounds, had almost entirely lost their reason; yet they had a share in the distribution of provisions, and might, before their death, consume thirty or forty bottles of wine, which were of inestimable value to us. We deliberated thus: to put the sick on half allowance would have been killing them by inches. So after a debate, at which the most dreadful despair presided, it was resolved to throw them into the sea. This measure, however repugnant it was to ourselves, procured the survivors wine for six days;

when the decision was made, who would dare to execute it? The habit of seeing death ready to pounce upon us as his prey, the certainly of our infallible destruction, without this fatal expedient, everything in a word, had hardened our hearts, and rendered them callous to all feeling except that of self preservation. Three sailors and a soldier took on themselves this cruel execution: we turned our faces aside, and wept tears of blood over the fate of these unhappy men. Among them were the unfortunate woman and her husband. Both of them had been severely wounded in the various combats: the woman had a thigh broken between the pieces of wood composing the raft, and her husband had received a deep wound with a sabre on his head. Everything announced their speedy dissolution. We must seek to console ourselves, by the belief, that our cruel resolution shortened, but for a few moments only, the measure of their existence.

This French woman, to whom soldiers and Frenchmen gave the sea for a tomb, had partaken for twenty years in the glorious fatigues of our armies; for twenty years she had afforded to the brave, on the field of battle, either the assistance which they needed, or soothing consolations ... It is in the midst of her friends; it is by the hands of her friends ... Readers, who shudder at the cry of outraged humanity, recollect at least, that it was other men, fellow countrymen, comrades, who had placed us in this horrible situation.

This dreadful expedient saved the fifteen who remained; for, when we were found by the *Argus*, we had very little wine left, and it was the sixth day after the cruel sacrifice which we have just described: the victims, we repeat it, had not above forty-eight hours to live, and by keeping them on the raft, we should absolutely have been destitute of the means of existence two days before we were found. Weak as we were, we considered it as certain that it would have been impossible for us to hold out, even twenty-four hours, without taking some food. After this catastrophe, which inspired us with a degree of horror not to be overcome, we threw the arms into the sea; we reserved, however, one sabre in case it should be wanted to cut a rope or piece of wood.

After all this, we had scarcely sufficient food on the raft, to last for the six days, and they were the most wretched imaginable. Our dispositions had become soured: even in sleep, we figured to ourselves the sad end of all our unhappy companions, and we loudly invoked death.

A new event, for everything was an event for wretches for whom the universe was reduced to a flooring of a few *toises* in extent, who were the sport of the winds and waves, as they hung suspended over the abyss; an event then happened which happily diverted our attention from the horrors of our situation. All at once a white butterfly, of the species so common in France, appeared fluttering over our heads, and settled on our sail. The first idea which, as it were, inspired each of us made us consider this little animal as the harbinger, which brought us the news of a speedy approach to land, and we snatched at this hope with a kind of delirium of joy. But it was the ninth day that we passed upon the raft; the torments of hunger consumed our entrails; already some of the soldiers and sailors devoured, with haggard eyes, this wretched prey, and seemed ready to dispute it with each other. Others considered this butterfly as a messenger of heaven, declared that they took the poor insect under their protection, and hindered any injury being done to it. We turned our wishes and our eyes towards the land, which we so ardently longed for, and which we every moment fancied we saw rise before us. It is certain that we could not be far from it: for the butterflies continued, on the following days, to come and flutter about our sail, and the same day we had another sign equally positive: for we saw a seagull flying over our raft. This second visitor did not allow us to doubt of our being very near to the African shore, and we persuaded ourselves that we should soon be thrown upon the coast by the force of the currents. How often did we then, and in the following days, invoke a tempest to throw us on the coast, which, it seemed to us, we were on the point of touching.

The hope which had just penetrated the inmost recesses of our souls, revived our enfeebled strength, and inspired us with an ardour, an activity, of which we should not have thought ourselves capable. We again had recourse to all the means which we had before employed, to catch fish. Above all, we eagerly longed for the seagull, which appeared several times tempted to settle on the end of our machine. The impatience of our desire increased, when we saw several of its companions join it, and keep following us till our deliverance; but all attempts to draw them to us were in vain; not one of them suffered itself to be taken by the snares we had laid for them. Thus our destiny, on the fatal raft, was to be incessantly tossed between transitory illusions and continued torments, and we never experienced an agreeable sensation without being, in a manner, condemned to atone for it, by the anguish of some new suffering, by the irritating pangs of hope always deceived.

Another care employed us this day; as soon as we were reduced to a small number, we collected the little strength we had remaining; we loosened some planks on the front of the raft, and with some pretty long pieces of wood, raised in the centre a kind of platform, on which we reposed: all the effects which we had been able to collect, were placed upon it, and served to render it less hard; besides, they hindered the sea from passing with so much facility through the intervals between the different pieces of the raft; but the waves came across, and sometimes covered us entirely.

It was on this new theatre that we resolved to await death in a manner worthy of Frenchmen, and with perfect resignation. The most adroit among us, to divert our thoughts, and to make the time pass with more rapidity, got their comrades to relate to us their passed triumphs, and sometimes, to draw comparisons between the hardships they had undergone in their glorious campaigns, and the distresses we endured upon our raft. The following is what Lavillette the sergeant of artillery told us:

"I have experienced, in my various naval campaigns, all the fatigues, all the privations and all the dangers, which it is possible to meet with at sea, but none of my past sufferings, is comparable to the extreme pain and privations which I endure here. In my last campaigns in 1813 and 1814, in Germany and France, I shared all the fatigues which were alternately caused us by victory and retreat, I was at the glorious days of Lutzen, Bautzen, Dresden, Leipzig, Hanau, Montmirail, Champaubert, Montereau.... Yes, all that I suffered in so many forced marches, and in the midst of the privations which were the consequences of them, was nothing in comparison with what I endure on this frightful machine. In those days, when the French valour showed itself in all its lustre, and always worthy of a free people, I had hardly anything to fear, but during the battle; but here, I often have the same dangers, and what is more dreadful, I have to combat Frenchmen and comrades. I have to contend, besides, with hunger and thirst, with a tempestuous sea, full of dangerous monsters, and with the ardour of a burning sun, which is not the least of our enemies. Covered with ancient scars and fresh wounds, which I have no means of dressing, it is physically impossible for me to save myself from this extreme danger, if it should be prolonged for a few days."

The sad remembrance of the critical situation of our country also mingled with our grief; and certainly, of all the afflictions we experienced, this was not the least, to us, who had almost all of us left it, only that we might no longer be witnesses of the hard laws, of the afflicting dependence, under which, it is bowed down by enemies jealous of our glory and of our power. These thoughts, we do not fear to say so, and to boast of it, afflicted us still more than the inevitable death which we were almost certain of meeting on our raft. Several of us regretted not having fallen in the defence of France. At least, said they, if it had been possible for us to measure our strength once more, with the enemies of our independence, and our liberty! Others found some consolation in the death which awaited us, because we should no longer have to groan under the shameful yoke which oppresses the country. Thus passed the last days of our abode on the raft. Our time was almost wholly employed in speaking of our unhappy country: all our wishes, our last prayers were for the happiness of France.

CHAPTER 6

Miraculously Saved

During the first days and nights of our being abandoned, the weather was very cold, but we bore the immersion pretty well; and during the last nights that we passed on the raft, every time that a wave rolled over us, it produced a very disagreeable sensation, and made us utter plaintive cries, so that each of us employed means to avoid it: some raised their heads, by means of pieces of wood, and made with whatever they could find a kind of parapet, against which the wave broke: others sheltered themselves behind empty casks which were placed across, alongside each other; but these means often proved insufficient; it was only when the sea was very calm that it did not break over us.

A raging thirst, which was redoubled in the daytime by the beams of a burning sun, consumed us: it was such, that we eagerly moistened our parched lips with urine, which we cooled in little tin cups. We put the cup in a place where there was a little water, that the urine might cool the sooner; it often happened that these cups were stolen from those who had thus prepared them. The cup was returned, indeed, to him to whom it belonged, but not till the liquid which it contained was drank. Mr. Savigny observed that the urine of sum of us was more agreeable than that of others. There was a passenger who could never prevail on himself to swallow it: in reality, it had not a disagreeable taste; but in some of us it became thick, and extraordinarily acrid: it produced an effect truly worthy of remark: namely, that it was scarcely swallowed, when it excited an inclination to urine anew. We also tried to quench our thirst by drinking sea-water. Mr. Griffon, the governor's secretary, used it continually, he drank ten or twelve glasses in succession. But all these means only diminished our thirst to render it more severe a moment afterwards.

An officer of the army, found by chance, a little lemon, and it may be imagined how valuable this fruit must be to him; he, in fact, reserved it entirely for himself; his comrades, notwithstanding the most pressing entreaties, could not obtain any of it; already emotions of rage were rising in every heart, and if he had not partly yielded to those who surrounded him, they would certainly have taken it from him by force, and he would have perished, the victim of his selfishness. We also disputed for about thirty cloves of garlic, which had been found accidentally in a little bag: all these disputes were generally accompanied with violent threats, and if they had been protracted we should, perhaps, have come to the last extremities.

We had found, also, two little phials which contained a spirituous liquor to clean the teeth; he who possessed them, kept them carefully, and made many difficulties to give one or two drops of this liquid in the hollow of the hand. This liquor, which we believe was an essence of guaiacum, cinnamon, cloves, and other aromatic substances, produced on our tongues a delightful sensation, and removed for a few moments the thirst which consumed us. Some of us found pieces of pewter, which, being put into the mouth produced a kind of coolness.

One of the means generally employed, was to put some sea-water into a hat, with which we washed our faces for some time, recurring to it at intervals; we also moistened our hair with it, and held our hands plunged in the water. Misfortune rendered us ingenious, and everyone thought of a thousand means to alleviate his sufferings; extenuated by the most cruel privations, the smallest agreeable sensation was to us a supreme happiness; thus we eagerly sought a little empty phial, which one of us possessed, and which had formerly contained essence of roses: as soon as we could get hold of it we inhaled, with delight, the perfume which issued from it, and which communicated to our senses the most soothing impressions. Some of us reserved our portion of wine in little tin cups, and sucked up the wine with a quill; this manner of taking it was very beneficial to us, and quenched our thirst much more than if we had drunk it off at once. Even the smell of this liquor was extremely agreeable to us. Mr. Savigny observed that many of us, after having taken their small portion, fell into a state approaching to intoxication, and that there was always more discord among us after the distribution had been made.

The following is one instance, among many, which we could adduce. The tenth day of our being on the raft, after a distribution of wine, Messrs. Clairet, Coudin, Charlot, and one or two of our sailors, conceived the strange idea of destroying themselves, first intoxicating themselves with what remained in our barrel. In vain Captain Dupont, seconded by Messrs. Lavillette, Savigny, Lheureux, and all the others, opposed their purpose by urgent remonstrances, and by all the firmness of which they were capable—their disordered brains persisted in the mad idea which governed them, and a new combat was on the point of commencing; however, after infinite trouble, we were beginning to bring back Messrs. Clairet and Coudin to the use of their reason; or rather he who watched over us dispelled this fatal quarrel, by turning our attention to the new danger which threatened us, at the moment when cruel discord was, perhaps, about to break out among wretches already a prey to so many other evils—it was a number of sharks which came and surrounded our raft. They approached so near, that we were able to strike them with our sabre, but we could not subdue one of them, notwithstanding the goodness of the weapon we possessed, and the ardour with which the brave Lavillette made use of it. The blows which he struck these monsters, made them replunge into the sea; but a few seconds after, they re-appeared upon the surface, and did not seem at all alarmed at our presence. Their backs rose about 30 centimetres above the water: several of them appeared to us to be at least 10 metres in length.

Three days passed in inexpressible anguish; we despised life to such a degree that many of us did not fear to bathe in sight of the sharks which surrounded our raft; others placed themselves naked on the front part of our machine which was still submerged: these means diminished, a little, their burning thirst. A kind of *polypus* (*mollusques*), known by seamen under the name of *galere*, was frequently driven in great numbers on our raft, and when their long arms clung to our naked bodies, they caused us the most cruel sufferings. Will it be believed, that amidst these dreadful scenes, struggling with inevitable death, some of us indulged in pleasantries which excited a smile, notwithstanding the horror of our situation? One, among others said, joking, "If the brig is sent to look for us, let us pray to God that she may have the eyes of *Argus*," alluding to the name of the vessel, which we presumed would be sent after us. This consolatory idea did not quit us an instant, and we spoke of it frequently.

During the day of the 16th, reckoning ourselves to be very near land, eight of the most determined of us, resolved to try to reach the coast: we unfastened a strong fish of a mast, which made part of the little parapet of which we have spoken, we fixed boards to it at intervals, transversely, by means of great nails, to hinder it from upsetting; a little mast and sail were fixed in the front; we intended to provide ourselves with oars made of barrel staves, cut out with the only sabre we had remaining: we cut pieces of rope, we split them, and made smaller ropes, that were more easy to manage: a hammock cloth, which was by chance on the raft, served for a sail; the dimensions of which, might be about 130 centimetres in breadth and 160 in length: the transverse diameter of the fish was 60 or 70 centimetres, and its length about 12 metres. A certain portion of wine was assigned to us, and our departure fixed for the next day, the 17th. When our machine was finished, it remained to make a trial of it: a sailor wanting to pass from the front to the back of it, finding the mast in his way, set his foot on one of the cross boards; the weight of his body made it upset, and this accident proved to us the temerity of our enterprise. It was then resolved that we should all await death in our present situation; the cable winch fastened the machine to our raft, was made loose, and it drifted away. It is very certain that if we had ventured upon this second raft, weak as we were, we should not have been able to hold out six hours, with our legs in the water, and thus obliged continually to row.

Mean time the night came, and its gloomy shades revived in our minds the most afflicting thoughts; we were convinced that there were not above twelve or fifteen bottles of wine left in our barrel. We began to feel an invincible disgust at the flesh which had till then, scarcely supported us; and we may say that the sight of it inspired us with a sentiment of terror, which was doubtless produced by the idea of approaching destruction.

On the 17th, in the morning, the sun appeared entirely free from clouds; after having put up our prayers to the Almighty, we divided among us, a part of our wine; everyone was taking with delight his small portion, when a captain of infantry looking towards the horizon, descried a ship, and announced it to us by an exclamation of joy: we perceived that it was a brig; but it was at a very great distance; we could distinguish only the tops of the masts. The sight of this vessel excited in us a transport of joy which it would be difficult to describe; each of us believed his deliverance certain, and we gave a thousand thanks to God; yet, fears mingled with our hopes: we straitened some hoops of casks, to the end of which we tied handkerchiefs of different colours. A man, assisted by us all together, mounted to the top of the mast and waved these little flags.

For above half an hour, we were suspended between hope and fear; some thought they saw the ship become larger, and others affirmed that its course carried it from us: these latter were the only ones whose eyes were not fascinated by hope, for the brig disappeared. From the delirium of joy, we fell into profound despondency and grief; we envied the fate of those whom we had seen perish at our side, and we said to ourselves, when we shall be destitute of everything, and our strength begins to forsake us, we will wrap ourselves up as well as we can, we will lay ourselves down on this platform, the scene of so many sufferings, and there we will await death with resignation. At last, to calm our despair, we wished to seek some consolation in the arms of sleep; the day before we had been consumed by the fire of a burning sun; this day, to avoid the fierceness of his beams, we made a tent with the sails of the frigate: as soon as it was put up, we all lay down under it, so that we could not perceive what was passing around us. We then proposed to inscribe upon a board an account of our adventures, to write all our names at the bottom of the narrative, and to fasten it to the upper part of the mast, in the hope that it would reach the government and our families.

After we had passed two hours, absorbed in the most cruel reflections, the master gunner of the frigate wishing to go to the front of the raft, went out of our tent; scarcely had he put his head out, when he turned towards us, uttering a loud cry; joy was painted on his countenance, his hands were stretched towards the sea, he scarcely breathed: all that he could say, was, "Saved! see the brig close upon us."

And in fact, it was, at the most, half a league distant, carrying a press of sail, and steering so as to come extremely close to us; we precipitately left the tent: even those whom enormous wounds, in the lower extremities, had confined for some days past, always to lie down, crawled to the back part of the raft, to enjoy the sight of this vessel, which was coming to deliver us from certain death. We all embraced each other with transports that looked like delirium, and tears of joy rolled down our cheeks, shrunk by the most cruel privations. Every one seized handkerchiefs, or pieces of linen to make signals to the brig, which was approaching rapidly. Others prostrating themselves, fervently thanked Providence for our miraculous preservation. Our joy redoubled when we perceived a great white flag at the foremast head, and we exclaimed "It is then to Frenchmen that we shall owe our deliverance." We almost immediately recognised the brig to be the *Argus*: it was then within two musket shot: we were extremely impatient to see her clue up her sails; she lowered them at length, and fresh cries of joy rose from our raft. The *Argus* came and lay-to on our starboard, within half a pistol shot. The crew, ranged on the deck and in the shrouds, showed, by waving their hats and handkerchiefs, the pleasure they felt at coming to the assistance of their unhappy countrymen. A boat was immediately hoisted out; an officer belonging to the brig, whose name was Mr. Lemaigre, had embarked in it, in order to have the pleasure of taking us himself from this fatal machine. This officer, full of humanity and zeal, acquitted himself of his mission in the kindest manner, and took himself, those that were the weakest, to convey them into the boat. After all the others were placed in it, Mr. Lemaigre came and took in his arms Mr. Correard, whose health was the worst, and who was the most excoriated: he placed him at his side in the boat, bestowed on him all imaginable cares, and spoke to him in the most consoling terms.

In a short time we were all removed on board the *Argus*, where we met with the lieutenant of the frigate, and some others of those who had been shipwrecked. Pity was painted on every face, and compassion drew tears from all who cast their eyes on us.

Let the reader imagine fifteen unfortunate men, almost naked; their bodies and faces disfigured by the scorching beams of the sun; ten of the fifteen were hardly able to move; our limbs were excoriated, our sufferings were deeply imprinted on our features, our eyes were hollow, and almost wild, and our long beards rendered our appearance still more frightful; we were but the shadows of ourselves. We found on board the brig some very good broth, which had been got ready; as soon as they perceived us, they added some excellent wine to it; thus they restored our almost exhausted strength; they bestowed on us the most generous care and attention; our wounds were dressed, and the next day several of our sick began to recover; however, some of us had a great deal to suffer; for they were placed between decks, very near the kitchen, which augmented the almost insupportable heat of these countries; the want of room in a small vessel, was the cause of this inconvenience. The number of the shipwrecked was indeed too great. Those who did not belong to the marine, were laid upon cables, wrapped in some flags, and placed under the kitchen fire, which exposed them to perish in the night; fire having broken out between decks, about ten o'clock, which had like to have reduced the vessel to ashes; but timely assistance was afforded, and we were saved for the second time. We had scarcely escaped when some of us again become delirious: an officer of the army wanted to throw himself into the sea, to go and look for his pocket book; which he would have done had he not been prevented; others were seized in a manner equally striking.

The commander and officers of the brig were eager to serve us, and kindly anticipated our wants. They had just snatched us from death, by rescuing us from our raft; their reiterated care rekindled in us the flame of life. Mr. Renaud, the surgeon, distinguished himself by indefatigable zeal; he passed the whole day in dressing our wounds; and during the two days that we remained on board the brig, he exerted all the resources of his art, with a degree of attention and gentleness which merit our eternal gratitude.

It was, in truth, time that our sufferings should have an end: they had already lasted thirteen days; the strongest among us might, at the most, have lived forty-eight hours more. Mr. Correard, felt that he must die in the course of the day; yet he had a foreboding that we should be saved; he said that a series of events so extraordinary was not destined to be buried in oblivion: that providence would preserve some of us at least, to present to mankind the affecting picture of our unhappy adventures.

Through how many terrible trials have we past! Where are the men who can say that they have been more unfortunate than we have?

The manner in which we were saved is truly miraculous: the finger of heaven is conspicuous in this event.

Chapter 7

Senegal at Last

The *Argus* had been dispatched, from Senegal, to assist the shipwrecked people belonging to the boats, and to look for the raft; for several days it sailed along the coast without meeting us, and gave provisions to the people from the boats who were crossing the great desert of Zaara; the captain, thinking that it would be useless to look for our raft any longer, steered his course towards the harbour from which he had been dispatched, in order to announce that his search had been fruitless; it was when he was running towards Senegal that we perceived him. In the morning he was not above forty leagues from the mouth of the river, when the wind veered to the south west; the captain, as by a kind of inspiration, said that they ought to go about, the winds blew towards the frigate; after they had run two hours on this tack, the man at the mast head, announced a vessel: when the brig was nearer to us, by the aid of glasses, they perceived that it was our raft. When we were taken up by the *Argus*, we asked this question: Gentlemen have you been long looking for us? We were answered yes; but that, however, the captain had not received any positive orders on the subject; and that we were indebted to chance alone, for the good fortune of having been met with. We repeat with pleasure the expression of Mr. Parnajon, addressed to one of us.

"If they were to give me the rank of captain of a frigate, I should feel a less lively pleasure, than that which I experienced when I met your raft."

Some persons said to us without reserve, "We thought you were all dead a week ago."

We say that the commander of the brig had not received positive orders to look for us. The following were his instructions:

"Mr. de Parnajon, commanding the brig *Argus*, will proceed to the side of the desert with his vessel, will employ every means to assist the shipwrecked persons, who must have reached the coast; and will supply them with such provisions and ammunition as they may want; after having assured himself of the fate of these unfortunate persons, he will endeavour to continue his course to the *Medusa*, to see whether the currents have carried the raft towards her."

This is all that was said of our wretched machine. It is very certain, that, at the Island of St. Louis, we were given up; our friends believed we had perished: this is so true, that some, who were going to send letters to Europe, wrote that one hundred and fifty unfortunate people had been placed on a raft, and that it was impossible they should have escaped. It will not, perhaps, be out of place, to mention here a conversation which took place respecting us. In a pretty large company, some persons said:

"It is a pity that the raft was abandoned; for there were many brave fellows on board; but their sufferings are over; they are happier than we, for who knows how all this will end."

In short, as we were now found, the frigate steered again for Senegal, and the next day we saw the land, for which we had been longing for thirteen days: we cast anchor in the evening off the coast, and in the morning, the winds being favourable, we directed our course to the road of St. Louis, where we cast anchor on the 19th of July, about three o'clock in the afternoon.

Such is the faithful history of one hundred and fifty persons, who were left upon the raft; only fifteen of whom were saved; and five of that number were so reduced, that they died of fatigue, shortly after arriving at St. Louis; those who still exist are covered with scars, and the cruel sufferings which they have endured have greatly impaired their constitution.

In terminating this recital of the unparalleled sufferings, to which we were a prey for thirteen days, we beg leave to name those who shared them with us:

Alive when we were saved		Notice of their fate
Dupont	captain of foot	In Senegal
L'Heureux	lieutenant	In Senegal
Lozach	sub-lieutenant	Dead
Clairet	sub-lieutenant	Dead
Griffon du Bellay	ex-clerk of the navy	Out of employment
Coudin	*eleve de marine*	Midshipman
Charlot	sergeant major	In Senegal
Courtade	master gunner	Dead
Lavillette		In France
Coste	sailor	In France
Thomas	pilot	In France
Francois	hospital keeper	In the Indies
Jean Charles	black soldier	Dead
Correard	engineer geographer	Without employment
Savigny	surgeon	Resigned

The governor having been apprised of our arrival, sent a large-decked vessel to convey us ashore. This vessel also brought us wine and some refreshments; the master, thinking the tide sufficiently high to enable him to pass the bar of sand, which lies at the mouth of the river, resolved to land us at once upon the island. Those who were the most feeble among us, were placed below deck, together with a few of the least skilful of the negroes, who composed the crew, and the hatches closed upon us, to prevent the sea from coming in between decks, while the dangers occasioned by the surf running over the bar, was passed. The wretched condition to which we were reduced, was such as to awaken a feeling of sympathy, even among the blacks, who shed tears of compassion for our misfortunes; during this time, the most profound silence reigned on board; the voice of the master alone was heard; as soon as we were out of danger, the negroes recommenced their songs, which did not cease till we arrived at St. Louis.

We were received in the most brilliant manner; the governor, several officers, both English and French, came to meet us, and one of the officers in this numerous train, held out to us a hand, which a fortnight before, had, as it were, plunged us in the depth of despair by loosening the tow-rope which made our raft fast to the boat. But such is the effect produced by the sight of wretches who have just been miraculously delivered, that there was not a single person, either English or French, who did not shed tears of compassion on seeing the deplorable condition to which we were reduced; all seemed truly affected by our distress, and by the intrepidity which we had shown on the raft. Yet we could not contain our indignation, at the sight of some persons in this train.

Some of us were received by two French merchants, who bestowed on us every attention, and rendered every assistance in their power. Messrs. Valentin and Lasalle stimulated by that natural impulse which incites man to assist a fellow creature in distress, is, on that account, entitled to the highest praise. We are extremely sorry to say that they were the only colonists who gave assistance to the shipwrecked people belonging to the raft.

Before we proceed to the second part of our work, in which we shall include the history of the Camp of Daccard and of the unfortunate persons shipwrecked in the *Medusa*, who remained in the hospitals of St. Louis, let us cast our eyes back, and examine what were the operations of the boats after the tow-lines had been loosened, and the raft abandoned.

The long-boat was the last which we lost sight of. It descried the land and the Isles of Arguin, the same evening before sun-set: the other boats must, therefore, necessarily, have seen it sometime before, which proves, we think, that when we were abandoned, we were at a very small distance from the coast. Two boats succeeded in reaching Senegal without accident; they were those in; which were the governor and the commander of the frigate. During the bad weather, which forced the other boats to make the land, these two had a great deal of difficulty to resist a heavy sea and an extremely high wind. Two young seamen gave proofs of courage and coolness in these critical moments, in the barge. Mr. Barbotin, *eleve* of the marine: and in the captain's barge, Mr. Rang, also an *eleve* of the marine, as deserving of praise for his knowledge, as for the courage he displayed on this occasion; both of them, as long as the bad weather lasted, remained at the helm, and guided the boats. One Thomas, steersman, and one Lange, the boatswain's mate, also showed great courage, and all the experience of old seamen. These two boats, reached the *Echo* corvette, on the 9th, at 10 o'clock in the evening, which had been at anchor for some days, in the road of St. Louis. A council was held, and the most prompt and certain measures adopted to assist those who were left on board the boats and the raft.

The *Argus* brig was appointed for this mission. The commander of this vessel, burning with eagerness to fly to the assistance of his unfortunate countrymen, wanted to set sail that very moment; but causes, respecting which we shall be silent, fettered his zeal; however, this distinguished officer executed the orders which he received with uncommon activity.

Let us return to the history of the four other boats; and first, that of the principal, which was the long-boat. As soon as it descried the land, it tacked and stood out in the open sea; because it was on the shallows, and it would have been imprudent to pass the night in one metre, or one metre 30 centimetres of water; it had already grounded two or three times. On the 6th, about four o'clock in the morning, finding itself too far from the coast, and the sea very hollow, it tacked, and in a few hours saw the coast for the second time. At eight o'clock, they were extremely near, and the men ardently desiring to get on shore, sixty-three of the most resolute were landed; arms were given them, and as much biscuit as could be spared; they set out in search of Senegal, following the sea-coast. This landing was effected to the north of Cape Meric, eighty or ninety leagues from the Isle of St. Louis. This vessel then stood out to sea. We will leave, for the present, these sixty-three poor people who have been landed on the sands of Cape Meric; and shall return to them in the sequel.

CHAPTER 8

Misfortunes of Other Vessels

We will now proceed to describe the motions and fate of the other vessels. At noon, after having proceeded some miles, the long-boat saw the other vessels, and endeavoured to fall in with them; but everyone distrusted the other: the long-boat did its utmost to rally them; but they employed all the means they could to avoid the meeting; even the officers assisted in working them, because some persons had asserted that the crew of the long-boat had mutinied, and had even threatened to fire on the other boats. The long-boat, on the other hand, which had just landed a part of its people, advanced to inform the other boats that it was able to relieve them, in case they were too much loaded. The captain's boat and the *pirogue*, were the only ones that came within hail: at five o'clock in the afternoon the sea became hollow, and the wind very high, when the *pirogue*, unable to hold out against it, asked the assistance of the long-boat, which tacked and took on board the fifteen persons which that frail boat contained. At two o'clock in the afternoon, of the 8th, the men, tormented by a burning thirst, and a violent hunger which they could not appease, obliged the officer, by their reiterated importunities, to make the land, which was done the same evening. His intention was to proceed to Senegal: he would doubtless have succeeded; but the cries of the soldiers and sailors, who murmured loudly, induced the measure that was taken, and the crew landed about forty leagues from the Island of St. Louis. The great-boat, which had approached very near the coast, and had not been able to resist the violence of the weather, being besides, destitute of provisions, had also been obliged to make the land on the 8th: the first, at five in the afternoon; the second, at eleven in the morning. The officers joined their crews, ranged them in order, and proceeded towards Senegal; but they were in distress, destitute of resources of every kind: without a guide, on a coast inhabited by barbarians: hunger and thirst cruelly tormented them; the beams of a scorching sun, reflected from the immense sandy plains, aggravated their sufferings. In the day, oppressed by excessive heat, they could scarcely move a step: it was only in the cool of the morning and the evening, that they could pursue their painful march. Having, after infinite pains, crossed the downs, they met with vast plains, where they had the good fortune to find water, by digging holes in the sand: this refreshing beverage gave them fresh life and hope.

This manner of procuring water is mentioned by many travellers, and practised in various countries. All along the coasts of Senegambia, and for some distance in land, they find, by digging in the sand to the depth of five or six feet, a white and brackish water, which is exclusively used in these countries, both for the ordinary beverage and domestic purposes; the water of the Senegal, may, however, be used at St. Louis at the time of the rise or inundation.

The Moors have signs, which they have agreed upon among themselves, to inform each other at a distance when they have found water. As the sands of the desert lie in undulations, and the surface of these plains has the appearance of a sea, broken in large waves, which, by some sudden enchantment, had been fixed and suspended before they could fall back; it is on the ridges of these motionless waves, that the Moors in general travel, unless they run in a direction too different from that of their intended route, in which case they are obliged to traverse them; but besides, as these ridges themselves are not always ranged parallel to each other, but frequently cross each other, the Moors always have some of their party before, to serve as guides, and to point out by signs with their hands, at every crossing, on which side they ought to go; and also everything which prudence requires they should know beforehand, as well as the water, or rather the moisture and verdure which are to be perceived. In general, these people who approach the sea-coast during the winds and hurricanes of the summer solstice, rarely keep on the breach properly so called, because they and their cattle are too much tormented by myriads of flies which never quit the sea-coast. In this same season the appearance of the gnats, or mosquitoes, induces them to remove from the Senegal, for their cattle being incessantly stung by these animals, become mad and sick.

Our people met with some of these Moors, and in some measure forced them to serve as guides; after continuing their march along the sea-coast, they perceived on the morning of the 11th, the *Argus* brig, which was cruising to assist those who had landed; as soon as the brig perceived them, it approached very near to the coast, lay-to, and sent a boat on shore with biscuit and wine.

On the 11th, in the evening, they met with more of the natives, and an Irish captain of a merchant ship, who, of his own accord, had come from St. Louis with the intention of assisting the sufferers: he spoke the language of the country, and had put on the same dress as the Moors. We are sorry that we cannot recollect the name of this foreign officer, which we should take particular pleasure in publishing; but since time has effaced it from our memory, we will at least publish his zeal and noble efforts, which are an unquestionable title to the gratitude of every man of feeling. At last, after the most cruel sufferings and privations, the unfortunate men who composed the crews of the great-boat, and of that which we called the Senegal boat, twenty-five men from the long-boat, and fifteen persons from the *pirogue*, arrived at Saint Louis, on the 13th of July, at seven o'clock in the evening, after having wandered above five whole days, in the midst of these frightful deserts, which on all sides presented to their eyes only the most profound solitude, and the prospect of inevitable destruction.

During their progress, they had to struggle with the most dreadful extremes of hunger and thirst; the latter was such, that the first time that several of them discovered water in the desert, such selfishness was manifested that those who had found these beneficent springs, knelt down four or five together, near the hole which they had just dug, and there, with their eyes fixed on the water, made signs to their comrades not to approach them; that they had found the springs, and that they alone had a right to drink at them; it was not till after the most urgent supplications that they granted a little water to their wretched companions, who were consumed by a raging thirst. When they met with any Moors, they obtained some assistance from them; but these barbarians carried their inhumanity so far as to refuse to show them the springs which are scattered along the shore: sordid avarice made them act in this manner to these unhappy people; for when the latter had passed a well, the Moors drew water from it, which they sold to them at a gourd for a glass; they exacted the same price for a small handful of millet. When the brig approached the coast, to assist these unfortunate men, a great many of the natives of the country immediately crowned the heights; their number was so great, that it caused some fear in the French, who immediately formed, in order of battle, under the command of a captain of infantry. Two officers went to ask the chiefs of the Moors what were their intentions? whether they desired peace or war? They gave the officers to understand that far from wishing to act as enemies, they were willing to afford the shipwrecked people all the assistance in their power; but these barbarians showed, on all occasions, a perfidiousness which is peculiar to the inhabitants of these climates; when the brig had sent biscuit on shore, they seized the half of it, and a few moments after, sold it at an exorbitant price, to those from whom they had stolen it. If they met with any soldiers or sailors who had had the imprudence to stray from the main body, they stripped them entirely, and then ill treated them; it was only numbers united, which, inspiring them with fear, that did not receive any insult from them; besides, there exists between the chiefs of these tribes and the government of the Isle of St. Louis, a treaty, in which it is stipulated that a large reward shall be given to the Moors, who meet in the desert with persons that have been shipwrecked, and bring them to the European factory: these barbarians were therefore induced by their interest, and if they brought back those who went astray, it was only in hope of obtaining a reward.

The women and young children inspired the greatest pity. These feeble beings could not put their delicate feet on the burning sands, and were besides incapable of walking for any length of time. The officers themselves assisted the children, and carried them in turn: their example induced others to imitate them; but having met with some Moors, who never travel in these deserts without having their camels and their asses with them, all that were not able to walk, mounted these animals: to obtain this indulgence, it was necessary to pay two gourds for a day; so that it was impossible for Mr. Picard, who had a numerous family, to bear so great an expense: his respectable young ladies were therefore obliged to walk.

One day at noon, which was the hour for halting, the eldest of these young ladies, exhausted with fatigue, withdrew to a solitary place to take some moments rest. She fell asleep upon the beach; to guard herself from the mosquitoes, she had covered her breast and face with a large shawl. While everybody was sleeping, one of the Moors who served as guides, either from curiosity, or some other motive, approached her softly, attentively examined her appearance, and not content with this, lifting up the shawl, looked at her with fixed eyes, remained for a few moments like one profoundly astonished, approached her then very near, but did not venture to touch her. After having looked at her for some time, he let fall the veil, and returned to his place, where he joyfully related to his comrades what he had just seen. Several Frenchmen who had perceived the Moor, informed Mr. Picard, who resolved, on the obliging offers of the officers, to dress these ladies in a military dress, which, for the future, prevented all attempts of the inhabitants of the desert.

Before they arrived at the Senegal, the Irish officer, of whom we have already spoken, bought an ox: it was immediately killed;

they collected such combustibles as they could find, and when the animal was divided into as many portions as there were persons, each fixed his portion to the end of his sabre or bayonet, and thus they prepared a repast which they found delicious.

During the whole time they remained in the desert, biscuit, wine and brandy, in very small quantities, had been their principal nourishment; sometimes they procured by money, from the Moors, milk and millet; but what most distressed them was, that in the midst of these sandy plains, it was absolutely impossible for them to shelter themselves from the rays of a burning sun, which inflames the atmosphere of these desert regions. Scorched by insupportable heat, almost destitute of the first necessaries of life, some of them partly lost their senses; a spirit of mutiny even showed itself for some moments, and two officers, whose conduct is, however, irreproachable, were marked as the first victims: happily they did not proceed to open violence. Many of those who crossed the desert, have assured us that there were moments when they were quite beside themselves.

An officer of the army in particular, gave signs of the most violent despair; he rolled himself in the sand, begging his comrades to kill him, because he could no longer bear up against so many sufferings. They succeeded in calming him; he arrived at St. Louis with the caravan.

The sixty-three who embarked near the Moles of Angel, had a longer series of fatigue to endure: they had to go between eighty and ninety leagues, in the immense desert of Zaara. After their landing, they had to cross downs that were extremely elevated, in order to reach the plain, in which they had the good fortune to meet with a vast pond of fresh water, where they quenched their thirst, and near which they lay down to rest. Having met with some Moors, they took them for guides, and after long marches, and the most cruel privations, they arrived at the Senegal, on the 23rd of July, in the evening. Some of them perished for want: among this number was an unhappy gardener, and the wife of a soldier: this poor woman, exhausted with fatigue, told her husband to abandon her, for, that it was impossible for her to proceed; the soldier in despair, said to her in a rage: "well, since you cannot walk, to hinder you from being devoured alive by wild beasts, or carried into captivity among the Moors, I will run you through the body with my sabre;" he did not execute this threat, which he had probably conceived in a moment of despair; but the poor woman fell, and died under the most cruel sufferings.

Some persons having strayed from the main body, were taken by the natives of the country, and carried into the camp of the Moors; an officer remained above a month with them, and was afterwards brought to the Isle of St. Louis. The naturalist, Kummer, and Mr. Rogery, having separated from the troops, were forced to wander from one horde to another, and were at last conducted to Senegal. Their story, which we are now going to give, will complete the narrative of the adventures of our shipwrecked companions who traversed the desert.

After the stranding of the long-boat, Mr. Kummer quitted the caravan, formed by the persons wrecked, and proceeded in an easterly direction, in the hope of meeting with some Moors, who would give him food, to appease the hunger and thirst which he had endured for two days. Shortly after his departure, Mr. Rogery took the same resolution as our naturalist, and followed a route parallel to that taken by Mr. Kummer. This latter walked the whole day without meeting with anybody; towards the evening he perceived, at a distance, some fires on the heights which generally lie round the ponds. This sight filled him with joy, and with hopes of meeting, at length, with some Moors who would conduct him to the Isle of St. Louis, and give him food of which he was much in need; he advanced with a firm and rapid step, went up to the Moors, who were under their tents, with much assurance, pronouncing as well as he could, a few words in Arabic, in which language he had taken some lessons while in France, and which he accompanied with profound salutations: "Receive," said he, "in your tents, the son of an unfortunate Mahometan woman, whom I am going to join in Upper Egypt; a shipwreck has thrown me on your coast, and I come in the name of the great prophet, to ask you for hospitality and assistance." At the name of the great prophet, Mr. Kummer bowed his face to the earth, and made the customary salutation: the Moors did the same, and doubted not but that they saw, before them, a follower of Mahomet.

They received him with joy, asked him to enter their tents, and to give a short account of his adventures. Milk, and flour of millet, were given him, and this food revived his strength. Then the Moors made him promise to conduct them to the place where the long-boat had stranded; they hoped to get possessions of the numerous effects, which they supposed the persons shipwrecked to have abandoned on the shore. Having made this promise, Mr. Kummer went to examine the tents, and the flocks of the chief of this tribe who conducted him himself, and boasted of his wealth and his dignity: he told him that he was the Prince Fune Fahdime Muhammed, son of Liralie Zaide, King of the Moors, called Trazas, and that, when he returned from the sea coast, he would take him to the King, his father, and that he would see there, his numerous slaves, and his innumerable flocks. While they were walking about the camp, Prince Muhammed perceived that Mr. Kummer had a watch: he desired to see it; of course, he could not refuse to show it; the prince took it, and told Mr. Kummer that he would return it him when they should arrive at Andar, which promise he punctually performed. They arrived at last at the head of the flock, and our naturalist was astonished at the extraordinary care which these people take of their beasts. The horses and camels were in a separate place, and the whole flock was on the border of a large salt pond; behind them, the slaves had formed a line of fires of great extent, to drive away the mosquitoes and other insects, which torment these animals: they were all remarkably beautiful. While traversing, with the chief, the various quarters of the camp, Mr. Kummer beheld with surprise, their manner of cleaning their beasts. Upon an order of the Prince, the men, charged with this employment, take the strongest oxen by the horns, and throw them down on the sand with astonishing ease; the slaves then take the animal, and clear its whole body from the insects, which, notwithstanding the fires that surround the flocks, get among the hair of the cattle, which they torment cruelly. After this first operation, they are washed with care, particularly the cows, which are then milked. These various operations generally employ the slaves, and even the masters, till eleven o'clock at night. Mr. Kummer was afterwards invited to repose in the Prince's tent; but before, he could go to sleep, he was assailed with a multitude of questions. The history of the French Revolution has penetrated to these people; and they put questions to our naturalist which surprised him much; they afterwards asked him why our vessels no longer came to Portendick and the Isles of Arguin; after this, they allowed him to take a few moments' repose; but the poor *Toubabe*, (the name which the Moors give to the whites) did not dare to indulge himself in sleep; he feared the perfidy of the Moors, and their rapacious spirit; however, exhausted by three days incessant fatigue, he fell asleep for a few moments; he had but a very disturbed slumber; during which, the barbarians took away his purse, which still contained thirty pieces of 20 *francs* each, his cravat, pocket handkerchief, greatcoat, shoes, waistcoat, and some other things which he carried in his pockets: he had nothing left but a bad pair of pantaloons and a hunting jacket; his shoes were, however, returned to him.

The next morning, at sun-rise, the Moors made their *salam*, (a Mahometan prayer): then about eight o'clock, the Prince, four of his subjects, Mr. Kummer, and a slave, set out for the sea-coast, in order to look for the wreck of the long-boat. They proceeded first towards the south, then to the west, then to the north, which made Mr. Kummer imagine that they were conducting him to Morocco. The Moors have no other method of finding their way, than to go from one eminence to another, which obliges them to take all sorts of directions; after they had proceeded five or six leagues to the east, they again turned to the west, then to the south west. After walking a considerable time longer, they arrived at the shore, where they found but few things. What particularly attracted their attention, was pieces of copper: they took them away, resolving to return and fetch the fragments of the long-boat, and several barrel, which the currents had driven on the coast. After taking whatever they could carry away, they set out towards the east, and at the end of about two leagues, they met some other Moors, also subjects of Prince Muhammed; they stopped and lay down under their tents: the Prince lay down under the finest, and ordered refreshments to be given to the *Toubabe*, who was worn out with fatigue and want of nourishment. Here Mr. Kummer was tormented by the women and children, who came every moment to touch and feel the fineness of his skin, and to take away some fragments of his shirt, and the few things which he had left. During the evening, fresh questions were put to him respecting the cruel wars which desolated France; he was obliged to trace the account of them, on the sand in Arabic letters. It was this extreme complaisance, and his pretended quality of the son of a Christian and of a Mahometan woman, which caused him to be upon very good terms with Prince Muhammed, and in general, with all the Moors whom he met with, on his journey. Every moment of the day, the Prince begged Mr. Kummer, to make the wheels of his watch go, the motions of which, much astonished the Moors; our traveller was on his side equally surprised, to see among the hordes, children five or six years of age, who wrote Arabic perfectly well.

The next day, July 8th, at day-break, the Moors went and stationed themselves on the summit of a hill. There, prostrated with their faces turned towards the east, they waited for the rising of the sun, to perform their *salam*, which they begin the moment he appears in the horizon. Mr. Kummer followed them, imitated them in all their ceremonies, and never failed in the sequel, to perform his devotions at the same time as they did. The ceremony being over, the prince and his suite, continued their route in the direction of the south east, which again frightened the poor *Toubabe*; he thought that the Moors were going to resume their course to the north, and that in the end they would take him to Morocco; then he endeavoured to impart his uneasiness to Prince Muhammed, who at last comprehended him; but to make it quite clear, Mr. Kummer drew upon the sand, a part of the map of Africa; meantime, he heard them continually pronounce the word *Andar*, which did not at all diminish his alarms; but by the lines which he traced, he soon understood that the Moors meant the Isle of St. Louis; of which he was convinced when he had written the name of the European factory, by the side of that of Andar. The Moors let him know that they had comprehended him; and showed great joy that a white could understand their language.

At noon, they stopped on the side of a great pond or lake. Mr. Kummer, who was extremely fatigued, lay down on the sand, and fell asleep immediately. During his sleep, the Moors went to look for a fruit, produced by a tree which generally grows on the sides of these lakes (*marigots*). They are bunches of little red berries, and very refreshing: the Moors are very fond of them, and make great use of them.

During this time, chance ordered it, that Mr. Rogery, who had also been taken by the Moors, stopped at the same place: he was brought by some of the natives, who were taking him also to their sovereign Zaide: he soon perceived Mr. Kummer lying with his face to the earth, and thought he was dead; at this sight, a mortal chillness pervaded all the limbs of the unfortunate Rogery; he deplored the loss of a friend, of a companion in misfortune: he approached him trembling; but his grief was soon changed into joy, when he perceived that his friend still breathed; he took hold of him, and embraced him eagerly. These two unfortunate men were transported with mutual joy, at meeting in the midst of their distress, with a fellow countryman. Mr. Rogery had lost everything; they had taken from him about forty pieces of 20 *francs* each, his watch, and all his effects: he had nothing left but his shirt, a very bad pair of pantaloons, and a hat. The wives of the Moors, and still more the children, had greatly tormented him; the latter, continually pinched him, and hindered him from taking a moment's sleep. His character was remarkably soured by this treatment, and his faculties rather impaired. These two unfortunate men, after having related their distresses to each other, fell asleep close together; some hours after, the Moors returned, and gave them some of the berries we have before mentioned. The caravan soon set forward again, and took a south west direction, which led to the camp of King Zaide: they reached it in the evening, but the monarch was absent; the report of our shipwreck had reached his camp, and Zaide, who desires to see everything himself, had gone to the sea-shore to have assistance given to such of the persons shipwrecked, as he should meet with. The King did not return till twenty-four hours after, which gave time for our travellers to repose, and for Prince Muhammed to make a bargain with the two whites: to conduct them to the Isle of St. Louis; the Prince demanded for his trouble, including the expenses of provisions and travelling, 800 *gourdes* for each, and obliged them before they set out, to sign an agreement in the Arabic language: Mr. Kummer consented to it, and said to Mr. Rogery, when we have once got to St. Louis, we will give them what we please. The latter hesitated, being much more scrupulous on that point, he would not at first accede to an agreement which he feared he should not be able to perform; but seeing that the Moors were resolved to keep him among them, he consented to accept the absolute proposal of the Prince, and the conventions were signed.

Our two travellers passed a part of their time in examining the customs of these people; we shall mention some circumstances which particularly struck them. They observed, that the children imperiously command their fathers and mothers: but especially the latter, who never oppose their inclinations; hence, doubtless comes that despotic spirit, which is carried to the extreme; a refusal, or a delay, in the executions of their orders irritates them, and their anger is so violent that in the first transport, the unhappy slave who may have excited their fury, runs the risk of being stabbed on the spot. Hence, too doubtless the manly boldness which characterises them, and which seems to inspire those who surround them, with respect and submission. The Moors are, in every respect, much superior to the Negroes: braver than they are, they reduce them to slavery, and employ them in the hardest labour; they are, in general, tall and well made, and their faces are very handsome, and full of expression.

However, it may also be observed that the Moors of both sexes, appear at the first sight, like a people composed of two distinct races, which have nothing in common, except, the extremely brown, or tanned colour of their skin, and the shining black of their hair. The greater part of them, it is true, are endowed with the stature, and the noble, but austere features, which call to mind some of the great Italian painters, but there are several, (indeed the smaller number) whose cranium and profile form a singular contrast with the others. Their head is remarkably elongated, the ears small: the forehead, which, in the first, is very high and finely formed, is contracted in the latter, and becomes at the top disagreeably protuberant; their eyes are sunk, and placed as it were obliquely, which gives them the savage look with which they are reproached, and their lower jaw has a tendency to be elongated. Some of them have, it is true, the high forehead of the former: but it always differs by being sunk in at the base. These latter are, perhaps, the descendants of the aborigines of this country, whose characteristic features are still discernible, notwithstanding their alliance with so many strangers? History has, indeed, transmitted to us some of the customs of the Numidians, who were by turns, the enemies, and the allies of the Romans; but it has not condescended to draw their portrait. Juvenal somewhere speaks of the withered hands of the Moors: *manus ossea Mauri*. But, besides, that this is general in hot countries, this description may be understood of ill-fed slaves.

The travellers remarked that there was no difference between the very frugal diet of the slaves, who are all blacks, and that of their masters. The fathers and mothers, as well as the marabous, (a kind of priests) pass their leisure moments in teaching the principles of their religion, as well as instructing them in reading and writing on the sand; the wives of King Zaide, the number of whom is considerable, passively obey Fatima, who is the favourite, or chief wife of the sovereign.

Our travellers estimated the number of men, women, children and slaves, at seven or eight hundred persons; their flocks appeared to them very numerous: they constitute part of the wealth of Zaide, who possesses a great many besides, in different parts of the kingdom, the extent of which is pretty considerable; it has about sixty leagues of coast, and stretches to a great depth in the interior of the desert. The people, as we have said, call themselves Trasas, and profess the Mahometan religion; they hunt lions, tigers, leopards, and all other ferocious animals, which abound in this part of Africa. Their commerce is in furs or skins, and ostrich feathers: they manufacture the leather called basil, in French, *basane*, which they prepare very well; they make this leather into pocketbooks, to which they give different forms, but in general, that of a *sabretache*. They also dress goats skins, and join several together to give them more breadth; they are known under the name of *peaux de maures*, are excellent, and afford a complete defence against the rain: in form, they nearly resemble the dress of a Capuchin; they sell all these articles in the interior, as well as goldsmiths work, which they manufacture with only a hammer, and a little anvil; but their chief commerce, which is very extensive, is in salt, which they carry to Tombuctoo, and to Sego, large and very populous cities, situated in the interior of Africa. Sego is built on both sides of the river Niger, and Tombuctoo not far from its banks, the former about five hundred, and the latter about six hundred leagues east of the Island of Goree. The Marabous, who are almost all traders, frequently extend their journeys into Upper Egypt. The Moors and the Negroes, have an extraordinary respect for these priests, who manufacture leather, into little etuis, perfumed bags, and pocketbooks, to which they give the name of *gris-gris*. By means of magic words spoken over the *gris-gris*, and little notes written in Arabic, which they enclose in them, he who carries such a one about him, is secure against the bite of wild beasts; they make them to protect the wearer against lions, crocodiles, serpents, &c. They sell them extremely dear, and those who possess them set a very high value on them; the king and the princes are not less superstitious than those whom they command. There are some who wear as many as twenty of these *gris-gris* fixed to the neck, the arms, and the legs.

After a day's stay, King Zaide arrived: he had no ornament which distinguished him; but he was of a lofty stature, had an open countenance, and three large teeth in the upper jaw, on the left side, which projected at least two lines over the under lip, which the Moors consider as a great beauty. He was armed with a large sabre, a poniard and a pair of pistols; his soldiers had *zagayes* or lances, and little sabres in the Turkish fashion. The King has always at his side, his favourite negro, who wears a necklace of red pearls, and is called Billai. Zaide received the two whites kindly, ordered that they should be well-treated, and that Mr. Rogery should not be molested, he being continually tormented by the children. Mr. Kummer was much more lively, and did not mind his misfortunes; he wrote Arabic, and had passed himself off for the son of a Mahometan woman; all this greatly pleased the Moors, who treated him well; while Mr. Rogery, deeply affected by his misfortunes, and having just lost his last resources, did not much rely on the good faith of the Moors.

In the course of the day, the King ordered Mr. Kummer to relate to him the events of the last French revolution; he was already acquainted with those of the first. Mr. Kummer did not exactly comprehend what the king wanted of him. Zaide ordered his chief minister, to draw upon the sand, the map of Europe, the Mediterranean, and the coast of Africa, along that sea: he pointed out to him the Isle of Elba, and ordered him to relate the circumstances which had taken place in the invasion of 1815, from the moment that Bonaparte left it. Mr. Kummer took advantage of this favourable moment, to ask for his watch; and the King ordered his son to return it to the *Toubabe*, who then commenced his narrative; and as in the course of it he called the Ex-Emperor, sometimes Bonaparte, and sometimes Napoleon, a Marabou, at the name of Bonaparte, interrupted him, and asked if he was the general whose armies he had seen in Upper Egypt, when he was going on his pilgrimage to Mecca, to which Mr. Kummer answering in the affirmative, the king and his suite were quite delighted; they could not conceive how a mere general of army had been able to raise himself to the rank of Emperor: it seems that these people had, till then, believed that Napoleon and Bonaparte were two different persons. Mr. Kummer was also asked if his father belonged to the army of Egypt; he said no, but that he was a peaceable merchant, who had never borne arms. Mr. Kummer continued his narrative, and astonished more and more, the King of the Trasas, and all his court. The next day, Zaide desired to see the two whites again, from whom he always learnt something new. He sent away the Moors, his subjects, who had brought Mr. Rogery, and ordered his son, Prince Muhammed, accompanied by one of his ministers, two other Moors of his suite, and a slave, to conduct the two whites to Andar. They had camels to carry them, as well as their provisions. Zaide, before he dismissed them, made them take some refreshments, gave them provisions, for a part of the journey, and advised Mr. Kummer to entrust his watch to his son; because, by that means, he would be secure from its being taken from him by the Moors; and that it would be returned to him at Saint Louis. Mr. Kummer immediately obeyed. The prince faithfully executed his father's orders.

Before the departure of the two Frenchmen, the King wished to show them his respect for the laws which govern his dominions; knowing that this quality is that which nations always desire to find in those who govern them; he therefore thought, with reason, that he could not give a higher idea of his virtues, and show his character in a more honourable light, than by convincing them that he was the protector and most faithful observer of the laws: to prove it, he related the following anecdote:

"Two princes, my subjects, had had an affair, for a long time, in litigation: to terminate it, they resolved to ask me to be arbitrator between them; but the proposals which I made, though I thought them reasonable, were not approved by them; so that after my proposals, a violent quarrel arose between the two parties: a challenge ensued, and the two princes left my tent to decide their cause by arms. In fact, they fought in my presence; one of them, the weakest, who was my friend, was thrown down by his adversary, who stabbed him immediately. I had the grief to see my friend die, and notwithstanding all my power, it was impossible for me, as our laws allow duelling, and on account of the respect which I have for them, to avenge the death of the prince whom I esteemed. You may judge, by this, how scrupulously I observe the laws by which I govern my dominions, and which regulate the rights of the princes, as well as those of the citizens, and of the slaves."

CHAPTER 9

The English Keep the Colony

The third and fourth day, after they had quitted the camp of King Zaide, our travellers were reposing as usual, till the greatest heat of the day should be passed. During the repast, the minister, who had the contracts between the Prince and the two Frenchmen, took from his great *gris-gris*, or pocket book, that of Mr. Rogery, who snatched it from him, and tore it into a thousand pieces; immediately one of the Moors rushed upon him, seized him by the throat, with one hand threw him on the ground, and was going to stab him with a dagger which he held in the other; happily, the Prince, out of regard for Mr. Kummer, whom he particularly esteemed, pardoned him who had dared, so seriously, to insult one of his ministers. But, during the four or five days that the journey continued, they incessantly tormented him; and did not give him a fourth part of what was necessary for his support, so that the unfortunate man was frequently obliged to gnaw the bones which the Moors had thrown away; they also forced him to make the whole journey on foot; it was pretty long; for these gentlemen, on their arrival at St. Louis, estimated it at a hundred and forty leagues at the least, because the Moors made them go so much out of their way.

The respectable Mr. Rogery, a man of rare probity, was disturbed by the recollection of the agreement which he had made with Muhammed, in a moment of difficulty, knowing very well that he could never fulfil it; he thought his honour implicated, and strictly bound by this contract, though he had destroyed it.

This recollection, and his inability to pay, affected his nerves; to this was added fear, lest the contract should be known to his countrymen; and this was what induced him to that act of desperation which had nearly cost him his life, and deprived humanity of one of the most zealous partisans of liberty, and of the abolition of the slave trade.

On the 19th, in the morning, they arrived at a village situated on the bank of one of the arms of Senegal, which is called Marigot of the Maringouins, and which appears to have been the ancient mouth of the river, when it flowed directly to the sea, before it turned aside and flowed to the south. This position may one day become important, if Senegambia should ever be colonised.

The gentlemen remarked, that the banks of this arm of the river, are very well cultivated; the fields are covered with plantations of cotton-trees, with maize and millet; one meets, at intervals, with tufts of wood, which render it agreeable and healthy. Mr. Kummer thinks that this country could be adapted to the cultivation of colonial productions. Here begins Nigritia, and one may say, the country of good people; for, from this moment, the travellers were never again in want of food, and the negroes gave them whatever they wanted.

In the first village, which is called Vu, they met with a good negress, who offered them milk and *cous-cous*, (flour of millet). She was affected, and shed tears when she saw the two unhappy whites almost naked, and particularly when she learned that they were Frenchmen. She began by praising our nation; it is the custom of these people; and then, she gave them a short account of the misfortunes she had experienced. This good negress had been made a slave by the Moors, who had torn her from the arms of her mother; she consequently detested them, and called them the banditti of the desert; she said to the two whites, in very good French: "are they not very villainous people?" "Yes," answered our unhappy countrymen. "Well," continued she, "these robbers carried me off, notwithstanding the efforts of my unhappy father, who defended me with courage; they then carried desolation into our village, which a moment before enjoyed tranquillity and happiness; on this sad day we saw whole families carried off, and we were all conducted to that horrible market at St. Louis, where the whites carry on the execrable trade of dealers in men; chance favoured me, and saved me from being sent to find death in America, amidst the tempests which cover the ocean that separates it from Africa. I had the good fortune to fall into the hands of the respectable General Blanchot, whose name and memory will be ever dear to the inhabitants of St. Louis. This worthy governor kept me some years in his service; but seeing that I always thought of my country and my relations, and that, in short, I could not habituate myself to your customs, he gave me my liberty, and from that moment I have vowed eternal friendship to everything that bears the French name." Our two whites were much affected by this interesting meeting; from that moment they fancied themselves among their own countrymen.

After some hours repose they continued their journey, and in fact, they had every reason to praise the negroes, who did not let them want for anything. In proportion, as they approached the town, the Moors became much more civil, and when they were going to pass the river, to enter St. Louis, Prince Muhammed returned Mr. Kummer his watch. The French governor received the Prince and his suite, very well; he caused them to be paid about sixty *francs* in two *sous*-pieces; this sum seemed enormous to them; for they were extremely satisfied with it: this gives ground to suppose that they were not acquainted with the value of the gourde, when they demanded eight hundred for the ransom of each of the two travellers. It was on the 22nd of July, that they arrived, after having wandered sixteen days in the burning desert of Zaara, and having endured all the horrors of hunger and thirst, particularly the unfortunate Mr. Rogery, who had to bear all the caprices of the Moors.

All the shipwrecked persons who had escaped these disasters being assembled at St. Louis, we thought we should immediately take possession of our establishments. But the English governor, Mr. Beurthonne, having learned our shipwreck, either of his own authority, or having received orders to that effect, from his government, refused to give up the colony. This difficulty obliged the commander of the French expedition to take measures, to wait for fresh orders from France. He was enjoined to send away immediately all the shipwrecked persons who arrived in the town of St. Louis.

Everything induces us to believe that the delay in the restitution of these settlements depended on the English governor, who threw obstacles in the way, whenever circumstances permitted him. He alleged at first, that he had not received orders to give up the colony, and that besides he was in want of vessels to remove his troops, and all the effects belonging to his nation. This last allegation of wanting vessels is, of itself, sufficient to show, that he was not much inclined to retire from the Isle of St. Louis; for the French governor, in order to remove all difficulties, proposed the *Loire* to serve as a transport, and this offer was refused. We think we have guessed the cause of this delay in the restitution of the colony, for two reasons, which seem to us the better founded, as they take their origin in the British policy, which is constantly to follow no other rule than its political or commercial interest. We give them, however, only as suppositions; but these suppositions seem so well confirmed by the events to which they relate, that we do not hesitate to lay them before our readers.

We think then that Mr. Beurthonne had received orders to give up the Islands of St. Louis and Goree, to the French squadron, which should come to take possession of them; but we think also, that he was desired to evacuate them as late as possible, in case the English merchants or government could derive any advantage from a delay.

In fact, if Mr. Beurthonne had not received any instructions to deliver up the colony, it was certainly, useless to allege that he was in want of vessels. To the desires of the French governor, he had only to make the plain and unanswerable objection, that his government had not given him any orders. It is therefore, by the kind of vacillation which appears in his answers, that himself, leads us to the opinion which we have formed. But it will be said, what advantage could the English government derive from this delay? The following, is what we conjecture on this subject.

The gum trade was on the point of commencing; it was very just that the English merchants, who were in Senegal, should carry off this crop, which would have belonged to the French merchants if the colony, had been restored.

A second motive, not less powerful, is, that we were just at the entrance of the bad season, and that the English settlements, on the river Gambia, (to which, a part of the English, garrison were to go) are extremely unhealthy: diseases that are almost always mortal, prevail during the winter-season, and generally carry off two thirds of the Europeans, who are newly arrived. Every year the mortality is the same; because, every year it is necessary to send fresh garrisons: those who have the good fortune to resist these terrible epidemics, come, to recover, to the Isle of Goree, where the air is salubrious. Such are the reasons which, as we think, caused the delay in the restitution of our settlements on the coast of Africa.

Without losing ourselves farther in conjectures, we will conclude with one remark: namely, them on this occasion the English governor was influenced more by the usual policy of his government than by local and particular considerations. Let us remember what passed on the restitution of our colonies at the peace of 1802 and that of 1814; and it will be seen that the British Government, without giving itself much trouble to assign reasons, has adopted and faithfully followed the principle, of not willingly giving up what it possessed.

The shipwreck of the *Medusa* favoured the designs of the governor; for, what sensation could be produced by the arrival of an expedition, of which the principal vessel no longer existed, and the three others appeared one after the other? If the English had had the intention to restore the colony on our arrival, the disorder in which we appeared, would alone have sufficed; to make them conceive the idea of delaying as much as possible to withdraw from the Island of St. Louis. But what we cannot conceive is, that the governor, after giving the French a good reception for some days, should have required their troops to be sent away from the colony: and what were these troops? wretches almost naked, worn out by the long fatigues and privations which they had had to bear in the deserts; they were almost all without arms. Did he fear the spirit of the colonists, and even that of the negroes, which was not in his favour, and who saw with the greatest pleasure the arrival of the French? This is not at all probable.

All the shipwrecked persons being assembled at St. Louis, as we have already said, the governor, two days before his departure for Cape Verde, thought of sending a vessel on board the *Medusa*, to look for a sum of 100,000 *francs*, which was intended to form the treasure of the colony, as well as provisions, which were in abundance on board, and of which there was some scarcity in the colony. Very little was said about the men, who had remained on board, and to whom their companions had solemnly promised to send for them as soon as they should arrive at St. Louis; but these unfortunate men were already hardly thought of any more. Mr. Correard says that the first day that he took a walk in the town, he went to pay a visit to the family of the governor. During the conversation, the vessel was mentioned, that was going to be sent to the *Medusa*, as also the possibility of recovering the 100,000 *francs*, provisions, and effects. Seeing that they said nothing of the seventeen men who had remained on board the frigate, he said, "but a more precious object, of which nothing is said, is the seventeen poor men who were left!" "Pooh," answered somebody, "seventeen! there are not three left." "And if there remained but three, but one," replied he, "yet, his life is more valuable than all that can be recovered from the frigate;" and left the company in anger.

When in the first part of this work, we represented Mrs. and Miss Schmalz, as alone unmoved when the frigate ran aground; and seeming to rise above the general consternation, our readers may have given them credit for uncommon greatness of soul, and more than manly courage. Why are we obliged to destroy this honourable illusion which we may have caused? Why, when these ladies, have carried indifference so far as to dispense themselves from the most common duties of humanity, by refraining from paying the smallest visit to the poor wretches, placed in the hospital at St. Louis, have they themselves discovered to, us that their composure on board the frigate was nothing but profound insensibility?

We could, however, if not excuse, at least explain this last mark of their hard-heartedness: what sight, in fact, awaited them in this melancholy abode, on the new theatre, where the sad victims of a first act of inhumanity, had to struggle with the fresh miseries prepared for them by the indifference, the inattention of their fellow-creatures? The sight of men, who all bore in their hearts, the remembrance of the faults, of a husband, of a father, could not be an object which they would be desirous of seeking, or meeting with; and in this point of view, the care, which they took to avoid the hospital, seems to us almost pardonable. But what is not, what cannot be excused, what we have not learned without the greatest surprise is, that Miss Schmalz, judging of us doubtless, after a manner of thinking which was not ours, and not supposing it possible that the faults of her father, and the inhuman conduct of herself and her mother, should not be one day known in France, should have hastened to anticipate this publication, by writing to her friends at Paris, a letter justifying her relations with the shipwrecked persons belonging to the raft, and trying to devote these unfortunate men to public hatred and contempt. In this singular letter, which has been circulated in Paris, she confessed that the sight of the shipwrecked persons inspired her with a degree of horror, which she could not suppress. "It was really impossible for me," said she, "to endure the presence of these men, without feeling a sentiment of indignation."

What then was our crime in the eyes of Miss Schmalz? Doubtless that of knowing too well the persons really guilty of our misfortunes. Yes, on this account, whenever Miss Schmalz saw us, which was extremely seldom, our presence must have been a thunder-bolt to her. She could say to herself, "these men have in their hands the fate of my father. If they speak, if they utter complaints which they suppress here, if they are listened to, (and how should they not be listened to in a country, where a charter, the noble present of our august Monarch, causes justice and the law to reign,) instead of being the daughter of a governor, I am but a wretched orphan; instead of these honours, with which it gives me so much pleasure to be surrounded, I fall into the degradation, and the oblivion which generally await the unhappy family of a great criminal."

It is certain that, if we had listened to our griefs, if we had called to legal account, the authors of our misfortunes, it is difficult to believe that they would have escaped the inflexible rigour of justice. But we have been generous, and it is we who are oppressed! Thus, as the historians of the human heart, have but too often observed, "It is more easy to pardon the injury we have received, than that we have inflicted."

The little vessel chosen to go to the frigate, was a schooner, commanded by a lieutenant of the navy; the crew was composed of some black-drivers, and some passengers. It sailed from St. Louis, on the 26th, of July, and had on board, provisions for eight days: so that having met with contrary winds, it was obliged to return to port, after having, in vain, endeavoured for seven or eight days, to get to the *Medusa*.

This schooner sailed again after having taken in provisions for about twenty-five days; but, as the sails were in a very bad condition, and the owner would not change them, till they were wholly unfit for service, she was obliged to sail again, with a few repairs only. Having experienced at sea, a pretty heavy gale, the sails were almost entirely destroyed, and she was obliged to return to port after having been a fortnight at sea, without having been able to accomplish her purpose. She was then furnished with new sails, which cost about ten days labour. As soon as she was ready, they sailed for the third time, and reached the *Medusa*, fifty-two days, after she had been abandoned.

A very obvious reflection here presents itself to the most inattentive mind: it is certain, that the reader must presume, that this was the only schooner in the colony; it is our duty to undeceive him: many other merchants offered their vessels; but their offers were declined. The governor liked better to treat with a single house, than to have accounts to regulate with a part of the merchants of the colony; who, however, were ready to place at his disposal, everything in their power. Mr. Durecur was the merchant favoured. This house carries on the whole trade of Senegal; its firm has taken place of the African company. He made the governor large advances, both of provisions and money, which amounted to 50,000 *francs*; he had continually, at his house, Mr. Schmalz, his family and a numerous suite. The general opinion was that, Mr. Durecur had got by his acts of generosity, a decent profit of a hundred per cent; he was, besides, recompensed, on the application of the governor, by that decoration, which it seems, ought to be conferred for some brilliant action, and not for a very profitable commercial transaction; but let us return to our schooner. What was the astonishment of those on board her, at still finding in the *Medusa*, three unfortunate men on the point of expiring! Most certainly, they were very far from expecting this meeting; but as we have said, 17 were abandoned. What became of the 14 others? We will try to relate the story of their unhappy fate.

As soon as the boats and the raft had left the frigate, these 17 men endeavoured to subsist till assistance should be sent them. They searched wherever the water had not penetrated, and succeeded in collecting sufficient biscuit, wine, brandy, and bacon, to enable them to subsist for some time. As long as their provision lasted, tranquillity prevailed among them: but forty-two days passed without their receiving the assistance which had been promised them; when twelve of the most resolute, seeing that they were on the point of being destitute of everything, determined to get to the land. To attain their object, they formed a raft with the pieces of timber which remained on board of the frigate, the whole bound together like the first, with strong ropes: they embarked upon it, and directed their course towards the land; but how could they steer on a machine, that was doubtless destitute of oars and the necessary sails. It is certain that these poor men, who had taken with them but a very small stock of provisions, could not hold out long, and that, overcome by despair and want, they have been the victims of their rashness. That such was the result of their fatal attempt, was proved by the remains of their raft, which were found on the coast of the desert of Zaara, by some Moors, subjects of King Zaide, who came to Andar to give the information. These unhappy men were doubtless the prey of the sea-monsters which are found in great numbers on the coasts of Africa.

Unhappy victims we deplore the rigour of your lot: like us, you have been exposed to the most dreadful torments: like us abandoned upon a raft, you have had to struggle with those pressing wants which man cannot subdue, hunger and thirst carried to the extreme! Our imagination carries us to your fatal machine; we see your despair, your rage; we appreciate the whole extent of your sufferings, and your misfortunes draw forth our tears. It is then true that misfortune strikes more forcibly him who has had already to struggle with adversity! The happy man scarcely believes in misfortune, and often accuses him whose distresses he has caused.

A sailor who had refused to embark upon the raft, attempted also to reach the shore some days after the first, he put himself on a chicken coop, but he sunk within half a cable's length of the frigate.

Four men resolved not to leave the *Medusa*, alleging that they preferred dying on board, to braving new dangers which it seemed impossible for them to surmount. One of the four had just died when the schooner arrived, his body had been thrown into the sea: the three others were very weak; two days later they would have been no more. These unhappy men occupied each a separate place, and never left it but to fetch provisions, which in the last days consisted only of a little brandy, tallow, and salt pork. When they met, they ran upon each other brandishing their knifes. As long as the wine had lasted with the other provisions, they had kept up their strength perfectly well; but as soon as they had only brandy to drink they grew weaker every day.

Every care was bestowed on these three men that their situation demanded, and all three are now in perfect health.

After having given the necessary succours to the three men of whom we have just spoken, they proceeded to get out of the frigate, everything that could be removed; they cut a large hole in her, (*on la saborda,*) and were thus able to save wine, flour, and many other things. Mr. Correa had the simplicity to think that the shipwrecked people were going to recover a part, at least, of their effects, since a vessel, belonging to the king, had reached the frigate. But far from it! Those who were on board declared themselves corsairs, and pillaged, as we may say, all the effects which they could get at. One of them Mr. ———, carried off several portmanteaus, and four hammocks, full of all kind of articles, the whole for his own use.

The schooner having quite completed its cargo, and all attempts to recover the 100,000 *francs*, of which we have spoken, being fruitless, returned to Senegal. We saw this little vessel arrive, and our hearts beat with joy; we thought we should see again our unfortunate companions, who had been abandoned on board the frigate, and recover some clothes, of which we were in much need. The schooner passed the bar, and in an hour or two had traversed the space which separated it from us. In an instant we ran to the port, and enquired if any of our unfortunate countrymen had been saved. We were answered, three are still living, and fourteen have died since our departure: this answer confounded us. We then asked if it had been possible to save any of our effects; and were answered, yes, but that they were a good prize; we could not understand this answer, but it was repeated to us, and we learnt for the first time that we were at war with Frenchmen, because we had been excessively unfortunate.

CHAPTER 10

Appalling Conditions

The next day the town was transformed into a public fair, which lasted at least a week. There were sold effects belonging to the State, and those of the unhappy crew who had perished; here, the clothes of those who were still living, a little further was the furniture of the captain's cabin: in another place were the signal flags, which the negroes were buying to make themselves aprons and cloaks; at one place they sold the tackling and sails of the frigate, at another bed-linen, frames, hammocks, quilts, books, instruments, &c. &c.

But there is one thing that is sacred, respected by every man who serves with honour, the rallying sign under which he ought to find victory or death, the flag; what it will be asked became of it?... It was saved ... Did it fall; into the hands of a Frenchman?... No! he who debases a respectable sign, which represents a nation, cannot belong to that nation. Well! this sign was employed in domestic uses. Vases which belonged to the captain of the frigate himself, were also saved, and were transferred from his side-board to the table of the Governor, where Mr. de Chaumareys recognized them, and it is from him we have received these details. It is true that the ladies of the Governor had received them, as a present, from those who went on board the schooner.

Nothing was now seen in the town but negroes dressed, some in jackets and pantaloons, some in large grey great coats; others had shirts, waistcoats, police-bonnets, &c. everything, in short, presented the image of disorder and confusion. Such was a part of the mission of the schooner: the provisions, which it brought, were of the greatest choice to the French Governor, who began to be in want of them.

Some days after, the Merchants of St. Louis, were authorized to go on board the *Medusa* with their vessels, on the following conditions: they were to equip the vessels at their own expense, and all the effects which they could save out of the frigate were to be divided into two equal parts, one for the government, the other for the owners of the vessels. Four schooners sailed from St. Louis, and in a few days reached their destination: they brought back to the colony a great quantity of barrels of flour, salt, meat, wine, brandy, cordage, sails, &c. &c. This expedition was terminated in less than twenty days. As the schooners arrived in the Senegal, the proper way would have been to unload them, and deposit the things saved, in a magazine, till the arrival of the French Governor, who was absent; it appears to us, that, in making the division, his presence, or that of some other competent authority was necessary. But whether the ship-owners, would not wait for the return of the Governor, or whether they were in haste to possess their share of the cargo, they went to Mr. Potin Agent, or Partner of the house of Durecur, and begged him to divide the articles saved from the frigate. We are ignorant whether Mr. Potin was authorized to make this division; but whether he was authorised or not, we think he could not make it, without the co-operation of one or more officers of the administration, since he was himself one of the ship-owners. It would have been the more easy to have this division superintended by an officer of the government, as there were then three or four at St. Louis; among whom were the secretary and the paymaster. Yet neither of them was called in to be present at these operations, though they lasted some days. However, those to whom the vessels belonged, showed themselves much more generous to the shipwrecked people, than those who went on board the frigate, with the first schooner: the few books and effects which they had been able to save were restored to such of the crew as claimed them.

A short time after these depredations were ended, some French officers and soldiers, belonging as well to the land as the sea-service, and who were still at St. Louis, received orders from the English Governor to go immediately to the camp of Daccard: it was about the first of October. At this time Mr. Correard remained the only Frenchman in the hospital at St. Louis, till he should be entirely recovered. We are entirely ignorant of the reasons which induced this Governor to employ such severe measures towards about twenty unhappy persons, among whom three officers had been part of the crew of the fatal raft. He however, allowed the civil officers to remain in the city.

Let us take a rapid survey of the new misfortunes which overtook some of the unfortunate persons who escaped from the raft and the desert, and remained plunged in a horrid hospital without assistance, and without consolation, before we proceed to the history of the camp at Daccard, which will terminate this account. Our readers will remember that it was on the 23rd of July, that the men, who escaped from the raft, were united to the sixty-three landed by the long boat, near the Moles of Angel.

Mr. Coudin, commander of the raft, and Mr. Savigny, were received at Senegal by Mr. Lasalle, a French Merchant, who, on all occasions, bestowed on them the most generous care, which spared them the new sufferings, to which their companions in misfortune were exposed, and gives Mr. Lasalle a title to their lasting gratitude.

As for Mr. Correard, as soon as he was at the isle of St. Louis, he and some others of our companions covered with wounds, and almost without life, were laid upon truck-beds, which, instead of mattresses, had only blankets doubled in four, with sheets disgustingly dirty; the four officers of the troops were also placed in one of the rooms of the hospital, and the soldiers and sailors in another room, near the first, and lying in the same manner as the officers. The evening of their arrival, the Governor, accompanied by the captain of the frigate, and by a numerous suite, came to pay them a visit: the air of compassion, with which he addressed them, much affected them; in this first moment, they were promised a guinea, linen to clothe them, wine to restore their strength, and ammunition to amuse them when they should be able to go out. Vain promises! It is to the compassion of strangers, alone, that they were indebted for their existence for five months. The Governor announced his departure for the camp at Duccard, saying to these poor men who were left behind, that he had given orders that they should want for nothing during his absence. All the French, able to embark, departed with the Governor.

Left to themselves in the horrid abode which they inhabited, surrounded with men in whom their cruel situation inspired no pity, our countrymen again abandoned, gave vent to their distress in useless complaints. In vain they represented to the English physician that the ordinary ration of a common soldier, which had been hitherto given them, was wholly unfit for them, first, because their health required, if it was indeed wished to recover them, better nourishment than is given to a soldier in good health in his barracks: that, besides, officers enjoyed in all countries some preference, and that, in consequence, he was requested to have regard to the just desires of the sick.

The doctor was inexorable: he answered that he had received no orders and that he should make no change. They then addressed their complaints to the English Governor, who was equally insensible. It is, however, probable that the French Governor, before his departure, had requested this officer to afford all the assistance which the situation of those whom he left required, under the protection of his generosity. If this request was made it must be allowed that this Mr. Beurthonne has a heart but little accessible to sentiments of humanity.

What a contrast between the conduct of this Lieutenant-Colonel, and that of the other officers of his nation, belonging to the expedition for exploring the interior of Africa, with whom the officers of the garrison joined. It is to their generous efforts that the officers saved from the raft, owed assistance and perhaps life. It is not, in fact, rare to see the same circumstances give rise to the same observation. On occasions of this kind, a great number of private Englishmen excite astonishment by the excess of their generosity to their enemies, while on the other hand the agents of the government, and individuals, who doubtless believe that they enter into its views, seem to glory in a conduct diametrically opposite.

These gentlemen, some days after the arrival of our unfortunate comrades, having been informed of their melancholy situation, came to the hospital and took away with them the four officers who were already able to go out; they invited them to share their repast with them, till the colony should be given up. Forty days had passed, since the compassionate English had come to the relief of these four companions in misfortune, without the distressed Correard's having personally felt the effects of their kindness. His health was greatly impaired, in consequence of the unheard-of sufferings which he had experienced on the raft; his wounds gave him great pain, and he was obliged to remain in the infirmary: add to this the absolute want of clothes, having nothing to cover him except the sheet of his bed, in which he wrapped himself up. Since the departure of the governor, he had heard nothing of the French, which made him very uneasy, and doubled his desire to join his countrymen, hoping to find from them, consolation and relief; for he had friends among the officers and passengers who were at the Camp of Deccard. He was in this temper of mind, and in the melancholy situation which we have just described, reduced to the ration of a common soldier, during the forty days which had just elapsed, when he caused the captain of an American merchant vessel to be asked whether he would do him the pleasure to take him to Cape Verde, to which place he was to go; the answer was affirmative, and the departure fixed for two days after. In this interval, Mr. Kummer, the naturalist, happened to express, in the presence of Major Peddy, commander in chief of the English expedition for the interior of Africa, the fears which he felt at the departure of his friend, alleging that he was very uneasy respecting the effects of the bad air of the camp of Deccard, on a constitution so shaken as that of Mr. Correard. Scarcely had the sensible Mr. Kummer ceased speaking, when Major Peddy hastily went away, returned to his apartment, and immediately got ready linen, clothes and money, and while he was thus employed, this genuine philanthropist shed tears at the fate of the unhappy man, whom he did not know, cursing those who had cruelly abandoned him. His indignation was excited, because he had been assured that ever since the departure of the French governor, Mr. Correard had heard nothing farther, either of him, or of his countrymen. Respectable Major! worthy friend of humanity! in departing for the interior of Africa, you have carried with you the regret and the gratitude of a heart, on which your noble beneficence is indelibly engraved.

While this unexpected relief was preparing Mr. Correard, seated at the foot of his truck bed, was overwhelmed by the thoughts of his wretchedness, and plunged in the most heart-rending reflections. All that he saw affected him still more deeply, than the dreadful scenes which had passed upon the raft. "In the very heat of battle," said he, "the pain of my wounds was not accompanied by the gloomy despondency which now depresses me, and by a slow, but sure progress, is conducting me to death. Only two months ago, I was strong, intrepid, capable of braving every fatigue: now, confined to this horrid abode, my courage is vanished, everything forsakes me. I have, in vain, asked some assistance of those who have come to see me, not from humanity, but from unfeeling curiosity: thus, people went to Liege to see the brave Goffin, after he had extricated himself by his courage, from the coal-pit which had fallen in and buried him. But he, happier than I, was rewarded with the cross of the legion of honour, and a pension which enabled him to subsist. If I were in France," he continued, "my relations, my countrymen, would mitigate my sufferings; but here, under a burning climate, where everything is strange to me, surrounded by these Africans, who are hardened by the habitual sight of the horrors produced by the slave trade, nothing relieves me; on the contrary, the length of the nights, the continuance of my sufferings, the sight of those of my companions in misfortune, the disgusting filth by which

I am surrounded, the inattention of a soldier who acts as nurse, and is always drunk or negligent, the insupportable hardness of a wretched bed, scarcely sheltered from the inclemency of the air, all announce to me an inevitable death. I must resign myself to it, and await it with courage! I was less to be pitied on the raft; then my imagination was exalted, and I scarcely enjoyed my intellectual faculties! but here, I am only an ordinary man, with all the weaknesses of humanity. My mind is continually absorbed in melancholy reflections; my soul sinks under incessant sufferings, and I daily see those who shared my unhappy fate, drop before me into the grave."

While he was wholly absorbed in this distressing soliloquy, he saw two young officers enter the room, followed by three or four slaves, carrying various effects. These two officers approached, with an air of kindness, the mournful and motionless Correard, "Accept," said they, "these trifling presents, they are sent to you by Major Peddy, and Captain Cambpell: we, sir, have desired the happiness of bringing you this first assistance; we were commissioned by all our comrades, to obtain from you accurate information respecting your wants; you are, besides, invited to partake of our table, all the time we shall pass together: the Major, and all the officers, beg you to remain here, and not to go to the pestilential camp at Deccard, where a mortal distemper would carry you off in a few days." It would be ungrateful not to name these two young officers: one bears the name of Beurthonne, without being a relation of the Governors; the name of the other is Adam.

While these generous officers were fulfilling, with so much politeness and kindness, these acts of humanity, Major Peddy entered the room, followed by other slaves, also loaded with things, which he came to offer to the friend of the naturalist, Kummer, by whom he was accompanied. The Major approached the unfortunate Correard, who seemed as if awaking from a dream; he embraced him, shedding tears, and vowing to him a friendship which never abated during the whole time that he remained with him. What a sublime image is a fine man, almost two metres in height, who sheds tears of pity at the sight of an unfortunate man, who was not less affected, and, shed them in abundance, penetrated with the most delicious feelings of gratitude and admiration. After he had recovered from the emotion excited in him by the sight of the melancholy situation of the stranger, whom he had just snatched from misery, the Major made him the most obliging offers: and that Mr. Correard might not decline them, he assured him, beforehand, that he himself and many of his comrades had received similar assistance from Frenchmen; and that their countrymen ought to allow him the honour of discharging, if it were possible, his debt to their nation, for the generous treatment which he had received from them. Offers so nobly made, could not but be accepted by Mr. Correard, who expressed to his benefactor, how happy he should esteem himself to be able to merit the friendship that he had just offered him, and that he wished nothing so much as to be able, one day, to show his gratitude in a manner worthy of himself, and of a Frenchman. From that time Mr. Correard received all imaginable assistance from the Major and his officers, and it may be said with truth, that he owes them his life, as do the four French officers who were with him.

On the 24th of August, Mr. Clairet paid the debt of nature. It was thirty-four days after our arrival at St, Louis. Mr. Correard had the grief to see him die at his side, and to hear him say before his death, that he died satisfied, since he had had time to recommend to his father a natural son whom he loved. At this time Major Peddy had not yet relieved Mr. Correard; he was without clothes, so that he could not attend the funeral of his comrade, who had just expired, worn out by the sufferings which he had experienced on the raft.

The remains of this young officer received the honours due to them. The English officers, and especially Major Peddy, acted on this occasion in a manner worthy of praise.

Perhaps our readers will not be sorry to be made acquainted with some of the details of this mournful ceremony. They are drawn up by Mr. Correard, who still feels a sad pleasure in calling to mind the moments which necessarily made upon him so great an impression.

The body of the unfortunate Clairet was laid out in a subterranean apartment of the hospital, whither immense crowds repaired to see once more the mortal remains of one who was almost regarded as an extraordinary man; and who, at this moment, owed to his cruel adventures, the powerful interest, which the public favour attached to him and to those, who had so miraculously escaped from all the combined afflictions sustained on the fatal raft.

"About four o'clock in the afternoon," says Mr. Correard, "I heard the mournful sounds of martial instruments under the windows of the hospital. This was a dreadful blow to me, not so much because it warned me of the speedy fate which infallibly awaited me, as because this funeral signal announced to me the moment of eternal separation from the companion of my sufferings: from the friend, whom our common misfortunes had given me, when I passed with him the most dreadful moments of my life. At this sound I wrapped myself in my sheet, and crawled to the balcony of my window, to bid him the last farewell, and to follow him with my eyes as far as possible. I know not what effect the sight of me may have produced, but when I now reflect upon it myself, I imagine that the people must have believed it was a spectre welcoming a corpse to the abode of the grave.

"As for me, notwithstanding my emotion, the sacrifice which I supposed I had made of my life, permitted me to contemplate and to follow in detail the sad spectacle on which my almost extinguished eyes eagerly dwelt. I distinguished a crowd of slaves who had obtained permission from their masters to be present at the ceremony. A body of English soldiers was placed in a line; after them came two lines of French soldiers and sailors. Immediately after, four soldiers bore the coffin on their shoulders, after the manner of the ancients. A national flag covered it, and hung down to the ground; four officers, two French and two English, were placed at the angles, diagonally opposite, and supported the corners; on the coffin were laid the uniform and the arms of the young soldier, and the distinctive marks of his rank. On the right and left French officers of the army and navy, and all the officers of the administration, ranged in two files, formed the procession. The band of music was at their head: afterwards, came the English staff with the respectable Major Peddy at its head, and the corps of citizens, led by the mayor of the town; lastly, the officers of the regiment, and a detachment, commanded by one of them, closed the procession. Thus was conducted to his last repose, this other victim of the fatal raft, snatched in the flower of his age, from his friends and his country, by the most fatal death, and whose fine qualities and courage rendered him worthy of a less deplorable fate."

This brave officer, who was only twenty-eight years of age, had been eight years in the service; he had received the cross of the Legion of Honour at the Champ de Mai, as a reward for the services which he had performed at Talavera de la Reina, Sierra Morena, Saragossa, Montmiraill, Champaubert, and Montereau; he was present, also, at the too deplorable day of Waterloo; he was then ensign-bearer of his regiment.

Such were the events that passed in the isle of St. Louis. The bad season, which, in these countries is so fatal to the Europeans, began to spread those numerous and dreadful maladies, which are so frequently accompanied by death. Let us now turn to the unhappy persons assembled in the camp at Daccard, not far from the village of that name, situated on the Peninsula of Cape Verde.

CHAPTER 11

Despair at Camp Daccard

The French Governor, as we have already observed, being unable to enter into the possession of the colony, resolved to go and remain upon Cape Verde, which had been recognized to be the property of France. On the 26th of July the *Argus* brig, and a three-roasted vessel belonging to Messrs. Potin and Durecur, took on board the remains of the crew of the *Medusa*, that is, the men who had landed near Portendick, and some persons from the raft: those whose health were the most impaired remained in the hospital at St. Louis. These two vessels set sail; the Governor embarked on board that with three masts, and they arrived in the Goree Roads at nightfall. The next day the men were removed to Cape Verde: several soldiers and sailors had already repaired to it; these were those who had first crossed the desert: the flute, la *Loire*, had conveyed them thither some days before, with the commander of the frigate. It had also landed the troops it had on board, consisting of a company of colonial soldiers. The command of the camp was confided to Mr. de Fonsain, a respectable old man, who died there the victim of his zeal. What procured him this fatal distinction was the resolution taken by the Governor to go and reside in the island of Goree, to be able to superintend the camp, and the ships, and doubtless for the sake of his health.

The shipwreck of the frigate having much reduced the number of the garrison, and occasioned the loss of a great quantity of provisions which she had on board, it was necessary to dispatch a vessel to France, to obtain assistance and fresh orders, on account of the difficulties that had been raised by the English Governor. The *Echo* corvette was chosen for this purpose, which sailed on the 29th of July, in the evening. She had on board fifty-five of those who had been shipwrecked, three of whom were officers of the navy, the head surgeon, the accountant, three *eleves* of the marine, and an under surgeon. After a passage of thirty-four days, this corvette anchored in Brest Roads. Mr. Savigny says, that during the six years he has been in the navy, he has never seen a vessel so well kept, and where the duty was done with so much regularity as on board the *Echo*. Let us return to the new establishment, which collected the remnant of us on Cape Verde.

A camp was formed there to receive them near a village inhabited by negroes, and called Daccard, as has been stated above. The natives of the country appeared to be pleased at seeing the French found an establishment on their coast. A few days after, the soldiers and sailors having had some misunderstanding, the latter were removed, and distributed between the *Loire* and the *Argus*.

The men who formed this camp were soon attacked with the diseases of the country. They were ill fed, and many of them had just endured long fatigues. Some fish, very bad rum, a little bread, or rice, such were their provisions. The chase also contributed to supply their wants; but the excursions which they made to procure game, frequently impaired their health. It was in the beginning of July that the bad season began to be felt. Cruel diseases attacked the unhappy French; who being exhausted by long privations, these terrible maladies spread with dreadful rapidity. Two thirds of them were attacked by putrid fevers, the rapid progress of which hardly allowed the physicians time, to administer that precious remedy, the produce of Peru, of which, by some mismanagement, the hospitals were nearly destitute. It was in these distressing circumstances that Mr. de Chaumareys came to take the command of the camp. Other measures were taken, and the hospitals were no longer in want of bark; but dysenteries, which frequently proved mortal, spread everywhere.

On all sides there were none but unhappy men who gave themselves up to despair, and who sighed after their country: it was scarcely possible to find men enough for the duty of the camp. It is remarkable, that the crews of the vessels, which were in the roads of Goree, were hardly sensible of the influence of the bad season: it is true these crews were better fed, better clothed, and sheltered from the inclemency of the air; it is, besides, pretty certain, that this road is healthy, while the maladies of the country prevail on shore. Such was the situation of the camp of Daccard, when, on the 20th of November, the French Governor, was authorized, by Mr. Macarty, Governor General of the English settlements, to inhabit, on the former coast of the French possessions, the place which should suit him the best. Mr. Schmalz chose St. Louis.

As we were neither of us at the camp of Daccard we have not been able to detail all that passed there, and to speak only of things, with which we are perfectly acquainted, we have been obliged to pass over this part of our narrative rather slightly.

Mr. Correard, who had remained at the isle of St. Louis, hastened to pay his respects to the governor, when he came, in consequence of the permission of Mr. Macarty to inhabit that town. He relates, that on this occasion, the governor received him very well, pitied him much, and protested that if he had not been taken better care of, it was not his fault: Mr. Schmalz, allowed, that he had been the worst treated of all the shipwrecked persons, a thing which he had long known; "But, added he, your misfortunes are terminated, and henceforward you will want for nothing. I will send you, every day, very good rations of rice, meat, good wine, and excellent bread; besides, in a short time, I will put you to board with Mr. Monbrun, where you will be extremely well off." These last promises were as unavailing as the first had been. One day, however, in a fit of the fever, Mr. Correard sent his servant to the governor with a note, in which he asked for a bottle of wine, and one of brandy; he, in fact, received what he had asked for; but when he was recovered from his delirium, he was going to send back these two bottles; however, on reflection, he thought it would not be proper, and he resolved to keep them. This is all that he was able to obtain from the French authorities, during five month's time that he remained at Saint Louis. It is even probable that he would have returned to France without having cost his government the smallest trifle, but for that fit of the fever, which deprived him of his reason, and during which, be made the request which he afterwards thought to be indiscreet and improper.

On the 23rd, or 24th of November, he again saw his two benefactors Major Peddy and Captain Campbell, who were about to depart on their great expedition to the interior of Africa.

At the moment of their separation, Major Peddy was eager to give to Mr. Correard the last marks of true friendship, not only by his inexhaustible generosity, but also by good advice, which the event has rendered very remarkable, and which, for this reason, we think it necessary to mention here. The following is pretty nearly the discourse which the good Major addressed to Mr. Correard at their last interview:

"Since your intention," said he, "is to return to France, allow me, first of all, to give you some advice; I am persuaded that, if you will follow it, you will one day have reason to congratulate yourself on it. I know mankind, and without pretending exactly to guess how your Minister of the Marine will act towards you, I, nevertheless, think myself justified in presuming that you will obtain no relief from him; for, remember that a minister, who has committed a fault, never will suffer it to be mentioned to him, nor the persons or things presented to him, that might remind him of his want of ability; therefore, believe me, my friend; instead of taking the road to Paris, take that to London; there you will find a number of philanthropists, who will assist you, and I can assure you that henceforward, you will want for nothing. Your misfortunes have been so very great that there is no Englishman who will not feel a pleasure in assisting you. Here, Sir, are 300 *francs*, which will suffice for the expenses of your voyage, whether you go to Paris or to London. Reflect a moment on what I propose to you, and if your resolution is such as

I wish you to take, let me know it immediately, that I may give you letters of recommendation to all my friends, as well as to my patrons, who will be truly happy to serve you."

Mr. Correard was deeply affected by what he had just heard; the noble generosity of the excellent man to whom he already owed his life, and who entered with such perfect readiness, into all the details which he thought the most proper to finish his work, and insure the happiness of his poor friend, filled the heart of the latter with emotion and gratitude; yet, shall we say it? The advice to go to London, which the Major had just given him, had in it something that distressed him; he had not heard it without recollecting that he was a Frenchman, and some secret suggestions of self-love and national pride, told him that a Frenchman who had served his country, and to whom unparalleled misfortunes had given so many claims to the justice, as well as to the kindness of his own government, could not, without offering a kind of insult to his fellow countrymen, begin by going to England, and there throwing himself on the public compassion. These sentiments, therefore, suggested much more by his heart than by his understanding, dictated his answer to the Major.

It was not difficult for him to express, with warmth, all the gratitude which he owed him, for the noble and delicate manner in which he had sought him out, and relieved him in his misfortune.

"As for the pecuniary assistance which you still offer me," continued he, "I accept it with great pleasure, because benefits conferred by you, can only do honour to him who receives them, and because I hope, one day, to repay this debt with interest, to your countrymen, if I can meet with any who have need of my assistance. As for your other proposal, Major, allow me not to be of your opinion, and to have a little more confidence in the generosity of my government, as well as in that of my countrymen. If I acted otherwise, would you not be authorised to have a bad opinion of the French character and then, I appeal to yourself, generous Englishman, should not I have lost my claims to your esteem? Believe me, Major, France can also boast of a great number of men, whose patriotism and humanity may rival those which are so frequently found in Great Britain. Like you we are formed to the sentiments, to the duties which compose the true love of our country and of liberty. In returning to France, I firmly believe that I return into the bosom of a great family. But if, contrary to my expectation, it were possible that I should find myself, one day, abandoned by my government, as we were by some men who have nothing French about them but their dress; if France, which so often and so nobly welcomes the unfortunate of other countries, should refuse pity and assistance to her own children, then, Major, should I be obliged to seek, elsewhere, a happier fate and a new country: there is no doubt but that I should choose that of my generous benefactors in preference to every other."

Major Peddy answered Mr. Correard only by tears. The transport of patriotism, in which the latter had naturally indulged himself, had found, as may be supposed, the heart of the noble Briton, in harmony with that of him whom he protected; he felt a visible satisfaction, and an emotion which he did not attempt to dissemble. The Major closely embraced Mr. Correard, bidding him farewell for ever; it seemed that this worthy man foresaw his approaching end.

He was in fact destined to sink beneath the fatigues of the journey which he was about to undertake.

This expedition was composed, besides the Major, who commanded in chief, and the Captain, who was the second in command, and charged with the astronomical observations, of a young Physician, who was third in command; of Mr. Kummer, the naturalist (a Saxon naturalized in France); of a Mulatto, who acted as interpreter; of thirty white soldiers, almost all workmen; of a hundred black soldiers, and of about ten camels, a hundred and fifty horses, as many asses, and a hundred oxen to carry burdens; so that there were above a hundred and thirty men, and four hundred animals. All the equipages were embarked on board six small vessels, which ascended the Rio Grande to the distance of about fifty leagues up the country. The respectable commander of this expedition could not resist the influence of the climate; he was attacked by a cruel disease, which terminated his existence a few days after his departure from the island of St. Louis. Such men ought to be imperishable.

The English physicians finding that the health of Mr. Correard far from improving, seemed on the contrary, to decline more and more, persuaded him to return to France. These gentlemen gave him a certificate of such a nature, that the French governor could not object to his departure; he received his request perfectly well, and two days after his passage was secured; but we shall see in the sequel what was the motive of this favourable attention to his request.

On the 28th of November, in the morning, he embarked on board of a coasting vessel, which conveyed him first on board the *Loire*, which was bound for France: he was no sooner embarked, than the fever seized him, as it did almost every day; he was in a dreadful situation, weakened by five months' illness, consumed by a burning fever, added to the heat of the noon-day sun, which struck perpendicularly on his head; he thought he was going to die; he had, besides, painful vomitings, produced by the heat, and by an indisposition caused by the fish on which he had breakfasted before his departure. The little vessel crossed the bar; but it falling a dead calm, it could not proceed: they perceived this on board the *Loire*, and immediately dispatched a large boat to fetch the passengers out of the heat of the sun. While this boat was coming, Mr. Correard fell asleep upon a coil of cables that were on the deck of the little vessel; but before he fell quite asleep, he heard someone say, "There's one who will never get to France."

The boat came in less than a quarter of an hour; all those who were about my sick friend, embarked on board the boat, without any one's having the generosity to awaken him; they left him asleep, exposed to the beams of the sun; he passed five hours in this situation, after the departure of the boat. In his life he had never suffered so much, except during the thirteen days on the raft. When he asked, on awaking, what was become of the other gentlemen, he was told that they were gone, and that not one of them had showed any intention of taking him with them. A breeze springing up, his vessel at last reached the *Loire*, and there on the deck, in the presence of the sailors, he reproached in the bitterest manner, those who had abandoned him, and even said offensive things to them. These sallies, the consequence of his exasperation, caused him to be looked upon as out of his mind, and nobody troubled himself about the severe truths which he had thus publicly uttered. The *Loire* sailed on the 1st of December, and arrived in France on the 27th of the same month.

When Mr. Correard got to Rochefort, he waited on the Intendant of the Marine, who received him kindly, and authorised him to remain in the hospital as long as he should think necessary for his recovery. He was placed in the officers' ward, where he received the utmost attention from the medical gentlemen, who besides the aid of their art, showed him the greatest regard and mitigated his misfortunes by kind consolations. Mr. Savigny saw every day his companion in misfortune, and he often repeated, "I am happy, I have at length met with men sensible to my misfortunes." After having passed thirty-three days in this fine hospital, he judged his health sufficiently recovered, and desired to leave it, in order to go to his family.

We shall here conclude the nautical part of our history; but as, since our return to France, particular circumstances and a series of events, which we were far from foreseeing, have, as it were prolonged the chain of our adventures, we think it will not be amiss to add another article, respecting what has happened to us since we have returned to our country.

Mr. Savigny thought, that after having undergone unexampled misfortunes, he had a right to describe all the sufferings to which he and his companions in misfortune had been exposed for thirteen days. Was it ever heard that the unhappy were forbidden to complain? Well, the fresh misfortunes which have befallen him, and which he is going to lay before our readers, have arisen, from his not having buried in silence these disastrous events.

During his passage on board the *Echo*, he wrote the account of our unhappy adventures; his intention was to deliver his narrative to the Minister of the Marine. When he arrived in France, in the month of September, some persons advised him to go to Paris, where, said they, "Your misfortunes will procure you the favour of the Ministry," and it was considered as an absolute certainty, that some recompense would make him forget the considerable losses which he had sustained, the dangers which he had just escaped; and the pain arising from his wounds, for at that time he still wore his right arm in a sling. He listened to the advice which was given him, because it came from very sensible persons, and set out for the capital, carrying his manuscript with him. He arrived at Paris on the 11th of September: his first care was to go to the office of the Minister (of the Marine), where he deposited all the papers which he had drawn up respecting the shipwreck of the *Medusa*. But what was his astonishment to see the day after, the *Journal des Debats* of the 13th of September, an extract from his narrative, copied almost literally: he then endeavoured to discover whence the editors could have obtained these details; it cost him but little time to solve the riddle.

We shall not here explain by what means his manuscript became known to the editor of the *Journal*. We shall here content ourselves with saying, that while Mr. Savigny was still at Brest, a person, who has connexions with the officer of the marine, with the intention of serving him, asked him for a copy of his memoir, saying, that by the medium of a person in office, he could get it conveyed to the minister of the marine. This copy of our adventures was entrusted to this person, and by him sent to Paris. Mr. Savigny had acted in this manner, because his intention, at that time, was to go to his family, without passing through the capital. It appears that this copy was not discreetly kept, since it reached the editor of the *Journal des Debats*: certainly, he who received it from Brest, was very far from wishing to injure the author of the memoir. If he had had the smallest idea of all the disagreeable consequences arising from the publicity which he gave to the narrative, by showing it to several persons, he would have kept it more carefully, or at least, he would have delivered it immediately to the minister of the marine for whom it was intended. This publicity, by means of the *Journal*, drew upon Mr. Savigny the most serious remonstrances. The very same day he was sent for to the office; he was told that His Excellency was discontented, and that, he must immediately prove, that he was innocent of the publication of our misfortunes, which affected all France, and excited a lively interest in the fate of the victims. But for Mr. Savigny, everything was changed; instead of the interest, which his situation ought to inspire, he had called down upon himself the severity of the minister, and was to justify himself, for having dared to write that he had been very unfortunate, by the fault of others. The reception he met with at the office affected him so much, that but, for the advice of some persons, he would have resigned his commission at once. There was but one means to prove, that it was not he, who had given his narrative to the editor of the *Journal des Debats*: this was to obtain the certificate of the editor himself. Conscious of the truth, he went to him, and that honourable writer, without hesitation, did homage to the truth, by the following certificate:

> I certify that it is not from Mr. Savigny, that I have the details of the shipwreck of the *Medusa* inserted in the journal of the 13th of September, 1816.
> (Signed)—The Editor of the *Journal des Debats*

This certificate was put into the hands of M. —— and by him presented to His Excellency, who, however, did not appear satisfied, because this certificate, though it proved, that Mr. Savigny was not the person who had rendered public the history of our adventures, threw no light on the means by which the manuscript had become known to the editor. One of the principal persons in the office, having signified to him the opinion of His Excellency, who found this justification insufficient, Mr. Savigny again had recourse to the editor of the journal, who gave a second certificate as follows.

I certify, that it is not from Mr. Savigny, that I have the details inserted in the Number of the 13th of September, but from the office of the Minister of the Police.

After this new proof, it was no longer doubted, but that Mr. Savigny had been the victim of an indiscretion, and he was told that he might return to his post. He therefore left the capital, after having experienced many vexations; but those, which the publication of our misfortunes was to cause him, were not yet at an end.

The English translated the details contained in the *Journal* of the 13th of September, and inserted them in one of their Journals which reached Senegal. In this amplified translation, there were some pretty strong passages, which were far from pleasing the governor, and M. ———, one of the officers of the frigate. They perceived that there was but one means to combat the narrative; this was to endeavour to make it believed, that it was false in many particulars. A report was therefore drawn up at St Louis; it was brought to Mr. Correard to be signed, who, after perusing it, refused, because he found it contrary to the truth. The governor's secretary came several times to the hospital, to urge him for his signature; but he persisted in his refusal: the governor himself pressed him very earnestly one day that he went to solicit leave to depart; he answered, that he would never consent to sign a paper quite at variance with the truth, and returned to his hospital. The next day, his friend, Mr. Kummer, went to him, and invited him to return to the governor's, in order, at length, to sign this paper, because he had been informed, that if he persisted in his refusal, he should not return to France. These gentlemen, must therefore, have felt themselves deeply interested, to be reduced to employ such measures towards an unfortunate man, exhausted by a long sickness, and whose recovery depended on his return to Europe, which they thought not to grant him, except on condition of his signing a false narrative, contrary to what he had himself seen; for one paragraph was employed to prove that the towrope had broken; could he sign it, who was himself an eye witness, and who had been assured by more than twenty persons, that it had been made loose. Besides this falsehood, it was stated one passage, that, when the raft was left, the words we abandon them, were not pronounced; in another passage, that Mr. Savigny, in publishing his account, had shown himself ungrateful to his officers, who had done everything to serve him personally; there were, besides, some improper personalities: he was in particular much surprised to see at the bottom of this paper, the signature of a man, whose life Mr. Savigny had saved with his own hand. Mr. Correard's perseverance in withholding his signature, triumphed over injustice, and his return to Europe was no longer retarded. But the same manoeuvres had more success in another quarter, and Messrs. Dupont, Lheureux, Charlot, Jean Charles, and Touche-Lavilette could not escape the snare which was laid for them. They were labouring under that terrible fever which carried off the French with so much rapidity, when they were invited by the governor to sign this narrative. Some yielded to the fear of displeasing His Excellency; others conceived hopes of obtaining his protection, which, in the colonies is no trifling advantage; others again were so weak, that they were not even able to make themselves acquainted with the paper to which they were desired to put their names. It was thus, that our companions were induced to give testimony against themselves, to certify the contrary of what they had seen respecting all that had been done, to bring about our destruction. Our readers have just seen the noble disavowal of Mr. Griffon, of the false impressions which had deceived him in respect to us: in order that the reader may be able to form a just opinion of the report directed against us, we insert here a document equally precise and decisive: it is a declaration of Mr. Touche-Lavillette, who acknowledges, that he signed in confidence, a paper, the contents of which were unknown to him, as well as the purpose for which it was drawn up.

Thus supported by authorities, the value of which anybody can now appreciate, this tardy and inexact report was addressed to the minister of the marine. Mr. Correard, when he landed at Rochefort, informed Mr. Savigny of it, and gave him a certificate of what has been just related. The latter procured two others, which were delivered to him, by those of his companions in misfortune, who were in France.

Provided with these three certificates, Mr. Savigny solicited permission to go to Paris, in order to be able to let His Excellency see, that they were seeking to deceive him. Two months passed without information. Mean time, Mr. Correard departed for the capital, taking a letter from his comrade, for a person in the office, to whom it was delivered, and who did not give a decisive answer to what was asked of him. At length, Mr. Savigny received a letter from Paris, in which he was informed, "That not only he would not receive the permission which he solicited, but that, as long as the present minister was at the head of affairs, he would have no promotion."

This letter, which he had so long expected, was dated May 10, 1817. Mr. Savigny disgusted by all that he had just experienced, gave in his resignation, after having served six years, and made as many expeditions by sea. On leaving the service, this medical officer, who had several times narrowly escaped perishing in the waves, was honoured by the regret of the superiors under whom he has been employed, as may be judged by the copy of the certificate, which they gave him when he resigned his situation. Fresh misfortunes have also befallen Mr. Correard, from the time that he left Rochefort, till the moment that he was able to join his companion in misfortune, to write together the account of their shipwreck.

CHAPTER 12

Petitions

On the 4th of February 1817, thinking himself entirely recovered, he resolved to set out for Paris, where business rendered his presence necessary; but as his pecuniary resources were slender, and he had been at considerable expense to clothe himself, (for he was almost naked when he landed from the *Loire*) he thought he could make the journey on foot. On the first day he felt only a slight pain, on the second it increased, and on the third, the fever seized him. He was then three leagues from Poitiers, near a very little village: exhausted with fatigue, and weakened by the fever, he resolved to go to the mayor, and ask him for a billet; this functionary was from home, but his wife said, that at all events, it would be necessary first to obtain the consent of Monsieur the Marquis de ———— Colonel of the National Guard. The weary traveller thought there could be no impropriety in waiting on the Marquis: he was deceived in his expectation; the Colonel gave him a very bad reception, and was insensible to his entreaties; it was in vain that he showed him his certificates, his pass, his wounds, and even his arms which shook with the fever: nothing could move him. The unfortunate invalid, in despair, retired, cursing the inhumanity, which he had not expected to find in an officer of the National Guard, promising in his own mind, never to forget his illustrious name, and the unfeeling manner in which he had answered to his requests. Exhausted as he was, he was obliged to drag on another weary league on foot, in order to reach a public house where he might rest himself. The next day, with much difficulty, he got to Poitiers. He had the happiness to find a man of feeling in the Mayor, who was much affected by his melancholy situation; it was, indeed, calculated to excite interest; for a few minutes before he entered the town-hall, he fainted, but the most charitable assistance was bestowed on him by a respectable lady, and he soon recovered from this swoon. One of the clerks soon gave him a billet, assuring him that it was upon one of the best houses in the town; which was true; and the poor invalid owns, that in his life, he never has received more affectionate care than that which he met with in the house of Mr. Maury, proprietor of the hotel of the Roman Antiquities. Poitiers was therefore a place of happiness for him. It was soon known in the town, that one of the shipwrecked persons from the raft, was within its walls; and during the whole day nothing was spoken of but that melancholy event. Two persons, well known for their talents, and the high offices which they have filled, came to the relief of Mr. Correard: both had been formerly exiled; they knew what misfortune was, and knew how to pity that of an unhappy man, who had just experienced such extraordinary hardships; they invited him to spend the whole of the fine season at their country houses; but desiring to reach Paris as soon as possible, he refused the generous offer that was made him, and after having rested three days at Poitiers, he left it by the diligence, and at last arrived in the capital.

On his arrival, his first step was directed by gratitude; he recollected the signal services which he had received from the English officers, during his abode at Saint Louis; and his heart urged him to enquire of the ambassador of that nation, if he had not received any intelligence respecting his benefactors.

After he had thus discharged the duty which was imposed on him by their beneficence, he made all the necessary applications to the office of the Marine to obtain an employment in the capital. He was answered that it was impossible, advising him to make an application for a situation in the colonies, particularly

Cayenne. Three months passed in useless solicitations to obtain this employment, as well as the decoration of the legion of honour, which he had been led to hope for.

During this time he neglected nothing which he thought might conduce to enable him to attain the object which he thought he might propose to himself without being accused of extravagant pretensions. Excited by the advice of a great many persons, whose judgment, as well as their noble and generous sentiments, commanded implicit confidence, he resolved to go to the very fountain of favours, to carry into the royal palace the sight of his strange misfortune, to invoke that hereditary goodness, the bright patrimony of the Bourbons, which so many other unfortunate persons have not solicited in vain. But the malignant influence of the adverse star, which so long persecuted Mr. Correard, doubtless continued to manifest itself here. Neither he nor any other person will accuse the heart of the august personages to whom he addressed his petition; but whether timidity, the natural concomitant of misfortune, or a certain delicacy, hindered him from renewing his applications, for fear of seeming importunate, whether, as in the crowd of solicitors who surround princes, it is morally impossible that some should not be forgotten or less remarked, Mr. Correard's ill-fortune placed him among this less favoured number, or whether it be the effect of some other unknown adverse cause, he obtained on this side only vain hopes, as well as a just idea of the obstacles of every kind, with which the best princes are, as it were, surrounded without being conscious of it, and which keep back or turn aside the favour, which is always granted in their heart, just at the moment that it is on the point of being declared.

He first presented a petition to His Royal Highness Monsieur. He solicited the insignia of that order which was instituted to recompense all kinds of civil and military merit, to spread among all classes of society, the noble flame of emulation, of that order which was offered to Goffin, whose firmness forced his desponding companions, to hope for the assistance that was preparing for them: which has just been given to several of the shipwrecked crew of *La Caravane*, who in their disaster, showed themselves equally generous and intrepid; but who, however, had nothing to complain of but the elements, nothing to combat but the tempest.

He has every reason to believe that Monsieur had the goodness to sign his petition; but he has not been able to discover where, or how it has been lost on the way without reaching its destination. In the inquiries which he made at the office of the Prince's Secretary, he met with a young man eighteen or 20 twenty years of age, who already wore the same mark of merit which Mr. Correard desired, and who only expressed an astonishment which was more than disobliging, at the subject of his demand, asking him if he had been twenty-five years in the service. Mr. Correard, feeling on his side something more than surprise, thought it best to withdraw, but not till he had observed to this very young man, that he who appeared so difficult about the claims of others must, according to appearance, in order to obtain the cross of the legion of honour, have got the years of his ancestors services counted instead of his own.

His friends again persuaded him to petition the Duke d'Angouleme, from whom, as High-Admiral of France, these friends thought that Mr. Correard might expect an intervention more likely to promote the success of his application to the Minister of the Marine. He therefore went to the Tuileries on the 8th of May, and though his wounds still rendered walking painful to him, he had the good fortune to meet with the Prince as he was coming from a review, and to present him a memorial as he passed.

His Royal Highness received him graciously, expressed his satisfaction at seeing one of the persons who had escaped from the fatal raft, and pressing his hand in the most affable manner, said to him, "My friend, you have experienced very great misfortunes. It seems that amidst these disasters you have behaved well." After having run over the memorial, the Prince was pleased to add: "Thus it is that the King should be served; I will recommend you to His Majesty, and let him know your conduct and your situation."

These marks of kindness have hitherto been all that Mr. Correard has obtained by this memorial. However, His Royal Highness transmitted it to the navy-office, but there is every reason to suppose that it will remain buried there amidst the mass of papers; from which it might be presumed that the recommendations of princes are received with great indifference by the clerks of ministers, and that their offices are the shoals where the petitions of the unhappy are lost; in fact, a man of great experience, to whom Mr. Correard communicated this mischance, told him, that, in such an affair, he would rather have the protection of the meanest clerk, than that of the first prince of the blood.

We think it superfluous to detain the reader any longer, with two or three other attempts, which were still more unfortunate, and only revived painful recollections in the mind of Mr. Correard.

At last he received a letter from the Minister of the Marine, dated the 4th of June: it was a thunder-clap to him, for he was made to understand that all his applications would probably be in vain.

However, on the 20th of July, he received a note from Mr. Jubelin, inviting him to call at the Office of the Marine. His heart opened at this ray of hope; it was merely to know whether it were true, that he had received a pass to repair from Rochefort to his home. He answered in the affirmative, which seemed to cause much surprise, for one had just been refused to Mr. Richefort, who solicited it in vain, though he was also one of those shipwrecked. He profited by the opportunity to inquire whether the expedition to Cayenne was soon to depart? A vague answer being returned, he represented how unfortunate he and his companions on the raft were, that they could obtain nothing, while some officers of the frigate had been appointed to commands. Mr. Jubelin answered that the minister owed them nothing, and particularly to him: that he had gone of his own free will, and had engaged to ask nothing of the minister, except what was stipulated and mentioned in the treaty of May 16,

1816, by which His Excellency made to the explorers, numerous concessions (which it would be too long to mention here) on condition that they should correspond with His Excellency, through the Governor of Senegal; that they should be placed under the orders of that governor, and that they should undertake nothing without his approbation.

The impartial public will judge if, after such conventions, and having allowances, and passes from the government, it was to be presumed that he, who had been thus treated, would be told that they owed him nothing, not even assistance.

He learned, in the office, that the counsellor of State, Baron de Portal, had the intention to obtain for him, the decoration of the Legion of Honour, and that, for this purpose, he had had a memorial drawn up in his favour: but the minister had written in the margin, *I cannot lay this request before the King*. Thus the voice of the unfortunate Correard could not reach the throne; the minister would not permit it. Doubtless if His Majesty had been informed, that some unhappy Frenchmen, who had escaped from the raft of the *Medusa*, had long and in vain solicited his minister, his paternal goodness would have given them proofs of his justice and his benevolence. His kind hand which is extended even to the guilty, by conferring his favours upon us his faithful subjects, would have made us forget our misfortunes and our wounds; but no, an unfriendly power, between us and the throne, was an insuperable barrier, which stopped all our supplications.

Mr. Correard persuaded of the inutility of making fresh applications, gave up for the present all farther solicitation for what he had so well deserved by his courage and his services. The change in the ministry has revived his hopes: a letter from that department informs him that his Excellency would willingly embrace an opportunity to serve him.

A minister, when he is really so disposed, easily finds means to employ an unfortunate man who asks but little.

Such are the vexations which we have experienced since our return to France: now returned to the class of citizens, though reduced to inactivity, after having exhausted our resources in the service, disgusted, forgotten, we are not the less devoted to our country and our king. As Frenchmen, we know that we owe to them our fortune and our blood. It is with the sincere expression of these sentiments that we shall conclude the history of our adventures.

In fine, we think that the reader will not be sorry to have some notices concerning the French settlements on the coast of Africa. As they seemed to us very interesting, we shall examine, but briefly, the places themselves, and the advantages that might be derived from them.

These details will be a happy digression from the sad accounts of our misfortunes, and as the object of them is of great public utility, they will not be out of their place at the conclusion of a work, in which, we have thought it our duty, less for our own interest, than that of the public service, to employ our humble efforts for the disclosure of the truth.

The part of the coast beginning at Cape Blanco, and extending to the arm of the river Senegal, called the Marigot of the Maringouins; is so very arid, that it is not fit for any kind of cultivation; but from that Marigot, to the mouth of the river Gambia, a space, which may be about a hundred leagues, in length, with a depth of about two hundred, we meet with a vast country, which geographers call Senegambia.

Let us remark, however, before we go any further, that, notwithstanding the sterility of this part of the coast; it is not without importance, on account of the rich produce of the sea which bathes it. *The agriculture of the waters* as a celebrated naturalist has said, offers too many advantages, for the places that are adapted to it, to pass unobserved: this part of the sea, known by the name of the Gulf of Arguin, is especially remarkable for the immense quantity of fish which visit it, at different seasons, or which continually frequent these shores. This gulf, included between Capes Blanco and Merick and the coast of Zaara, on which, besides the isle of Arguin which was formerly occupied, there are several others at the mouth of what is called the river

St. John, is as it were closed towards the west, in its whole extent, by the bank which bears its name. This bank, by breaking the fury of the waves, raised by the winds of the ocean, contributes by securing the usual tranquillity of its waters, to render it a retreat for the fish, at the same time that it also favours the fishermen. In fact, it is from this gulf, that all the fish are procured which are salted by the inhabitants of the Canaries, and which constitute their principal food. They come hither every spring in vessels of about 100 tons burden, manned by 30 or 40 men, and they complete their operations with such rapidity, that they seldom employ more than a month. The fishermen of Marseilles and Bayonne might attempt this fishery. In short, whatever advantage may be sought to be derived from this gulf, so rich in fish, it may be considered as the African Bank of Newfoundland, which may one day contribute to supply the settlements of Senegambia, if the Europeans should ever succeed in establishing them to any extent. Among the species of fish found in this gulf, there is one, which seems peculiar to itself; it is that, which was caught on board the *Medusa*, and is the principal object of the fishery in these seas. An accurate description had been made of it, and Mr. Kummer made an exact drawing of it; but all was lost with the frigate. All that can be recollected of this description, is, that these fish which are from two to three feet long, are of the genus *Gade* or *Morue* (cod); that they do not appertain to any of the species mentioned by Mr. Lacepede, and that they belong to the section in which the Merlan is placed.

    Whence comes the name of Arguin? who gave it to this gulf? If we consider the heat of the sun which is experienced here, and the sparkling of the sandy downs which compose the coast, we cannot help remarking that *Arguia* in Phoenician means what is *luminous* and *brilliant*, and that in Celtic, *Guin* signifies *ardent*. If this name comes from the Carthaginians, who may have frequented these coasts, they must have been particularly struck with their resemblance to the famous Syrtes in their own neighbourhood, which mariners took so much care to avoid.

    Exercitas aut petit Syrtes Noto.

Some division of territory, or of pasturage among the hordes of the desert, was doubtless the cause, that the Europeans, who desired to carry on the gum trade, formerly chose the dangerous bay of Portendic, surrounded by a vast amphitheatre of burning sands, in preference to Cape Merick. Perhaps, the Trasas of the west, could not advance to the north of this bay, without quarrelling with the other Moors, who frequent Cape Blanco. This Cape Merick seems preferable for commerce, either as a factory, to trade with the Moors, or as a place of protection for the traders, and the fishery. Its elevation and nature, afford a facility of defence, which is not found at Portendic; where there is not at present the smallest appearance of vegetation.

The Estuary of the river, St. John, at the back of this Cape, is now entirely destitute of verdure, and humidity, and salt is abundant in the neighbourhood.

But, as we have said above, it is when we penetrate a little into the interior, that an immense country, rich in the gifts of nature, invites European cultivation, and offers the fairest prospect of success for the colonial productions.

The soil is in general good, and all colonists from the Antilles, who have visited these countries, think that they are well adapted to the cultivation of all kinds of colonial produce. This immense country is watered by the Senegal and the Gambia, which bound it to the north and south. The river Faleme crosses it in the eastern part, as well as many other less considerable rivers, which, flowing in different directions, water principally that part covered with mountains which is called the high country, or the country of Galam. All these little rivers fall at length into the two large ones, of which we have spoken above.

These countries are very thickly peopled, and are in general mild and hospitable. Their villages are so numerous, that it is almost impossible to go two leagues without meeting with some, that are very extensive and very populous. Nevertheless, we have no more than two settlements; those of St. Louis and Goree; the others, which were seven or eight in number, have been abandoned; either, because the French and the English, who have occupied them in turn, have wished to concentrate the trade in the two settlements which still exist; or because the natives no longer found the same advantage in bringing their goods and slaves. It is, however, true, (as we have been assured) that in consequence of the abolition of those factories, the considerable commerce which France carried on upon this coast before the revolution, has been reduced to one fourth of its former extent.

The town of St. Louis, the seat of the general government, is situated in longitude 18 deg. 48' 15" and in latitude 16 deg. 4' 10". It is built on a little island formed by the river Senegal, and is only two leagues distant from the new bar formed by the inundation of 1812. Its situation in a military point of view, is pretty advantageous, and if art added something to nature, there is no doubt, but this town might be rendered almost impregnable; but in its present state, it can hardly be considered as anything more than an open town, which four hundred resolute men, well commanded, might easily carry. At the mouth of the river is a bar, which is its strongest bulwark. It may even be said, that it would be impossible to pass it, if it were well guarded; but the coast of the point of Barbary, which separates the river from the sea is accessible; it would be even possible, without meeting with many obstacles, and with the help of flat bottomed boats, to land troops and artillery upon it. When this landing is once made, the place may be attacked on the side of the north, which is entirely destitute of fortifications. There is no doubt, but that, if it were attacked in this manner, it would be forced to surrender at the first summons. However, many have hitherto considered it as impregnable, believing that it was impossible to make a landing on the coast of Barbary. but as we are convinced of the contrary, because the English already executed this manoeuvre at the last capture of this place, we venture to call the attention of the government to the situation of St. Louis, which would certainly become impregnable if some new works were erected on different points.

This town has, in other respects, nothing very interesting in it, only the streets are strait, and pretty broad, the houses tolerably well built and airy. The soil is a burning sand, which produces but few vegetables: there are only eight or ten little gardens, containing from two to four *ares* of ground at the most, all cultivated, and in which, within these few years orange and lemon trees have been planted, so that there is reason to suppose, that, with some care, these trees would thrive perfectly well. Mr. Correard saw a fig-tree and an European vine, which are magnificent, and bear a large quantity of fruit. Since the colony has been restored to the French several kinds of fruit-trees have been planted, which thrive in an extraordinary manner. Five or six *palatuviers*, and a dozen palm trees are dispersed about the town.

The parade is tolerably handsome; it is situated opposite the castle, and what is called the fort and the barracks. On the west it is covered by a battery of ten or twelve twenty-four pounders, and two mortars; this is the principal strength of the island. On the east is the port, where vessels lie in great safety. The population of the town amounts to 10,000 souls, as the Mayor told Mr. Correard. The inhabitants of the island are both Catholics and Mahometans; but the latter are the most numerous, notwithstanding this, all the inhabitants live in peace and the most perfect harmony. There are no dissentions about religious opinions: every one prays to God in his own manner; but it is observed, that the men who have abjured Mahometanism, still retain the custom of having several wives. We think that it would not be very difficult to abolish it among the blacks, who are struck with the pomp of our religious ceremonies: they would be much more inclined to the Catholic religion, if it tolerated polygamy, a habit which will inevitably render all the efforts of the Missionaries abortive, as long as they commence their instruction by requiring its abolition.

The isle of St. Louis, by its important position, may command the whole river, being placed at the head of an Archipelago of pretty considerable islands: its extent is however small. Its length is 2,500 metres from north to south; and its breadth from east to west is, at the north part, 370 metres; in the middle of its length 28 metres; and at the south only 170 metres. The elevation of its soil is not more than 50 centimetres above the level of the river: in the middle it is however a little higher, which facilitates the running of the waters. The river dividing to form the isle of St. Louis has two arms, which reunite below the island: the principal situated on the east is about 1000 metres in breadth, and that on the west about 600. The currents are very rapid, and carry with them quantities of sand, which the sea throws back towards the coast; this it is that forms a bar at the mouth of the river; but the currents have opened themselves a passage, which is called the pass of the bar. This pass is about 200 metres broad and five or six metres in depth. Very often these dimensions are less; but at all times only such vessels can pass over it as draw four metres water at the utmost: the overplus is very necessary for the pitching of the vessel, which is always very considerable upon this bar. The waves which cover it are very large and short; when the weather is bad, they break furiously, and intimidate the most intrepid mariners.

The western arm of the river is separated from the sea by a point called the Point of Barbary. It is inconceivable how this slip of land, which is not above 250 metres in its greatest breadth, and is formed only of sand, should be able to resist the efforts of the river, which always tends to destroy it; and those of the sea, which breaks upon it sometimes with such fury, that it covers it entirely, and even crossing the arm of the river, comes and breaks on the shore of the island of St. Louis. Almost opposite the chateau and on the Point of Barbary, is a little battery of six guns at the most, which is called the Fort of Guetander; it is on the summit of a hill of sand which has been formed by the wind, and increases daily; it is even already pretty high, and is surrounded by a great number of huts of the blacks, which form a pretty extensive village: these buts tend to hold the sand together, and to prevent its sinking. The inhabitants of this village are very superstitious, as the following anecdote will prove.

Chapter 13
Exploring

In the course of the month of September, Messrs. Kummer and Correard crossed the arm of the river, to visit the coast of Barbary and the village of Guetander; when they landed on the point, they proceeded towards the north, and having gone three or four hundred paces along the shore, they found a turtle, the diameter of which was a metre at the least; it was turned upon its back and covered with a prodigious quantity of crabs, (*toulouroux*) which are found along the sea-coast. Mr. Correard stopped a moment, and remarked that, when he had wounded one of these animals with his cane, the others devoured it instantly. While he was looking at these crabs feeding on the turtle, Mr. Kummer went on towards the south, and visited the burying-places of the blacks. Mr. Correard joined him, and they saw that the natives erect over the tombs of their fathers, their relations and friends, little sepulchres, some made of straw, some of slight pieces of wood, and even of bones. All these frail monuments are consecrated much more by gratitude than by vanity. The blacks prohibit all approach to them in the strictest manner. Mr. Kummer, whom his companion had left to return to the shore, was examining very tranquilly these rustic tombs, when suddenly one of the Africans armed with a sabre, advanced towards him, crouching and endeavouring to surprise him; Mr. Kummer had no doubt but this man had a design upon his life, and retired towards Mr. Correard, whom he found again observing the crabs and the turtle. On relating to him what had just passed, as they were unarmed, they resolved immediately to pass the river, by throwing themselves into a boat; they had soon reason to congratulate themselves on having done so, for they perceived several men who had collected at the cries of the black, and, if they had not taken flight, it is probable that their innocent curiosity would have cost them their lives.

The left bank of the river, which is called Grande Terre, is covered with perpetual verdure, the soil is fertile, and wants only hands to cultivate it.

Opposite, and to the east of St. Louis, is the isle of Sor, which is four or five leagues in circumference; it is of a long and almost triangular form: there are two extensive plains in it, where habitations might be erected. They are covered with grass two metres in height, a certain proof of the advantages that might be derived from the cultivation of this island. Cotton and indigo grow there naturally, the ground is in some parts low and damp, which gives reason to suppose that the sugar-cane would succeed. It might be secured against the inundations which take place in the rainy season, by erecting little causeways a metre in height, at the most. There are in this island, principally on the east side, mangoes, *palatuviers*, a great quantity of gum trees, or mimosas, and magnificent Baobabs.

Let us stop for a moment before this colossus, which, by the enormous diameter to which it attains, has acquired the title of the Elephant of the vegetable kingdom. The Baobab often serves the negroes for a dwelling, the construction of which costs no further trouble than cutting an opening in the side to serve as a door, and taking out the very soft pith which fills the inside of the trunk. The tree, far from being injured by this operation, seems even to derive more vigour from the fire which is lighted in it for the purpose of drying the sap, by carbonising it. In this state it almost always happens, that the bark, instead of forming a ridge at the edge of the wound, as happens with some trees in Europe, continues to grow, and at length covers the whole inside of the tree, generally without any wrinkles, and thus presents the astonishing spectacle of an immense tree recompleted in its organisation, but having the form of an enormous hollow cylinder, or rather of a vast arborescent wall bent into a circular form, and having its sides sufficiently wide asunder to let you enter into the space which it encloses. If casting our eyes on the immense dome of verdure which forms the summit of this rural palace, we see a swarm of birds adorned with the richest colours, sporting in its foliage, such as rollers with a sky-blue plumage, *senegallis*, of a crimson colour, *soui-mangas* shining with gold and azure; if, advancing under the vault we find flowers of dazzling whiteness hanging on every side, and if, in the centre of this retreat, an old man and his family, a young mother and her children meet the eye, what a crowd of delicious ideas is aroused in this moment? Who would not be astonished at the generous fore-sight of nature? and where is the man who would not be transported with indignation if, while he was contemplating this charming scene, he beheld a party of ferocious Moors violate this peaceful asylum, and carry off some of the members of a family, to deliver them up to slavery? It would require the pencil of the author of the Indian Cottage, to do justice to such a picture.

This is not the only service which the blacks, who inhabit Senegambia, derive from the Adansonia or Baobab. They convert its leaves, when dried, into a powder which they call *lalo*, and use it as seasoning to almost all their food. They employ the roots as a purgative; they drink the warm infusion of its gummy bark, as a remedy for disorders in the breast; they lessen the inflammation of the *cutaneous* eruptions, to which they are subject by applying to the diseased parts cataplasms made of the parenchyma of the trunk: they make an astringent beverage of the pulp of its fruit; they regale themselves with its almonds, they smoke the calyx of its flowers instead of tobacco; and often by dividing into two parts the globulous capsules, and leaving the long woody stalk fixed to one of the halves, which become dry and hard, they make a large spoon or ladle.

It has been found that the substance, called very improperly, *terra sigillata* of *lemnos*, is nothing more than the powder made of the pulp of the fruit of the Baobab. The Mandingians and the Moors carry this fruit as an article of commerce into various parts of Africa, particularly Egypt; hence, it finds its way to the Levant. There it is that this pulp is reduced to powder, and reaches us by the way of trade. Its nature was long mistaken: Prosper Alpinus was the first who discovered that it was a vegetable substance.

After the Isle of Sor, towards the south is that of Babague, separated from the former and that of Safal, by two small arms of the river; this island, in an agricultural point of view, already affords a happy result to the colonists, who have renounced the inhuman traffic in slaves, to become peaceable planters. Many have already made plantations of cotton, which they call *lougans*. Mr. Artique, a merchant, has hitherto been the most successful. His little plantation brought him in 2400 *fr.* in 1814, which has excited in many inhabitants of St. Louis a desire to cultivate pieces of land there. After his example, we now see every where beginnings of plantations, which already promise valuable crops to those who have undertaken the cultivation of these colonial productions. The soil of Babague is more elevated than that of the surrounding islands. At its southern extremity, which is precisely opposite the new bar of the river, there is a very great number of huts of the blacks, a military post with an observatory, and two or three country houses.

The Isle of Safal, belonging to Mr. Picard, offers the same advantages. Its soil is fertile as that of the islands of which we have just spoken. No drinkable water is found in any of them; but it would be easy to procure excellent water by digging wells about two metres in depth.

Cotton and indigo grow everywhere spontaneously; what then is wanting, to these countries, to obtain in them what the other colonies produce? Nothing but some men, capable of directing the natives in their labours, and of procuring them the agricultural implements, and the plants of which they stand in need. When these men are found, we shall soon see numerous habitations arise on the banks of this river, which will rival those in the Antilles. The blacks love the French nation more than any other, and it would be easy to direct their minds to agriculture. A little adventure, which happened to Mr. Correard, will show to what a degree they love the French.

In the course of the month of September, his fever having left him for some days, he was invited by Mr. Francois Valentin, to join a hunting party in the environs of the village of Gandiolle, situated six leagues to the south, south east of St. Louis. Mr. Dupin, supercargo of a vessel from Bordeaux, who was then at Senegal, and Mr. Yonne brother of Mr. Valentin, were of the party. Their intention was to prolong the pleasures of the chase, for several days; in consequence, they borrowed a tent of the worthy Major Peddy, and fixed themselves on the banks of the gulf which the Senegal forms, since its ancient mouth is entirely stopped up, and a new one formed, three or four leagues higher up than the former. There they were only a short league from the village of Gandiolle. Mr. Correard directed his course, or rather his reconnaissances, a little into the interior, for he had conceived the idea of taking a plan of the coast, and of the islands formed by the Senegal. He was soon near to Gandiolle, and stopped some moments at the sight of an enormous Baobab tree, the whiteness of which much surprised him: he perceived it was covered with a cloud of the birds called aigrettes. He advanced across the village to the foot of this tree, and fired two shot successively, supposing he should kill at least twenty of these birds. Curiosity induced him to measure the prodigious tree, on which they were perched, and he found that its circumference was 28 metres. While he was examining this monstrous production of the vegetable kingdom, the report of his piece had caused a great many blacks to come out of their huts, who advanced towards Mr. Correard, doubtless, with the hope of obtaining from him some powder, ball, or tobacco. While he was loading his piece, he fixed his eyes upon an old man, whose respectable look announced a good disposition; his beard and hair were white, and his stature colossal; he called himself Sambadurand. When he saw Mr. Correard looking at him attentively, he advanced towards him, and asked him if he was an Englishman?

"No," replied he, "I am a Frenchman."

"How, my friend, you are a Frenchman! That gives me pleasure."

"Yes, good old man, I am."

Then the black tried to put on a certain air of dignity to pronounce the word Frenchman, and said, "Your nation is the most powerful in Europe, by its courage and the superiority of its genius, is it not?"

"Yes."

"It is true that you Frenchmen are not like the white men of other nations of Europe whom I have seen; that does not surprise me; and then, you are all fire, and as good tempered as we blacks. I think you resemble Durand in vivacity and stature; you must be as good as he was; are you his relation?

"No, good old man, I am not his relation; but I have often heard speak of him."

"Ah? You do not know him as I do: it is now thirty years since he came into this country with his friend Rubault, who was going to Galam. This Frenchman, whose language I learned at St. Louis, loaded us all with presents; I still keep a little dagger which he gave me, and I assure you that my son will keep it as long as I have done. We always remember those white men who have done us good, particularly the French whom we love very much."

"Well," answered Mr. Correard, "I am sorry I have nothing which can suit you, and be kept for a long time, or I would offer it you with pleasure, and you would join the remembrance of me with that of the philanthropic Durand, who had conceived plans which, if they had been executed, would, perhaps, have been the glory of my country, and the happiness of yours; but here, take my powder and ball, if that can do you pleasure."

"Ah! good Frenchman, I would willingly take them, for I know that you have as much as you please in your own country; but at this moment it would deprive you of the pleasure of the chase."

"No, take it all."

"Take my advice *Toubabe*: let us divide it, that will be better."

In fact, they divided. The black invited Mr. Correard to enter his hut to refresh himself. "Come *Toubabe*," said he, "come, my women shall give you some milk and millet flour, and you shall smoke a pipe with me."

Mr. Correard refused, in order to continue his sport, which was interrupted by the cries of the blacks, who pursued a young lion, which came from the village of Mouit, and attempted to enter that of Gandiolle; this animal had done no harm, but the natives pursued him in the hopes of killing him, and to sell his skin. Dinnertime being come, all the white hunters returned to their tent. A few moments after, they saw a young negro, twelve years of age at the most, whose mild and pleasant countenance was far from indicating the courage and the strength which he had just displayed; he held in his hands an enormous lizard quite alive, at least a metre and eighty centimetres in length. These gentlemen were astonished to see this child holding such a terrible animal, which opened a frightful pair of jaws. Mr. Correard begged Mr. Valentin to ask him how he had been able to take, and pinion it in this manner. The child answered as follows in the Yoloffe language:

"I saw this lizard come out of a hedge, I immediately seized it by the tail and hind feet: I raised it from the ground, and with my left hand took it by the neck; and holding it very fast, and at a distance from my body, I carried it in this manner to the village of Gandiolle, where I met one of my companions, who tied his legs, and persuaded me to come and present it to the *Toubabes* who are in the tent; he told me also that they were Frenchmen, and as we love them much, I have come to see them, and offer them this lizard."

After these details, Mr. Correard presented the butt end of his piece to the animal, which made a deep indenture with its teeth; having then presented it the end of the barrel, it immediately seized it furiously, and broke all its teeth, which made it bleed very much; nevertheless, it made no effort to disengage itself from its bonds.

The environs of Gandiolle appear to be extremely fertile; we find there grass two metres in height, fields of maize and millet. This country is full of large pieces of water, which the natives call *marigots*; the major part of which cover an immense space; but it would be easy to drain them by means of some little canals, particularly in the part near the coast. These lands would be very productive, and proper for the culture of the sugar cane: the soil is mud mixed with very fine sand.

After having examined the environs of St. Louis, let us cast a glance upon the rock called the Island of Goree, and its environs. This isle is nothing of itself; but its position renders it of the greatest importance: it is situated in longitude 19 deg. 5', and in latitude 14 deg. 40' 10", half a league from the main land, and thirty-six leagues from the mouth of the Senegal. The Cape de Verde Islands, are eighty leagues to the west. It is this position that renders it mistress of all the commerce of these countries. Its port is excellent; and so great a number of ships and boats are seen there that its road is continually covered; there is so much activity that some persons have said the Island of Goree was, perhaps, the point in the world, where there was most bustle and population. The number of its inhabitants is estimated at 5000 souls, which is by no means in proportion with its confined surface, which is not above 910 metres in length, and 245 in breadth. Its circumference is not above 2000 metres. It is only a very high rock, the access to the coasts, of which is very difficult. The numerous rocks, which surround it on all sides, have made some navigators give it the name of Little Gibraltar; and if nature were seconded by art, there is no doubt but like that, it would become impregnable. It was first taken possession of by Admiral d'Estrees, about the end of the year 1677. This isle lies in the direction of S.S.E and N.N.W. and is only about 2600 metres distant from Cape Verde. It is defended by a fort, and by some small batteries in very bad condition; but it is, nevertheless, impregnable by its position. In fact, it is not accessible, except on the E.N.E. where there is a pretty large and deep bay, capable of receiving the largest ships. Its road is immense; vessels are safe in it, and tolerably well sheltered. At two leagues from Goree is the bay of Ben, which affords the greatest facilities for the careening of vessels, and for the repairs of which they may stand in need.

The Island of Goree is cool during the evening, the night and the morning; but during the day, there prevails in the island an unsupportable heat, produced by the reflection of the sun's rays, which fall perpendicularly on the Basalt rocks which surround it. If we add to this the stagnation of the air, the circulation of which is interrupted by the houses, being very closely built, a considerable population, which continually fills the streets, and is beyond all proportion with the extent of the town, it will be readily conceived that all these reasons, powerfully contribute to concentrate here such insupportable heat, that one can scarcely breathe at noon day. The blacks too, who certainly know what hot countries are, find the heat excessive, and prefer living at St. Louis.

The Island of Goree may become of the greatest importance if the government should ever think proper to establish a powerful colony, from Cape Verde to the river Gambia; then this isle would be the bulwark of the settlements on the coast of Africa. But it will be objected that Goree is very small, and that great establishments can never be formed there; we think, only, that it is proper to be the central point, till a greater colony shall be established on Cape Verde, which nature seems to have intended for it, and the advantages of which, in a military and maritime point of view, are of the highest importance. Men of sound judgment who have examined it, have considered it calculated to become one day a second Cape of Good Hope. It is certain that, with time and by means of some works, this Cape would become highly interesting, and would serve as a depot, to accustom to the climate, such Europeans, as might wish to settle either in the projected colonies, or on those which might be founded, between this Cape and the Gambia, or on the islands of Todde, Reffo, Morphil, Bilbas, and even in the kingdom of Galam.

The position and figure of Cape Verde are such, that it would be easy to form there an excellent port at a small expense; perhaps it would not be impossible to make some use of the Lake or Marigot of Ben, which is but a short distance from the sea. Its road, which is the same as that of Goree, might almost serve as a port, even in its present state. The following is an extract from a Letter, written to Mr. Correard by a Physician, who has carefully examined Cape Verde:

> This Cape is very different from what we thought. Its surface is not above six or eight square leagues; its population is very numerous, and by no means in proportion with the part of this peninsula, proper for cultivation, which is not above one-third of its surface. Another third serves for pasture for the flocks of the blacks; and the other part is too much volcanised, too full of rocks, to afford any hope of advantage in an agricultural view. But its military position is admirable; all seems to concur to render it impregnable, and it would even be easy to insulate it entirely from the Continent, and to form upon it several ports, which nature seems to have already prepared.

This letter likewise speaks of the advantages offered by the environs of Rufisque, which are so well known, that we may dispense with speaking of them here. We shall only mention as among the principal points to be occupied, with the *mornes* of Cape Rouge, Portudal, Joal, and Cahone, this last on the river Salum near the Gambia; they are large villages, the environs of which are covered with magnificent forests, and the soil of which is perhaps the most fertile of any in Africa. For more ample accounts of these countries, we refer to the excellent works of Messrs. Durand and Geoffroy de Villeneuve, who have examined them like enlightened observers, and perfectly well described them in their travels, only that they have too much exaggerated the agricultural advantages of Cape Verde.

We shall not have the presumption to lay down plans, to propose systems, to enforce such or such means for putting them in execution. We shall merely terminate our task by some general considerations calculated to confirm what numerous and able observers have already thought, of the importance of the establishments in Africa, and of the necessity of adopting some general plan of colonisation for these countries.

However pride, prejudice and personal interest, may deceive themselves respecting the re-establishment of our western Colonies, nobody will be able longer to dissemble the inutility of attempts to persevere in a false route. Calculation will at length triumph over blind obstinacy and false reasonings. There is already a certain number of incontestable data, the consequences of which must be one day admitted. And first, though some persons who fancy that, like them the whole world have been asleep for these twenty-five or thirty years, still dream of the submission of St. Domingo, reasonably persons now acknowledge, that even were the final success of such an enterprise possible, its real result would be, to have expended, in order to conquer a desert, and ruins drenched in blood, ten times more men and money than would be sufficient to colonise Africa. It is well known, also, that the soil of Martinique is exhausted, and that its productions will diminish more and more; that the small extent of Guadaloupe confines its culture to a very narrow circle, and does not permit it to offer a mass of produce sufficient to add much to the force of the impulse, which a country like France, must give to all parts of its agricultural and commercial industry. It is not to be doubted, but that nature has given to French Guyana the elements of great prosperity; but this establishment requires to be entirely created; everything has hitherto concurred to prolong its infancy. There are not sufficient hands: and how will you convey thither the requisite number of cultivators, when you have proclaimed the abolition of the slave trade.

The Abolition of the Slave Trade: this is the principle, pregnant with consequences, which should induce every enlightened government speedily to change its whole colonial system. It would be in vain to attempt to prolong this odious trade by smuggling, and thus still to draw from it some precarious resources. This sad advantage would but keep open the wound which has struck the western colonies, without being able to effect their recovery, as is desired by those who seek to found their prosperity on the regular farming out of one of the races of mankind. The slave trade is abolished not only by religion, by treaties, by the consent of some powers, by the calculations and interest of some others, which will not permit it to be re-established; but it is abolished also by the light of the age, by the wish of all civilised nations; by opinion, that sovereign of the world, which triumphs over every obstacle, and subdues all that resist her laws. Without the slave trade, you cannot transport to the west Indies those throngs of men whose sweat and blood are the manure of your lands: on the other hand, you see the Genius of Independence hover over the New World, which will soon force you to seek friends and allies where you have hitherto reckoned only slaves. Why then do you hesitate to prepare a new order of things, to anticipate events, which time, whose march you cannot arrest, brings every day nearer and nearer? Reason, your own interest, the force of circumstances, the advantages of nature, the richness of the soil, everything tells you that it is to Africa, that you must carry culture and civilization.

Without entering into the question, whether the Government should reserve to itself, exclusively, the right of founding colonies on that continent, or whether it ought to encourage colonial companies, and depend on the efforts of private interest suitably directed, let us be permitted to offer some views, on the prudent and temperate course which ought to be laid down, to arrive at a satisfactory result, not only in respect to the civilization of the blacks, but even relatively to the commercial advantages which the colonist must naturally have in view.

Though the abolition of the slave trade has been proclaimed, yet the present slaves must be led to liberty only in a progressive manner. The whites who are possessed of negroes, should not be allowed to prolong their possession and their dominion over them, beyond the space of ten years, and without being permitted to resell them during that period. During these ten years, the negroes should be prepared for their new condition as well by instruction as by the successive amelioration of their situation; it would be necessary gradually to relax the chain of slavery; and by affording them means to lay up a part of the produce of their labour, inspire them with the desire, and the necessity of possessing something of their own.

After these ten years, which may be called a noviciate, it is to be presumed, that if lands were granted to them upon advantageous conditions, fixed before hand, if they were furnished in case of need, with the agricultural instruments, the use of which they would have learned, they would become excellent cultivators: it is needless to remark that the man who cultivates the soil, and whose labour the soil rewards, by its produce, becomes strongly attached to the land, which supplies both his wants and his enjoyments, and is soon led by family affections to the love of social order, and to the sentiments which constitute a good citizen.

The blacks have been too long encouraged to sell their fellow-creatures, for us to depend upon their soon forgetting this deplorable traffic. But doubtless we ought to begin by renouncing the perfidious means of inflaming their cupidity and their passions. The articles which they are the most desirous to obtain from us, ought to be the price of the produce of the soil, and no longer the means of exchange, and the aliment of this dreadful traffic in human flesh. It would, however, be proper that, as long as slaves should continue to arrive from the interior, the whites might buy them. This permission should be granted for a time, and in a certain extent of country. Their slavery should also be limited to ten years, as we have said above, and their moral and physical improvement, should be directed in such a manner as to attach them to the soil by exciting in them the love of property.

The laws and institutions which govern the mother country, would incontrovertibly be applicable to the new establishments. It would certainly be presumable, that on account of particular considerations of moral and political order, it would be proper to allow local regulations, in forming which, all proprietors enjoying the rights of citizenship, ought to participate, without any distinction of colour. It would especially be highly important, that the regulations for the government of the slaves, should be founded on mildness and humanity, that prudent and enlightened persons should superintend the execution of them, and have the necessary authority to prevent abuses, and to secure to the slave the protection of the law.

In order to obtain these results, it is evident that it would be no less essential to preserve the colonies from the scourge of arbitrary authority, from the excesses of power, which always accompany abuses, injustice, and corruption. When favour and caprice are the only laws that are attended to; when intrigue supplies the place of merit; when cupidity succeeds to honourable industry; when vice and meanness are titles to distinctions, and the true means of making a fortune; when honours are no longer synonymous with honour; then society presents only disorder and anarchy, then people renounce obscure virtue, and laborious acquisition to follow the easy ways of corruption; then enlightened men, for whom public esteem is a sterile recommendation, the true servants of the king, the faithful friends of their country, are forced to disappear, to withdraw from employments, and the interest of the public, as well as that of humanity, is miserably sacrificed to the basest calculations, to the most guilty passions.

He who desires the end, desires the means of attaining it. The end at present, should be to prepare everything beforehand, and rather sooner than later, in order to repair in Africa the past losses and disasters, which irremediable events have caused in the western Colonies, and to substitute for their riches their prosperity, the progressive decline of which is henceforward inevitable, new elements of wealth and prosperity: the means will be to carry into these countries, so long desolated by our relentless avarice, knowledge, cultivation, and industry. By these means we shall see in that vast continent numerous colonies arise, which will restore to the mother country all the splendour, all the advantages of her ancient commerce, and repay her with interest for the sacrifices she may have made in the new world. But to effect this, let there be no more secret enterprises; no more connivance at fraudulent traffic, no more unhappy negroes snatched away from their families; no more tears shed on that sad African soil, so long the witness of so many afflictions; no more human victims, dragged to the altars of the shameful, and insatiable divinities, which have already devoured such numbers: consequently, let there be no more grounds for hearing in the English Parliament, voices boldly impeaching our good faith, attacking the national honour, and positively asserting that France maintains in her African possessions, the system of the slave trade in the same manner as she did before she consented to its abolition.

Africa offers to our speculators, to the enterprises of our industry, a virgin soil, and an inexhaustible population peculiarly fitted to render it productive. It must be our business to form them according to our views, by associating them in these by a common interest. In conquering them by benefits, instead of subjugating them by crimes, or degrading them by corruption, let us lead them to social order and to happiness, by our moral superiority, instead of dragging them under scourges and chains to misery and death, we shall then have accomplished a useful and a glorious enterprise; we shall have raised our commercial prosperity on the greatest interest of those who have been the voluntary instruments of it, and above all, we shall have expiated, by an immense benefit, this immense crime of the outrages, with which we so long afflicted humanity.

APPENDIX

Notes by M. Bredif & An Officer of Merit

The following Notes were communicated to the authors, when the second edition was already so far advanced, as to render it impracticable to incorporate them with the body of the work, and they are therefore placed at the end. Some of them are extracted from the journal of Mr. Bredif, who belonged to the expedition, and were communicated by his uncle, Mr. Landry; the others are by an officer of merit, whose modesty prevents the publication of his name. Those of Mr. Bredif, are signed (B) the others (A).

On the route to Africa

In going from Europe to the western coasts of Africa, situated to the north of the line, it is better still, to pass between the Azores and Madeira, and not to come within sight of the coast, till you have nearly reached the latitude of the point where you desire to land. Nothing but the necessity of procuring refreshments can authorise vessels, bound to the Cape of Good Hope, or to the south of America, to touch at the Canaries, or at the Cape Verde Islands. Notwithstanding the depth of the channels between the first of these islands, these seas, which are subject both to calms and hurricanes are not without danger. By keeping at a distance, there is also the advantage of avoiding the current of Gibraltar, and of not running the risk of meeting with the north west winds, which generally prevail along the desert, (and hitherto insufficiently known.) Coasts of Zaara, along which the *Medusa* sailed to no purpose, and which winds also tend to impel vessels upon the dangerous bank of Arguin. (A)

On the manoeuvres before Funchal

The usual indecision, which the commander of the frigate displayed in all his resolutions, joined to a little accident, made him change the intention which he had expressed of presenting himself before Funchal. From a singularity which nothing justified, he appeared to have more confidence in one of the passengers, who had indeed, frequented these seas, than in any of his officers, in respect to the management of the vessel. As they approached Madeira, the vessel was worked almost entirely according to the advice of this passenger; but suddenly the breeze, which is always strong in the neighbourhood of these mountainous countries, fell when they got too near it, the sails flagged, the current seemed rapid; but after some hesitation in the manoeuvring of the vessel, which the officers soon put into proper order, they recovered the wind, and it was resolved to steer for Tenerife. (A)

On the islands of Madeira and Tenerife

Madeira and Tenerife seen on the side where their capital cities lie, have a very different appearance. The first is smiling with cultivation from its shores, almost to the summit of the mountains. Every where the eye discovers only little habitations surrounded by vineyards and orchards of the most delightful verdure: these modest dwellings surrounded by all the luxuriance of vegetation, placed under an azure sky, which is seldom obscured by clouds, seem to be the abode of happiness, and the navigator, long wearied by the monotonous prospect of the sea, cheerfully hailed this delightful prospect. Tenerife, on the contrary, shows itself with every mark of the cause by which it was formed. The whole south east side is composed of black sterile rocks, which are piled together in an extraordinary confusion; even to the environs of the town of Saint Croix, scarcely any thing is seen, on the greater part of these dry and burnt lands, but low plants, the higher of which are probably Euphorbia, or thorny Cereus; and those which cover the ground, the hairy lichen, *Crocella tinctoria*, which is employed in dying, and which this island furnishes in abundance. Seen from the sea, the town, which is in the form of an amphitheatre, appears to be situated in the recess, formed by two distinct branches of mountains, of which the one towards the south, forms the Peak properly so called; it is particularly remarkable at a distance for its slender towers, and for the steeples of its churches, the construction of which, calls to mind the Arabic architecture. (A)

On the mouth of the River St. John

There is probably an error in this account: the river St. John, is much more to the south, and on the north side of Cape Meric. The inlet, which was perceived during the ceremony of the tropic, which was a little tardy, is the gulf of St. Cyprian, into which the currents appear to set. Early in the morning, and to the north of this gulf, they passed a little island, very near the coast, and the black colour of which, owing doubtless to the marine plants that cover it, made a striking contrast with the whiteness of the sandy downs of the great desert, the abode of the Moors, and of wild beasts.—*Tellus leonum arida nutrix*. (A)

On the reconnaissance of Cape Blanco

Mr. de Chaumareys gave notice in the course of this day, that he had a mind to anchor at a cable's length from Cape Blanco. He talked of it till the evening, but on going to bed he thought no more about it; however, he continually repeated that the minister had ordered him to make that Cape; and therefore, when somebody said the next morning, that this Cape was supposed to have been seen at eight o'clock the preceding evening, it was from that time forbidden to doubt of it; and either from deference or persuasion it was agreed, but not without laughing, that the Cape had been seen at the hour mentioned. It was from the course of the vessel at this moment that the route was calculated till an observation was made at noon. (A)

On the refusal to answer the signals of the *Echo*

It would probably have been of no use to inform Mr. de Chaumarey's of the signals of the *Echo*. The commander of the *Medusa*, the chief of the division, had declared already in the roads of the island of Aix, his intention to abandon his vessels, and to proceed alone in all haste to the Senegal. Though he spoke of strictly following the pretended instructions of the minister respecting the route to be followed, it was, however, violating the principle one, since it is useless to form a division if it is not to go together. The corvette, commanded by Mr. Venancourt succeeded, it is true, several times in joining the commander; but soon, by the superior sailing of the *Medusa*, they lost sight of him again, and every time they rejoiced at it. This resolution, not to sail in company, was the chief cause of the loss of the principal vessel. The *Echo* having determined, as was proper, to follow its commander, alone passed to the north west of the bank. The two other vessels which had remained long behind and were much more at liberty, passed more than thirty leagues to the west of it, and thus proved that it was the safest and shortest route. (A)

On the stranding of the *Medusa*

From ten o'clock in the morning the colour of the water visibly changed, and the head pilot, calculating after his sea-torch before mentioned, declared, at half past eleven, that they were at the edge of the bank, and this was probable. From that moment the sailors were entirely employed in drawing up the lines thrown out alongside of the vessel, and the astonishing quantity of fish, all of the cod species, which were drawn on board, added to the weeds that floated on every side, were more than sufficient to make it believed that they were sailing upon a shoal. We shall speak below of the species of this fish; but as for the weeds, which were perceived on every side, besides that they gave reason to suppose that we were approaching the land, their appearance in this gulf, also gives ground to presume, that the currents of these seas, at this season, set north, since the plants, with exception of some *Zosteres*, were nothing but long stalks of grasses; most of them still furnished with their roots, and many even with their ears, belonging to the tall grasses of the banks of the Senegal, and the Gambia, which these rivers bring away at the time of the inundations. All those which could be observed were *Panios* or millets. (A)

Moment of the stranding of the frigate

The officers wanted to tack about, as the water became shallower every moment: but Mr. Richefort,(who enjoyed the confidence of Mr. de Chaumarey's,) declaring that there was no reason to be alarmed, the captain ordered more sail to be spread. Soon we had only fifteen fathoms, then nine, then six. By promptitude the danger might still have been avoided. They hesitated: two minutes afterwards a shock informed us that we had struck; the officers, at first astonished, gave their orders with a voice that showed their agitation: the captain was wholly deprived of his; terror was painted on the countenances of all those who were capable of appreciating the danger: I thought it imminent, and expected to see the frigate bilge. I confess that I was not satisfied with myself, at this first moment, I could not help trembling, but afterwards, my courage did not any more forsake me. (B)

Confusion on board the frigate

The frigate having stranded, the same thing happened, which usually does happen in critical circumstances, no decisive measures were taken: to increase our misfortunes the obedience of the crew to the officers was diminished for want of confidence. There was no concert. A great deal of time was spent, and the second day was lost without having done anything.

On the third, preparations were made to quit the frigate, and the efforts made the day before to get her afloat, were renewed, but only half measures were taken. The other preparations to insure our safety were not carried on with any activity. Everything went wrong. A list of the people was made, and they were distributed between the boats and the raft, in order that they might hold themselves ready to embark when it should be time. I was set down for the long boat. Our mode of living, during all this time, was extremely singular. We all worked either at the pump or at the capstan. There was no fixed time for meals, we eat just as we could snatch an opportunity. The greatest confusion prevailed, the sailors already attempted to plunder the trunks. (B)

The frigate lost

On the fourth the weather being fine, and the wind favourable to the motion which we wished to give to the vessel, we succeeded in it. The most ardent hope was excited among all the crew, we even supped very cheerfully; we flattered ourselves that we should free the vessel and sail the next day. A beautiful evening encouraged our hopes, we slept upon deck by moonlight; but at midnight the sky was overclouded, the wind rose, the sea swelled, the frigate began to be shaken. These shocks were much more dangerous than those in the night of the third. At three o'clock in the morning the master-caulker came to tell the captain that the vessel had sprung a leak and was filling; we immediately flew to the pumps, but in vain, the hull was split, all endeavours to save the frigate were given up, and nothing thought of but how to save the people. (B)

Embarkment of the crew

On the 5th, about seven o'clock in the morning, all the soldiers were first embarked on board the raft, which was not quite finished, these unfortunate men crowded together upon pieces of wood, were in water up to the middle.

Mrs. and Miss Schmalz went on board their boat. Mr. Schmalz, notwithstanding the entreaties of everybody, would not yet quit the vessel.

The people embarked in disorder, everybody was in a hurry, I advised them to wait patiently till every one's turn came. I gave the example, and was near being the victim of it. All the boats, carried away by the current, withdrew and dragged the raft with them: there still remained sixty of us on board. Some sailors, thinking that the others were going to abandon them, loaded their muskets, and were going to fire upon the boats, and particularly upon the boat of the captain, who had already gone on board. It was with the greatest difficulty that I dissuaded them from it. I had need of all my strength, and all the arguments I could think of. I succeeded in seizing some loaded muskets and threw them into the sea.

When I was preparing to quit the frigate, I had contented myself with a small parcel of things which were indispensable; all the rest had been already pillaged. I had divided, with a comrade, eight hundred *livres* in gold, which I had still in my possession; this proved very fortunate for me in the sequel. This comrade had embarked on board one of the boats. (B)

On Mr. Espiau

The name of this officer cannot be mentioned, in this memoir, without acknowledging the services which he performed on this occasion. To him we owe the lives of several sailors and soldiers who had remained on board. It is he who, notwithstanding the various dangers with which he was surrounded, following only the impulse of his courage, succeeded in saving them. In giving him a command, the minister has paid the debt which the State had contracted towards this officer for his honourable conduct. (A)

Embarkation of the Men Who Remained on Board the Frigate

I began to believe that we were abandoned, and that the boats, being too full, could take no more people on board. The frigate was quite full of water. Being convinced that she touched the bottom, and that she could not sink, we did not lose courage. Without fearing death it was proper to do everything we could to save ourselves: we joined all together, officers, sailors and soldiers. We appointed a master-pilot for our leader, we pledged our honour, either to save ourselves, or to perish all together; an officer and myself promised to remain to the last.

We thought of making another raft. We made the necessary preparations to cut away one of the masts, in order to ease the frigate. Exhausted by fatigue, it was necessary to think of taking some food; the galley was not under water; we lighted a fire; the pot was already boiling, when we thought we saw the long-boat returning to us; it was towed by two other lighter-boats, we all renewed the oath, either all to embark, or all to remain. It appeared to us that our weight would sink the long-boat.

Mr. Espiau, who commanded it, came on board the frigate, he said that he would take everybody on board. First, two women and a child were let down; the most fearful followed. I embarked immediately before Mr. Espiau. Some men preferred remaining on board the frigate to sinking, as they said, with the long-boat. In fact, we were crowded in it to the number of ninety persons; we were obliged to throw into the sea our little parcels, the only things we had left. We did not dare to make the least motion for fear of upsetting our frail vessel.

I had had some water-casks and a great many bottles of wine put on board: I had got all these things ready before hand. The sailors concealed in the long-boat what ought to have been for everybody; they drank the whole the first night, which exposed us to the danger of perishing with thirst in the sequel. (B)

Occurrences which took place after the raft was abandoned

About half-past six in the evening, and just at sun-set, the people in the boats descried the land: that is to say, the high downs of sand of the Zaara, which appeared quite brilliant and like heaps of gold and silver. The sea, between the frigate and the coast, appeared to have some depth; the waves were longer and more hollow, as if the bank of Arguin rose towards the west. But as they approached the land, the water suddenly became shallow, and finding only a depth of three or four feet, they resolved to cast anchor till day-break. Several scattered hills, a few rocky shoals nearly dry, made them presume that they were in the lagoons, formed by the River St. John; this opinion was verified by the sight of Cape Meric, which appears like the continuation of a high hill coming from the interior, but suddenly rising at its approach to the sea, like the torrents of Volcanic matter. In passing before this cape, out at sea and towards the west, the sea appeared to break over some shoals, which are suspected to be the southern end of the bank of Arguin, which, according to some persons at Senegal, is dry at low water. (A)

Forsaking the raft

When we had overtaken the raft, towed by the other boats, we asked the latter to take from us at least twenty men, or otherwise we should sink. They answered that they were already too much loaded. One of our movements, towards the boats, made them fancy that despair had inspired us with the idea of sinking them and ourselves at the same time.

How could the officers imagine that such a design was entertained by Mr. Espiau, who had just before displayed such a noble desire to assist his comrades? The boats, in order to avoid us, cut the ropes which united them together, and made all the sail they could from us. In the midst of this confusion, the rope which towed the raft, broke also, and a hundred and fifty men were abandoned in the midst of the ocean, without any hope of relief.

This moment was horrible. Mr. Espiau, to induce his comrades to make a last effort, tacked and made a motion to rejoin the raft. The sailors endeavoured to oppose it, saying that the men on the raft would fall upon us, and cause us all to perish.

"I know it, my friends," said he, "but I will not approach so near as to incur any danger; if the other vessels do not follow me, I will think only on your preservation, I cannot do impossibilities."

In fact, seeing that he was not seconded, he resumed his route. The other boats were already far off. "We shall sink," cried Mr. Espiau, "let us show courage to the very last. Let us do what we can: *vive le roi!*"

This cry a thousand times repeated rises from the bosom of the waters which are to serve us for a grave. The boats also repeated it, we were near enough to hear this cry of *vive le roi!* Some of us thought that this enthusiasm was madness: was it the fullness of despair which made them speak so, or was it the expression of the soul broken by misfortune? I know not, but for my part, this moment appeared to me sublime: this cry was a rallying cry, a cry of encouragement and resignation. (B)

On the sudden gale experienced by the raft

This strong gale was the same north west wind which in this season, as has been said before, blows every day with great violence after sun-set; but which, that day, began sooner, and continued till 4 o'clock the next morning, when it was succeeded by a calm. The two boats which resisted it, were several times on the point of being wrecked. The whole time that this gale lasted, the sea was covered with a remarkable quantity of *galeres* or *physalides*, (*physalis pelasgica*) which arranged, for the most part, in straight lines, and in two or three files, cut at an angle the direction of the waves, and seemed at the same time to present their crest or sail to the wind, in an oblique manner, as if to be less exposed to its impulse. It is probable that these animals have the faculty of sailing two or three abreast, and of ranging themselves in a regular or symmetrical order; but had the wind surprised these, so arranged on the surface of the sea, and before they had time to sink, and shelter themselves at the bottom, or did the sea, agitated on these shores, to a greater depth than is supposed, make them fear, in this situation, to be thrown upon the coast? However it be, the orders of their march; their disposition, in respect to the force which impelled them, and which they strove to resist; the apparent stiffness of the sail seemed equally admirable and surprising. Mr. Rang, who has been mentioned with praise in this work, having had the curiosity to catch one of these singular animals, soon felt a tingling in his hand, and a burning heat, which made him feel much pain till the next day. Bones of *seche gigantesque* (sepia, cuttlefish) already whitened by the sun, passed rapidly along the side of the ship, and almost always with some insects, which having, imprudently ventured too far from the land, had taken refuge on these floating islands. As soon as the sea grew calm, they perceived some large pelicans, gently rocking themselves on the bosom of the waves. (A)

Landing of the sixty-three men of the longboat

The sea was within two fingers breadth of the gunnels of the boat: the slightest wave entered; besides, it had a leak; it was necessary to empty it continually: a service which the soldiers and sailors, who were with me, refused. Happily the sea was pretty calm.

On the same evening, the 5th, we saw the land, and the cry of "land, land," was repeated by everybody. We were sailing rapidly towards the coast of Africa, when we felt that we had struck upon the bottom. We were again in distress: we had but three feet water; but would it be possible for us to get the boat afloat again, and put out into the open sea? There was no more hope of being able to reach the shore. As for myself, I saw nothing but danger on the coast of Africa, and I preferred drowning to being made a slave, and conducted to Morocco or Algiers. But the long-boat grounded only once; we proceeded on our route, and by frequent soundings we got into the open sea towards night.

Providence had decided that we should experience fears of every kind, and that we should not perish. What a night indeed was this! The sea ran very high, the ability of our pilot saved us. A single false manoeuvre, and we must all have perished. We, however, partly shipped two or three waves which we were obliged to empty immediately. Any other boat, in the same circumstances, would have been lost. This long and dreadful night was at length succeeded by day.

At day break we found ourselves in sight of land. The sea became a little calm. Hope revived in the souls of the desponding sailors, almost everybody desired to go on shore. The officer, in spite of himself, yielded to their wishes. We approached the coast and threw out a little anchor that we might not run aground. We were so happy as to come near the shore, where there was only two feet water. Sixty-three men threw themselves into the water and reached the shore, which is only a dry and burning sand, it must have been a few leagues above Portendic. I took care not to imitate them. I remained with about twenty-six others in the long-boat, all determined to endeavour to reach the Senegal with our vessel, which was lightened of above two-thirds of its burden. It was the 6th of July. (B)

THE FIFTEEN PERSONS IN THE YAWL TAKEN INTO THE LONGBOAT—SEQUEL OF THE DAY OF THE 6TH

An hour after landing the sixty-three men, we perceived behind us four of our boats. Mr. Espiau, notwithstanding the cries of his crew who opposed it, lowered his sails and lay-to, in order to wait for them. "They have refused to take any people from us, let us do better now we are lightened, let us offer to take some from them."

In fact, he made them this offer when they were within hail; but instead of approaching boldly, they kept at a distance. The smallest of the boats (a yawl) went from one to the other to consult them. This distrust came from their thinking, that, by a stratagem, we had concealed all our people under the benches, to rush upon them when they should be near enough, and so great was this distrust that they resolved to fly us like enemies. They feared everything from our crew, whom they thought to be in a state of mutiny: however, we proposed no other condition on receiving some people, than to take in some water, of which we began to be in want, as for biscuit we had a sufficient stock.

Above an hour had passed after this accident, when the sea ran very high. The yawl could not hold out against it: being obliged to ask assistance, it came up to us. My comrade de Chasteluz was one of the fifteen men on board of her. We thought first of his safety, he leaped into our boat, I caught him by the arm to hinder his falling into the sea, we pressed each other's hands, what language.

Singular concatenation of events! If our sixty-three men had not absolutely insisted upon landing, we could not have saved the fifteen men in the yawl; we should have had the grief of seeing them perish before our eyes, without being able to afford them any assistance: this is not all, the following is what relates to myself personally. A few minutes before we took in the people of the yawl, I had undressed myself in order to dry my clothes, which had been wet for forty-eight hours, from my having assisted in lading the water out of the long-boat. Before I took off my pantaloons I felt my purse, which contained the four hundred *francs*; a moment after I had lost it; this was the completion of all my misfortunes. What a happy thought was it to have divided my eight hundred *francs* with Mr. de Chasteluz who now had the other four hundred.

The heat was very violent on the sixth. We were reduced to an allowance of one glass of dirty or corrupted water: and therefore to check our thirst, we put a piece of lead into our mouths; a melancholy expedient!

The night returned; it was the most terrible of all: the light of the moon showed us a raging sea: long and hollow waves threatened twenty times to swallow us up. The pilot did not believe it possible to avoid all those which came upon us; if we had shipped a single one it would have been all over with us. The pilot must have let the helm go, and the boat would have sunk. Was it not in fact better to disappear at once than to die slowly?

Towards the morning the moon having set, exhausted by distress, fatigue, and want of sleep I could not hold out any longer and fell asleep; notwithstanding the waves which were ready to swallow me up. The Alps and their picturesque scenery rose before my imagination. I enjoyed the freshness of their shades, I renewed the delicious moments which I have passed there, and as if to enhance my present happiness by the idea of past evils, the remembrance of my good sister flying with me into the woods of Kaiserslautern to escape the Cossacks, is present to my fancy. My head hung over the sea; the noise of the waves dashing against our frail bark, produced on my senses the effect of a torrent falling from the summit of a mountain. I thought I was going to plunge into it. This pleasing illusion was not complete; I awoke, and in what a state! I raised my head with pain; I open my ulcerated lips, and my parched tongue finds on them only a bitter crust of salt, instead of a little of that water which I had seen in my dream. The moment was dreadful, and my despair was extreme. I thought of throwing myself into the sea, to terminate at once all my sufferings. This despair was of short duration, there was more courage in suffering.

A hollow noise, which we heard in the distance, increased the horrors of this night. Our fears, that it might be the bar of the Senegal, hindered us from making so much way as we might have done. This was a great error: the noise proceeded from the breakers which are met with on all the coasts of Africa. We found afterwards, that we were above sixty leagues from the Senegal. (B)

Stranding of the long-boat, and two other boats

Our situation did not change till the eighth; we suffered more and more from thirst. The officer desired me to make a list, and to call the people to distribute the allowance of water; every one came and drank what was given him. I held my list under the tin cap, to catch the drops which fell, and moisten my lips with them. Some persons attempted to drink sea water; I am of opinion that they did but hasten the moment of their destruction.

About the middle of the day, on the 8th of July, one of our boats sailed in company with the long-boat. The people on board suffered more than we, and resolved to go on shore and get water if possible; but the sailors mutinied and insisted on being landed at once: they had drank nothing for two days. The officers wished to oppose it; the sailors were armed with their sabres. A dreadful butchery was on the point of taking place on board this unfortunate boat. The two sails were hoisted in order to strand more speedily upon the coast, everybody reached the shore, the boat filled with water and was abandoned.

This example, fatal to us, gave our sailors an inclination to do the same. Mr. Espiau consented to land them; he hoped to be able afterwards with the little water that remained, and by working the vessel ourselves, to reach the Senegal. We therefore placed ourselves round this little water, and took our swords to defend it. We advanced near to the breakers, the anchor was got up, and the officer gave orders to let the boat's painter go gently, the sailors on the contrary, either let the rope go at once, or cut it. Our boat being no longer checked, was carried into the first breaker. The water passed over our heads, and three quarters filled the boat: it did not sink. Immediately we hoisted a sail which carried us through the other breakers. The boat entirely filled and sunk, but there was only four feet water; everybody leaped into the sea, and no one perished.

Before we thought of landing I had undressed myself, in order to dry my clothes; I might have put them on again, but the resolution to land having been taken, I thought that without clothes, I should be more able to swim in case of need. Mr. de Chasteluz could not swim: he fastened a rope round his middle, of which I took one end, and by means of which, I was to draw him to me as soon as I got on shore. When the boat sunk I threw myself into the water, I was very glad that I touched the bottom, for I was uneasy about my comrade. I returned to the boat to look for my clothes and my sword. A part of them had been already stolen, I found only my coat and one of the two pair of pantaloons which I had with me. A negro offered to sell me an old pair of shoes for eight *francs*, for I wanted a pair of shoes to walk in.

The sailors had saved the barrel of water; and as soon as we were on shore they fought for the drinking of it. I rushed in among them, and made my way to him who had got the barrel at his mouth. I snatched it from him and contrived to swallow two mouthfuls, the barrel was afterwards taken from me, but these two mouthfuls did me as much good as two bottles; but for them I could not have lived longer than a few hours.

Thus I found myself on the coast of Africa wet to the skin, with nothing in my pockets except a few biscuits, steeped in salt water, to support me for several days: without water, amidst a sandy desert inhabited by a ferocious race of men: thus we had left one danger to plunge into a greater.

We resolved to proceed along the sea coast, because the breeze cooled us a little, and besides the moist sand was softer than the fine moveable sand in the interior. Before we proceeded on our march, we waited for the crew of the other boat which had stranded before us.

We had proceeded about half an hour, when we perceived another boat advancing with full sail, and came with such violence on the beach that it stranded: it contained all the family of Mr. Picard, consisting of himself and his wife, three daughters grown up, and four young children, one of whom was at the breast. I threw myself into the sea to assist this unhappy family; I contributed to get Mr. Picard on shore, everybody was saved. I went to look for my clothes, but could not find them; I fell into a violent passion, and expressed in strong terms, the infamy of stealing in such circumstances. I was reduced to my shirt and my trousers. I know not whether my cries, and my complaints, excited remorse in the robber, but I found my coat and pantaloons again, a little further off upon the sand. (B)

We proceeded on our journey for the rest of the day on the 8th of July; many of us were overcome by thirst. Many with haggard eyes awaited only death. We dug in the sand, but found only water more salt than that of the sea.

At last we resolved to pass the sandy downs along the sea coast; we afterwards met with a sandy plain almost as low as the ocean. On this sand there was a little long and hard grass. We dug a hole three or four feet deep, and found water which was whitish and had a bad smell. I tasted it and finding it sweet, cried out "we are saved!" These words were repeated by the whole caravan who collected round this water, which everyone devoured with his eyes. Fire or six holes were soon made and every one took his fill of this muddy beverage. We remained two hours at this place, and endeavoured to eat a little biscuit in order to keep up our strength.

Towards evening we returned to the sea shore. The coolness of the night permitted us to walk, but Mr. Picard's family could not follow us. The children were carried, the officers setting the example, in order to induce the sailors to carry them by turns. The situation of Mr. Picard was cruel; his young ladies and his wife displayed great courage; they dressed themselves in men's clothes. After an hour's march Mr. Picard desired that we might stop, he spoke in the tone of a man who would not be refused; we consented, though the least delay might endanger the safety of all. We stretched ourselves upon the sand, and slept till three o'clock in the morning.

We immediately resumed our march. It was the 9th of July. We still proceeded along the sea shore, the wet sand was more easy to walk upon; we rested every half hour on account of the ladies.

About eight o'clock in the morning we went a little from the coast to reconnoitre some Moors who had shown themselves. We found two or three wretched tents, in which there were some Mooresses almost all naked, they were as ugly and frightful as the sands they inhabit. They came to our aid, offering us water, goat's milk, and millet, which are their only food. They would have appeared to us handsome, if it had been for the pleasure of obliging us, but these rapacious creatures wanted us to give them everything we had. The sailors, who were loaded with what they had pillaged from us, were more fortunate than we, a handkerchief procured them a glass of water or milk, or a handful of millet. They had more money than we, and gave pieces of five or ten *francs* for things, for which we offered twenty *sous*. These Mooresses, however, did not know the value of money, and delivered more to a person who gave them two or three little pieces of ten *sous*, than to him who offered them a crown of six *livres*. Unhappily we had no small money, and I drank more than one glass of milk at the rate of six *livres* per glass.

We bought, at a dearer price than we could have bought gold, two goats which we boiled by turns in a little metal kettle belonging to the Mooresses. We took out the pieces half boiled, and devoured them like savages. The sailors, for whom we had bought these goats, scarcely left the officers their share, but seized what they could, and still complained of having had too little. I could not help speaking to them as they deserved. They consequently had a spite against me and threatened me more than once.

At four o'clock in the afternoon, after we had passed the greatest heat of the day in the disgusting tents of the Mooresses, stretched by their side, we heard a cry of "To arms, to arms!" I had none; I took a large knife which I had preserved, and which was as good as a sword. We advanced towards some Moors and Negroes, who had already disarmed several of our people whom they had found reposing on the sea shore. The two parties were on the point of coming to blows, when we understood that these men came to offer to conduct us to Senegal.

Some timid persons distrusted their intentions. For myself, as well as the most prudent among us, I thought that we should trust entirely to men who came in a small number, and who, in fact, confided their own safety to us; though it would have been so easy for them, to come in sufficiently large numbers to overwhelm us. We did so, and experience proved that we did well.

We set off with our Moors who were very well made and fine men of their race; a Negro, their slave was one of the handsomest men I have ever seen. His body of a fine black, was clothed in a blue dress which he had received as a present. This dress became him admirably, his gait was proud and his air inspired confidence. The distrust of some of our Negroes, who had their arms unsheathed, and fear painted on the countenances of some made him laugh. He put himself in the middle of them, and placing the point of the weapons upon his breast, opened his arms, to make them comprehend that he was not afraid, and that they also ought not to fear him.

After we had proceeded some time, night being come, our guides conducted us a little inland, behind the downs where there were some tents inhabited by a pretty considerable number of Moors. Many persons in our caravan cried out, that they were going to be led to death. But we did not listen to them, persuaded that in every way we were undone, if the Moors were resolved on our destruction, that besides, it was their true interest to conduct us to Senegal, and that in short, confidence was the only means of safety.

Fear caused everybody to follow us. We found in the camp, water, camels' milk, and dry, or rather rotten fish. Though all these things were enormously dear, we were happy to meet with them. I bought for ten *francs* one of these fish which stunk terribly. I wrapped it up in the only handkerchief I had left, to carry it with me. We were not sure of always finding such a good inn upon the road. We slept in our usual bed, that is to say stretched upon the sand. We had rested till midnight: we took some asses for Mr. Picard's family, and for some men whom fatigue had rendered incapable of going any further.

I observed that the men who were most overcome by fatigue were precisely those who were the most robust. From their look and their apparent strength they might have been judged indefatigable, but they wanted mental strength, and this alone supports man in such a crisis. For my part I was astonished at bearing so well so many fatigues and privations. I suffered, but with courage; my stomach, to my great satisfaction did not suffer at all. I bore everything in the same manner till the last.

Sleep alone, but the most distressing sleep possible, had nearly caused my destruction. It was at two or three o'clock in the morning that it seized me, I slept as I walked. As soon as they cried halt I let myself fall upon the sand and was plunged into the most profound lethargy. Nothing gave me more pain than to hear at the expiration of a quarter of an hour "up, march."

I was once so overcome that I heard nothing, I remained stretched upon the ground while the whole caravan passed by me. It was already at a great distance when a straggler happily perceived me; he pushed me, and at last succeeded in awaking me. But for him I should doubtless have slept several hours. If I had awoke alone in the middle of the desert, either despair would have terminated my sufferings, or I should have been made a slave by the Moors, which I could not have borne. To avoid this misfortune I begged one of my friends to watch over me, and to waken me at every stage, which he did.

On the 10th of July towards six o'clock in the morning, we were marching along the sea coast, when our guide gave us notice to be upon our guard and to take our arms. I seized my knife; the whole party was collected. The country was inhabited by a poor and plundering race of Moors, who would not have failed to attack those who had loitered behind. The precaution was good, some Moors showed themselves on the downs; their number increased and soon exceeded ours. To move them, we placed ourselves in a line holding our swords and sabres in the air. Those who had no arms waved the scabbards, to make them believe that we were all armed with muskets. They did not approach. Our guides went halfway to meet them. They left one man and retired: the Moors did the same on their side. The two deputies conversed together for some time, then each returned to his party. The explanation was satisfactory, and the Moors soon came to us without the least distrust.

Their women brought us milk which they sold horribly dear; the rapacity of these Moors is astonishing, they insisted on having a share of the milk, which they had sold us.

Mean time we saw a sail advancing towards us: we made all kinds of signals to be perceived by it, and we were convinced that they were answered. Our joy was lively and well founded: it was the *Argus* brig which came to our assistance. She lowered her sails and hoisted out a boat. When it was near the breakers a Moor threw himself into the sea, carrying a note which painted our distress. The boat took the Moor on board and returned with the note to the captain. Half an hour afterwards the boat returned laden with a large barrel, and two small ones. When it reached the place where it had taken in the Moor, the latter threw himself into the sea again to bring back the answer. It informed us that they were going to throw into the sea a barrel of biscuit and cheese, and two others containing brandy and wine.

Another piece of news filled us with joy; the two boats which had not stranded on the coast as we had done arrived at the Senegal, after having experienced the most stormy weather. Without losing a moment the governor had dispatched the *Argus*, and taken every measure to assist the shipwrecked people, and to go to the *Medusa*. Besides, he had sent by land camels loaded with provisions to meet us, lastly, the Moors were desired to respect us, and to render us assistance: so much good news revived us, and gave us fresh courage.

I learned also that Mr. Schmalz and his family, those very ladies, whom I had seen expose themselves with so much composure to the fury of the waves, and who had made me shed the only tears which our misfortunes had drawn from me, were well and in safety. I should have been sorry to die without having learned that they were preserved.

When the three barrels were thrown into the sea we followed them with our eyes; we feared lest the current, instead of bringing them to the coast, should carry them into the open sea. At last we saw, clearly, that they approached us. Our Negroes and Moors swam to them, and pushed them to the coast, where we secured them.

The great barrel was opened: the biscuit and cheese were distributed. We would not open those of wine and brandy. We feared lest the Moors, at this sight, would not be able to refrain from falling upon the booty. We continued our march, and about half a league farther on, made a delicious feast on the seashore. Our strength being revived, we continued our route with more ardour.

Towards the close of the day, the aspect of the country began to change a little. The downs were lower: we perceived, at a distance, a sheet of water: we thought, and this was no small satisfaction to us, that it was the Senegal which made an elbow in this place to run parallel to the sea. From this elbow runs the little rivulet called Marigot *des* Maringouins; we left the sea-shore to pass it a little higher up. We reached a spot where there was some verdure and water, and resolved to remain there till midnight.

We had scarcely reached this spot, when we saw an Englishman coming towards us with three or four Marabous, or priests; they had camels with them; they were doubtless sent by the English Governor of Senegal, to seek for the shipwrecked people. One of the camels, laden with provisions, is immediately dispatched; those who conduct it are to go, if necessary, to Portendic, to fetch our companions in misfortune; or at least to get some information respecting them.

The English envoy had money to buy us provisions. He informed us that we had still three days march to the Senegal. We imagined that we were nearer to it; the most fatigued were terrified at this great distance. We slept all together on the sand. Nobody was suffered to go to a distance for fear of the lions, which were said to haunt this country. This fear did not at all alarm me, nor hinder me from sleeping pretty well.

On the 11th of July, after having walked from one o'clock in the morning till seven, we arrived at a place where the Englishman expected to meet with an ox. By some misunderstanding there was none; we were obliged to *pinch our bellies*: but we had a little water.

The heat was insupportable; the sun was already scorching.

We halted on the white sand of these downs, as being more wholesome for a resting place than the sand, wetted by the sea-water. But this sand was so hot, that even the hands could not endure it. Towards noon we were broiled by the beams of the sun darting perpendicularly upon our heads. I found no remedy, except in a creeping plant, which grew here and there on the moving sand. I set up some old stalks, and spread over them my coat and some leaves: thus I put my head in the shade; the rest of my body was roasted. The wind overturned, twenty times, my slight scaffolding.

Meantime, this Englishman was gone, on his camel, to see after an ox. He did not return till four or five o'clock: when he informed us that we should find this animal, after we had proceeded some hours. After a most painful march, till night, we, in fact, met with an ox which was small, but tolerably fat. We looked at some distance from the sea, for a place where there was supposed to be a spring. It was only a hole, which the Moors had left a few hours before. Here we fixed ourselves, a dozen fires were lighted around us. A negro twisted the neck of the ox, as we should have done that of a fowl. In five minutes it was flayed and cut into pieces, which we toasted on the points of our swords or sabres. Every one devoured his portion.

After this slight repast, we all lay down to sleep. I was not able to sleep: the tiresome buzzing of the mosquitoes, and their cruel stings, prevented me, though I was so much in need of repose.

On the 12th, we resumed our march at three o'clock in the morning. I was indisposed; and to knock me up entirely, we had to walk over the moving sand of the point of Barbary. Nothing hitherto, had been more fatiguing: everybody complained; our Moorish guides assured us that this way was shorter by two leagues. We preferred returning to the beach, and walking on the sand, which the sea-water rendered firm. This last effort was almost beyond my strength, I sunk under it, and but for my comrades, I should have remained upon the sand.

We had absolutely resolved to reach the point, where the river joins the downs. There some boats, which were coming up the river, were to take us on board, and convey us to St. Louis. When we had nearly reached this spot, we crossed the downs, and enjoyed the sight of the river which we had so long desired to meet with.

Happily too, it was the season when the water of the Senegal is fresh: we quenched our thirst at our pleasure. We stopped at last; it was only eight o'clock in the morning. We had no shelter during the whole day, except some trees, which were of a kind unknown to me, and which had a sombre foliage. I frequently went into the river, but without venturing too far from the bank, for fear of the alligators.

About two o'clock, a small boat arrived; the master of it asked for Mr. Picard; he was sent by one of the old friends of that gentleman, and brought him provisions and clothes for his family. He gave notice to us all, in the name of the English Governor, that two other boats loaded with provisions, were coming. Having to wait till they arrived, I could not remain with Mr. Picard's family. I know not what emotion arose in my soul when I saw the fine white bread cut, and the wine poured out, which would have given me so much pleasure. At four o'clock we also were able to eat bread and good biscuit, and to drink excellent Madeira, which was lavished on us with little prudence. Our sailors were drunk; even those among us who had been more cautious, and whose heads were stronger, were, to say the least, very merry. How did our tongues run as we went down the river in our boats! After a short and happy navigation, we landed at Saint Louis, about seven o'clock in the evening.

But what should we do? whither should we go? Such were our reflections when we set foot on shore. They were not of long duration. We met with some of our comrades belonging to the boats who had arrived before us, who conducted us, and distributed us among various private houses, where everything had been prepared to receive us well. I shall always remember the kind hospitality which was shown to us, in general, by the white inhabitants of St. Louis, both English and French. We were all made welcome; we had all clean linen to put on, water to wash our feet; a sumptuous table was ready for us. As for myself, I was received, with several of my companions, in the house of Messrs. Potin and Durecur, Merchants of Bordeaux. Everything they possessed was lavished upon us. They gave me linen, light clothes, in short, whatever I wanted. I had nothing left. Honour to him, who knows so well how to succour the unfortunate; to him especially who does it with so much simplicity, and as little ostentation as these gentlemen did. It seemed that it was a duty for them to assist everybody. They would willingly have left to others no share in the good that was to be done. English officers eagerly claimed the pleasure, as they expressed it, of having some of the shipwrecked people to take care of. Some of us had feather beds, others good mattresses laid upon mats, which they found very comfortable. I slept ill notwithstanding, I was too much fatigued, too much agitated: I always fancied, myself either bandied about by the waves, or treading on the burning sands. (B)

On the manufactures of the Moors

The Moors tan skins with the dried pods of the *Gummiferous Accia*: thus prepared, they are impenetrable to the rain, and it may be affirmed that, for their suppleness, as well as for the brilliancy and fine quality of their grain, they might become a valuable fur in Europe, either for use or ornament. The most beautiful of these skins seemed to be those of very young goats, taken from the belly of the dam before the time of gestation is completed. The great numbers of these animals, which are found round all the inhabited places, allow the inhabitants to sacrifice many to this species of luxury, without any extraordinary loss. The cloaks, with a hood, which are mentioned in this memoir, are composed of several of these skins, ingeniously sewed together, with small and very fine seams. These garments, designed as a protection against the cold and the rain, are generally black, but some are also seen of a reddish colour, which are not so beautiful, and heavier these latter are made of the skins of the kind of sheep, known by the name of guinea-sheep, which have hair instead of wool. As for the goldsmiths work, made by these people, it is executed by travelling workmen, who are at the same time armourers, smiths and jewellers. Furnished with a leather bag which is provided with an iron pipe, and filled with air, which they press and fill alternately, by putting it under their thigh, which they keep in constant motion, singing all the while; seated before a little hole dug in the sand, and under the shade of some leaves of the date-tree laid upon their heads, they execute on a little anvil, and with the help of a hammer, and some small iron awls, not only all kinds of repairs necessary to fire-arms, sabres, &c. but manufacture knives and daggers, and also make bracelets, earrings, and necklaces of gold, which they have the art of drawing into very fine wire, and forming into ornaments for women, in a manner which, though it wants taste, makes us admire the skill of the workman, especially when we consider the nature, and the small number of the tools which he employs.

The Moors, like the Mahometan negroes, are for the most part, provided with a larger or smaller number of *gris-gris*, a kind of talisman consisting in words, or verses copied from the Koran, to which they ascribe the power of securing them against diseases, witchcraft and accidents, and which they buy of their priests or Marabous. Some Spaniards from Tenerife, who came to Cape Verde, at the time that the French Expedition had taken refuge there, struck us all, by their resemblance with these Africans. It was not only by their brown complexions that they resembled them; but it was also by their long rosaries, twisted in the same manner about their arms, resembling, except the cross, those of the Moors, and by the great number of Amulets, (*gris-gris* of another kind) which they wear round their necks, and by which they seemed to wish to rival the infidels in credulity. There is then, in the south of Europe, as well as in the north of Africa, a class of men, who would found their authority, upon ignorance, and derive their authority from superstition.

On the bark given to the sick

The bark, which began to be administered at that time, had been damaged, but an attempt was made to supply the want of it by the bark which the negroes use to cure the dysentery, and which they bring from the environs of Rufisque. This bark, of which they made a secret, seems to come from some *terebinthine* plant, and perhaps, from the *monbins*, which are common on this part of the coast. In the winter fevers which prevail at Goree, Cape Verde, &c. two methods of cure were employed which had different effects. These fevers were often attended with colic, spasms in the stomach, and diarrhoea. The first method consisted in vomiting, purging, and then administering the bark, to which musk was sometimes added, when the disorder grew worse. In this case, when the disease did not end in death, the fever was often succeeded by dysentery, or those who believed themselves cured, were subject to relapses. The second method, which Doctor Bergeron employed with more success, was opposite to the former; he vomited the patients but little, or not at all, endeavouring to calm the symptoms, to strengthen the patient by bitters, and at the last, he administered the bark.

The Negroes who, like all other people, have a *materia medica*, and *pharmacopeia* of their own, and who at this season, are subject to the same disorders as the Europeans, have recourse at the very beginning, to a more heroic remedy, and such of our soldiers encamped at Daccard, as made use of it, in general found benefit from it. The Priest or Marabous, who often offered them the assistance of his art, made them take a large glass of rum-punch, very warm, with a slight infusion of cayenne pepper. An extraordinary perspiration generally terminated this fit. The patient then avoided, for some days, walking in the sun, and eat a small quantity of roasted fish and *cous-cous*, mixed with a sufficient quantity of cassia leaves of different species, to operate as a gentle purgative. In order to keep up the perspiration, or according to the Negro Doctor, to strengthen the skin, he applied from time to time, warm lotions of the leaves of the *palma christi*, and of *cassia*, (*casse puante*.) The use of rum, which is condemned by the Mahometan religion, and is a production foreign to this country, gives reason to suppose that the remedy is of modern date, among the Negroes.

On the isle of St. Louis

St. Louis is a bank of scorching sand, without drinkable water or verdure, with a few tolerable houses towards the south, and a great number of low smoky straw huts, which, occupy almost all the north part. The houses are of brick, made of a salt clay, (*argile salee*) which the wind reduces to powder, unless they are carefully covered with a layer of chalk or lime, which it is difficult to procure, and the dazzling whiteness of which injures the eyes.

Towards the middle of this town, if it may be so called, is a large manufactory in ruins, which is honoured with the name of a fort, and of which the English have sacrificed a part, in order to make apartments for the governor, and to make the ground floor more airy, to quarter troops in it.

Opposite is a battery of heavy cannon, the parapet of which covers the square, on which are some trees, planted in strait lines for ornament. These trees are *oleaginous* Benjamins (*Bens Oleferes*) which give no shade, and ought to be replaced by tamarinds, or sycamores, which are common in this neighbourhood, and would thrive well on this spot. None but people uncertain of their privilege to trade on this river, merchants who came merely to make a short stay, and indolent speculators would have contented themselves with this bank of burning sand, and not have been tempted by the cool shades and more fertile lands, which are within a hundred *toises*, but which, indeed, labour alone could render productive. Everything is wretched in this situation.

Saint Louis is but a halting place in the middle of the river, where merchants who were going up it to seek slaves and gum, moored their vessels, and deposited their provisions, and the goods they had brought with them to barter.

What is said in the narrative of the means of attacking this port, is correct. When the enemy have appeared, the Negroes have always been those who have defended it with the most effect. But unhappily, there, as in the Antilles, persons are already to be found, who are inclined to hold out their hands to the English.

At Louis there are some palm-trees, and the *lantara flabelliformis*. Some little gardens have been made; but a cabbage, or a salad, are still of some value. Want, the mother of industry, obliged some of the inhabitants, during the war, to turn their thoughts to cultivation, and it should be the object of the government to encourage them.

On the islands of Goree and Cape Verde

At the distance of 1200 *toises* from the Peninsula of Cape Verde, a large black rock rises abruptly, from the surface of the sea. It is cut perpendicularly on one side, inaccessible in two-thirds of its circumference, and terminates, towards the south, in a low beach which it commands, and which is edged with large stones, against which the sea dashes violently. This beach, which is the prolongation of the base of the rock, bends in an arch, and forms a recess, where people land as they can. At the extremity of this beach is a battery of two or three guns; on the beach of the landing-place, is an *epaulement*, with embrasures which commands it. The town stands on this sand bank, and a little fort, built on the ridge of the rock, commands and defends it. In its present state, Goree could not resist a ship of the line. Its road, which is only an anchoring place in the open sea, is safe in the most stormy weather; but it is exposed to all winds except those that blow from the island, which then serves to shelter it.

The Europeans who desire to carry on the slave trade, have preferred this arid rock, placed in the middle of a raging sea, to the neighbouring continent, where they would find water, wood, vegetables, and in short, the necessaries of life. The same reason which has caused the preference to be given to a narrow and barren sand bank, in the middle of the Senegal to build St.

Louis, has also decided in favour of Goree: it is, that both of them are but dens, or prisons, intended as a temporary confinement for wretches who, in any other situation, would find means to escape. To deal in men, nothing is wanting but fetters and jails, but as this kind of gain no longer exists, if it is wished to derive other productions from these possessions, and not to lose them entirely, it will be necessary to change the nature of our speculations, and to direct our views and our efforts to the continent, where industry and agriculture promise riches, the production of which humanity will applaud.

The point which seems most proper for an agricultural establishment, is Cape Belair, a league and a half to the leeward of Goree: its soil is a rich black mould, lying on a bed of Lava, which seems to come from the Mamelles. It is there that other large vegetables, besides the Baobabs, begin to be more numerous, and which, farther on, towards Cape Rouge, cover, like a forest, all the shores. The wells of Ben, which supply Goree with water, are but a short distance from it, and the lake of Tinguage, begins in the neighbourhood. This lake, which is formed, in a great measure, by the rain water of the Peninsula, contains a brackish water, which it is easy to render potable; it is inhabited by the Guesiks, or Guia-Sicks of the Yoloffes, or Black Crocodiles of Senegal; but it would be easy to destroy these animals. In September, this lake seems wholly covered with white *nymphaea*, or water-lily, and in winter time it is frequented by a multitude of waterfowl, among which, are distinguished by their large size, die great pelican, the fine crested crane, which has received the name of the royal-bird, the gigantic heron, known in Senegambia by the venerable name of Marabou, on account of its bald head, with a few scattered white hairs, its lofty stature, and its dignified gait.

Considered geologically, the Island of Goree is a group of basaltic columns still standing, but a part of which seem to have experienced the action of the same cause of destruction and overthrow, as the columns of the same formation of Cape Verde, because they are inclined and overthrown in the same direction.

Cape Verde is a peninsula about five leagues and a half long; the breadth is extremely variable. At its junction, with the continent, it is about four leagues broad; by the deep recess which the Bay of Daccard forms, it is reduced, near that village, to 600 *toises*, and becomes broader afterwards. This promontory, which forms the most western part of Africa, is placed, as it were, at the foot of a long hill, which represents the ancient shore of the continent. On the sea-shore, and towards the north-east, there are two hills of unequal height, which serve as a guide to mariners; and which, from the substances collected in their neighbourhood, evidently show that they are the remains of an ancient volcano. They have received the name of Mamelles. From this place, to the western extremity of the Peninsula, the country rises towards the north-east, and terminates in a sandy beach on the opposite side.

Almost the whole north-side is composed of steep rocks, covered with large masses of oxide of iron, or with regular columns of basalt which, for the most part, still preserve their vertical position. Their summits, which are sometimes *scorified*, seem to prove that they have been exposed to a great degree of heat. The soil which covers the plateau, formed by the summit of the Basaltic columns, the sides of which assume towards the Mamelles, the appearance of walls of Trapp, but already, in a great degree, changed into turf, is arid and covered with briars. The soil of the Mamelles, like almost all that of the middle of the Peninsula, which appears to lie upon argillaceous lava, in a state of decomposition, is much better. There are even to be found, here and there, some spots that are very fertile; this is the arable land of the inhabitants. Towards the south, all resumes more or less, the appearance of a desert; and the sands, though less destitute of vegetable mould, extend from thence to the sea-shore. It is by manuring the land, with the dung of their cattle, that the Negroes raise pretty good crops of *sorgho*. The population of this peninsula may be estimated at ten thousand souls. It is entirely of the Yoloffe race, and shows much attachment to all the ceremonies of Islamism. The Marabous or Priests, sometimes mounted on the top of the Nests of the Termites, or on the walls surrounding their mosque, call the people several times a day to prayer.

The social state of this little people, is a kind of republic governed by a senate, which is composed of the chiefs of most of the villages. They have taken from the Koran the idea of this form of government, as is the case with most of those, established among the nations who follow that law.

At the time of the expedition of the *Medusa* this senate was composed as follows:

    Moctar, supreme chief resident of Daccard
    Diacheten, chief of the village of Sinkieur
    Diogheul, chief of the village of Gorr

Phall Yokedieff	Tjallow-Talerfour Graff
Mouim Bott	Bayemour Kaye
Modiann Ketdym	Mamcthiar Symbodioun
Ghameu Wockam	Schenegall Bambara
Baindonlz Yoff	Mofall Ben

This tribe was formerly subject to a Negro King in the neighbourhood; but having revolted against him, though very inferior in numbers, it defeated his army a few years ago. The bones of the vanquished, that still lie scattered on the plain, attest the victory. A wall, pierced with loop-holes, which they erected in the narrowest part of the Peninsula, and which the enemy was unable to force, chiefly contributed to their success. The Yolloffes are in general handsome and their facial angle has hardly anything of the usual deformity of the Negroes. Their common food is *couscous*, with poultry, and above all fish; their drink is brackish water, mixed with milk and sometimes with palm wine. The poor go on foot, the rich on horseback, and some ride upon bulls, which are always very docile, for the Negroes are eminently distinguished by their good treatment of all animals. Their wealth consists in land and cattle; their dwellings are generally of reeds, their beds are mats made of *Asouman* (*maranta juncea*) and leopards' skins; and their clothing broad pieces of cotton. The women take care of the children, pound the millet, and prepare the food; the men cultivate the land, go a hunting and fishing, weave the stuff for their clothes, and gather in the wax.

Revenge and idleness seem to be the only vices of these people; their virtues are charity, hospitality, sobriety, and love of their children. The young women are licentious, but the married women are generally chaste and attached to their husbands. Their diseases among the children, are worms, and umbilical hernia; among the old people, and particularly those who have travelled much, blindness and *opthalamia*; and among the adult, affections of the heart, obstructions, sometimes leprosy, and rarely elephantiasis. Among the whole population of the Peninsula, there is only one person with a hunch back, and two or three who are lame. During the day they work or rest; but the night is reserved for dancing and conversation. As soon as the sun has set, the tambourine is heard, the women sing; the whole population is animated; love and the ball set everybody in motion. *Africa dances all the night,"* is an expression which has become proverbial among the Europeans who have travelled there.

There is not an atom of calcareous stone in the whole country: almost all the plants are twisted and thorny. The *Monbins* are the only species of timber that are met with. The thorny asparagus, *A. retrofractus*, is found in abundance in the woods; it tears the clothes, and the centaury of Egypt pricks the legs. The most troublesome insects of the neighbourhood are gnats, bugs, and ear-wigs. The monkey, called cynocephalus, plunders the harvests, the vultures attack the sick animals, the striped hyena and the leopard prowl about the villages during the night; but the cattle are extremely beautiful, and the fish make the sea on this coast boil, and foam by their extraordinary numbers. The hare of the Cape and the gazelle are frequently met with. The porcupines, in the moulting season, cast their quills in the fields, and dig themselves holes under the palm trees. The guinea-fowl (*Pintada*), the turtle-dove, the wood-pigeon are found everywhere. In winter immense flocks of plovers of various species, are seen on the edges of the marshes, and also great numbers of wild ducks. Other species frequent the reeds, and the surface of the water is covered with geese of different kinds, among which is that whose head bears a fleshy tubercle like that of the cassowary. The fishing nets are made of date leaves; their upper edge is furnished, instead of cork, with pieces of the light wood of the *Asclepias*.—The sails of the canoes are made of cotton.

Several shrubs, and a large number of herbaceous plants of this part of Africa, are found also in the Antilles. But among the indigenous plants, are the Cape Jessamine, the *Amaryllis Rubannee*, the Scarlet *Hoemanthus*, the *Gloriosa Superba*, and some extremely beautiful species of *Nerions*. A new species of *Calabash*, (*Crescentia*) with *pinnated* leaves is very common. Travellers appear to have confounded it with the Baobab, on account of the shape of its fruits, the thickness of its trunk, and the way in which its branches grow. Its wood, which is very heavy and of a fallow colour, has the grain and smell of ebony: its Yoloffe name is *Bonda*, the English have cut down and exported the greatest part of it.

In short, Africa, such as we have seen it either on the banks of the Senegal or the Peninsula of Cape Verde, is a new country, which promises to the naturalist an ample harvest of discoveries, and to the philosophical observer of mankind, a vast field for research and observation. May the detestable commerce in human flesh, which the Negroes abhor, and the Moors desire, cease to pollute these shores! It is the only means which the Europeans have left to become acquainted with the interior of this vast continent, and to make this great portion of the family of mankind, by which it is inhabited participate in the benefits of civilization.

The Sufferings of the Picard Family After the Shipwreck of the *Medusa*

Charlotte-Adélaïde Dard [née Picard]

Translated by Patrick Maxwell

Translator's Preface

The following pages are translated from the "African Cottage," of Mad. Dard.[1] They contain no romance, but a well authenticated story, corroborated by the previous Narrative of MM. Corréard and Savigny. Those gentlemen have detailed their sufferings on the fatal raft, after the disastrous shipwreck of the *Medusa* frigate; but the account concerning those who escaped, by aid of their boats, to the shores of Sahara, deficient in their recital, is supplied by Madame Dard, who was present at all the scenes she relates. Interwoven with the Narrative, is an interesting account of the Picard Family, whose wrongs cannot fail to excite pity, and to engage those feeling hearts in her favour, to whom the fair authoress has addressed the story of her misfortunes.

There is not, on the records of misery, an instance of more severe and protracted suffering; and I trust there is not, nor ever will be any, where human nature was more foully outraged and disgraced. There are, nevertheless, some pleasing traits of character in the story, and, I am proud to say, some of the brightest of them belong to our own nation. These present a beautiful relief to the selfishness and brutality which so much abound in the dark picture; and are, to our minds, the green spots of the

---

1: *La Chaumière Africaine; ou, Histoire d'une Famille Française jetée sur la côté occidentale de l'Afrique, à la suite du naufrage de la Frégate la Meduse. Par Mme. Dard, née Charlotte Adelaide Picard, aînée de cette famille, et l'une des naufragés de la Meduse*, Dijon. 1824.

desert—the fountain and the fruit-tree—as they were in very truth, to the poor wretches they assisted with such genuine singleness of heart.

To the end of the Narrative I have subjoined an Appendix, translated and abridged from the work of MM. Corréard and Savigny, detailing at greater length the sufferings of those who were exposed upon the raft. I have also added some Notes, extracted from several Authors, illustrative of various matters mentioned in the course of the Narrative.

It may be satisfactory for some readers to know, that, in 1824, Madame Dard was living with her husband in comfort at Bligny-sous-Beaune, a short distance from Dijon. I have lately seen in a French catalogue, a dictionary and grammar of the Woloff and Bambara languages, by M. J. Dard, *Bachelier des Sciences, Ancien Instituteur de l'Ecole du Sénégal*, brought out under the auspices of the French Government.

Patrick Maxwell
Edinburgh
July 1827

Author's Preface

Those who have read the *Account of the Shipwreck of the Medusa*, by MM. Savigny and Corréard, are already acquainted with the Picard family.

Attracted to Senegal by a faint prospect of advantage, my father, head of that unfortunate family, could not, in spite of a good constitution and the strength of his spirits, resist that destiny, from the mortal influence of which none of us save three escaped out of a family of nine. On his deathbed, he expressed to me the desire that our misfortunes should not remain unknown. This then became my duty, and a duty sacred to the public. I feel a pleasure in fulfilling it, and consolation in the thought, that no feeling mind will read the story of our misfortunes without being affected; and that those who persecuted us will at least experience some regret.

The recital of the shipwreck of the *Medusa* was necessary, as much to explain the origin of our misfortunes, as the cause of the connexion between that disastrous event, and the terrible journey in the desert of Sahara, by which we at last reached Senegal. It will furnish me, also, with an opportunity of adverting to some errors in the work of Messrs Savigny and Corréard.

It only now remains for me to crave the indulgence of the reader for my style. I trust such will not be refused to one who has dared to take the pen, only in compliance with a father's dying request.

CHAPTER 1

Bound for Africa

About the beginning of 1800, my father solicited and obtained the situation of resident attorney at Senegal, on the west coast of Africa. My mother was then nursing my youngest sister, and could not be persuaded to expose us, at so tender an age, to the fatigue and danger of so long a voyage. At this period I was not quite two years old.

It was then resolved that my father should go alone, and that we should join him on the following year; but my mother's hopes were disappointed, war having rendered impossible all communication with our colonies. In despair, at a separation which placed her nearly two thousand leagues from her husband, and ignorant how long it might continue, she soon after fell into a languid condition; and death deprived us of her, at the end of five years of suffering. My grandfather, at whose house we had hitherto lived, now became both father and mother to us; and I owe it to the good old man to say, that his care and attention soon made us forget we were orphans. Too young to reflect, that the condition of happiness which we enjoyed under his guardianship would ever have an end, we lived without a care for the future, and our years glided on in perfect tranquillity.

Thus were we living when, in 1809, the English captured the colony of Senegal, and permitted our father to return to his family. But what a change did he meet with on his arrival at Paris! Wife, home, furniture, friends, had all disappeared; and nothing remained but two young daughters, who refused to acknowledge him for their father: so much were our young minds habituated to see and love but one in the world—the worthy old man who had watched over our infancy.

In 1810, our father thought fit to marry a second time; but a great misfortune befell his children in the death of their grandfather. Our tears were scarcely dry, when we were conducted home to her who had become our second mother. We would hardly acknowledge her. Our sorrow was excessive, and the loss we had sustained irreparable. But they strove to comfort us; dresses, playthings, amusements in abundance, were given to us to obliterate the loss of our best friend. In this state of perfect happiness we were living, when the armies of the Allies entered Paris in 1814.

France having had the good fortune to recover her King, and with him the blessing of peace, an expedition was fitted out at Brest to go and resume possession of Senegal, which had been restored to us. My father was instantly reinstated in his place of resident attorney, and went in the month of November to Brest.

As our family had become more numerous since the second marriage of my father, he could only take with him our stepmother and the younger children. My sister Caroline and myself were placed in a boarding school at Paris, until the Minister of Marine and the Colonies would grant us a passage; but the events of 1815 caused the expedition to Senegal to be abandoned, while it was still in the harbour of Brest, and all the officers dismissed. My father then returned to Paris, leaving at Brest my stepmother, who was then in an unfit condition for travelling.

In 1816, a new expedition was fitted out. My father was ordered to repair to Rochefort, whence it was to set off. He took measures also for taking along with him his wife, who had remained at Brest during the "hundred days." The design of our accompanying him to Africa, obliged him to address a new petition to the Minister of Marine, praying him to grant us all a passage, which he obtained.

The 23rd of May was the day on which we were to quit the capital, our relations and friends. In the meanwhile, my sister and myself left the boarding school where we had been placed, and went to take farewell of all those who were dear to us. One cousin, who loved us most tenderly, could not hear of our approaching departure without shedding tears; and as it was impossible for her to change our destiny, she offered to share it. Immediately she appeared before the minister, and M. le Baron Portal, struck with a friendship which made her encounter the dangers of so long a voyage, granted her request.

At last, a beautiful morning announced to us the afflicting moment when we were to quit Paris. The postilion, who was to convey us to Rochefort, was already at the door of the house in which we lived, to conduct us to his carriage, which waited for us at the Orléans gate. Immediately an old hackney coach appeared; my father stepped into it, and in an instant it was filled. The impatient coachman cracked his whip, sparks flashed from the horse's feet, and the street of Lille, which we had just quitted, was soon far behind us. On arriving before the garden of the Luxembourg, the first rays of the morning's sun darted fiercely through the foliage, as if to say, you forsake the zephyrs in quitting this beautiful abode.

We reached the Observatory, and in an instant passed the gate d'Enfer. There, as yet for a moment to breathe the air of the capital, we alighted at the Hotel du Pantheon, where we found our carriage. After a hasty breakfast, the postilion arranged our trunks, and off again we set. It was nearly seven in the morning when we quitted the gates of Paris, and we arrived that evening at the little village of d'Etampes, where our landlord, pressing us to refresh ourselves, almost burned his inn in making us an omelette with rotten eggs. The flames, ascending the old chimney, soon rose to the roof of the house, but they succeeded in extinguishing them. We were, however, regaled with a smoke which made us shed tears. It was broad day when we quitted d'Etampes; and our postilion, who had spent the greater part of the night in drinking with his comrades, was something less than polite. We reproached him, but he made light of the circumstance; for, in the evening, he was completely drunk. On the twenty-fifth of

May, at ten in the morning, my father told me we were already thirty-two leagues from Paris. Thirty-two leagues! cried I; alas, so far! Whilst I made this reflection, we arrived at Orléans. Here we remained about three hours to refresh ourselves as well as our horses. We could not leave the place without visiting the statue raised in honour of Joan of Arc, that extraordinary woman, to whom the monarchy once owed its safety.

On leaving Orléans, the Loire, and the fertile pastures through which it rolls its waters, excited our admiration. We had on our right the beautiful vineyards of Beaugency. The road, as far as Amboise, is delightful. I then began to think, that Paris and its environs might perhaps be forgotten, if the country of Senegal, to which we were going, was as fine as that through which we were journeying. We slept at Amboise, which, being situated at the confluence of the Loire and the Maise, presents a most agreeable appearance.

When we set off, the sun began to show us verdant groves, watered by the majestic course of the river. His disk looked like a glorious lustre suspended in the azure vault of heaven. Our road was studded on both sides with lofty poplars, which seemed to shoot their pyramidal heads into the clouds. On our left was the Loire, and on our right a large rivulet, whose crystal waters everywhere reflected the bright beams of the sun. The birds, with their songs, celebrated the beauty of the day, whilst the dews, in the form of pearls, quivering fell from the tender boughs, fanned by the zephyrs. A thousand picturesque objects presented themselves to our view. On the one hand were delightful groves, the sweet flowers of which perfumed the air we breathed; on the other, a clear fountain sprang bubbling from the crevice of a rock, and, after falling from the top of a little hill among a tuft of flowers, bent its devious course to join the waters of the river. More distant, a small wood of filbert trees served as a retreat to the ringdoves who cooed, and the nightingales who chanted the spring.

We enjoyed this truly enchanting spectacle till we arrived at Tours. But as our route from Orléans had been diversified and agreeable, from the latter place to Rochefort it was monotonous and tiresome. However, the towns of Chatellerault, Poitiers, and Niort made a slight change in the sameness of the scene. From Niort to Rochefort the road was nearly impassable. We were frequently obliged to alight from the carriage, in order to allow the horses to drag it out from the deep ruts which we met. In approaching to a hamlet, named Charente, we stuck so fast in the mud, that even after removing the trunks and other baggage, we found it almost next to an impossibility to drag it out. We were in the midst of a wood, and no village within view.

It was then resolved to wait till some good soul would be passing, who would assist to extricate us from our embarrassment. After vainly waiting a long hour for this expected succour, the first people who appeared were travelling merchants, who would not stay on any account to give us assistance. At length we saw a young lady upon a little path, which was at the extremity of the wood, walking with a book in her hand. My father instantly ran towards her, and acquainted her with our situation. This lady, far from acting like the travellers we formerly met, went to an adjoining field where were some farmers at work, and requested them to go with their oxen to free us from our jeopardy, and returned herself with them. When our carriage was put in a condition to continue our route, she invited us to refresh ourselves in her country seat, situated in the middle of the wood.

We then took the cross-way, and returned with our carriage at the instance of the amiable lady, who received us in the most affable and generous manner. She offered us at first some pears, which were already very good; after which we were served with an exquisite collation, at the end of which a child, beautiful as the loves, presented us with a basket filled with the fairest flowers of the spring. We accepted the gift of Flora, in testimony of our regard for our generous landlady and her charming child. Traversing after that the park of our hospitable hostess, we rejoined the route to Rochefort.

In paying this just tribute of remembrance to the offices of that person who gave us so great assistance, I cannot resist the pleasure of mentioning her name. She is the wife of M. Télotte, superior officer of the general magazine at Rochefort.

Already the masts of the ships appeared in the horizon, and we heard in the distance a hollow and confused sound, like that made by a multitude of people engaged in various occupations. On approaching nearer to Rochefort, we found that the tumult we heard was caused by the labourers in the wood-yards and the galley-slaves, who, painfully dragging their fetters, attended to the various labours of the port. Having entered the town, the first picture which presented itself to our eyes was that of these unfortunate creatures, who, coupled two and two by enormous chains, are forced to carry the heaviest burdens. It may be mentioned, in passing, that the sight is not very attracting to young ladies who have never been out of Paris; for, in spite of all the repugnance we can have for those who are condemned by the laws to live apart from society, we can never look with indifference on that crowd of thinking beings, degraded, by following their vicious actions, to a level with the beasts of burden.

My mind was yet occupied with these painful reflections, when my father, opening the door of the carriage, requested us to follow him into an hotel in the street Dauphine, where already were our stepmother and our young brothers and sisters, who had returned with her from Brest. Soon our numerous family were again united. What transports of joy, what saluting and embracing! O! there is nothing comparable to the pleasure of meeting with those we love after a long absence!

My father went to visit the officers who were to make the voyage to Senegal along with us. My step-mother busied herself in preparing supper, and my sister Caroline, my cousin, and myself, went to sleep; for any farther exercise but ill accorded with the fatigue we had already undergone; otherwise we could easily have sat till supper, after having eat of the good things we had had at the farm of Charente.

We spent the morrow, the 3rd of June, in running about the

town. In the space of two hours we had seen everything worth seeing. What a fine thing a maritime town is for a maker of romances! But as I have neither talents nor desire to write one, and as I have promised to the reader to adhere strictly to the truth, I will content myself by telling him, that in nine days I was tired of Rochefort.

CHAPTER 2

We Begin Our Voyage

Early on the morning of the 12th of June, we were on our way to the boats that were to convey us on board the *Medusa*, which was riding at anchor off the island of Aix, distant about four leagues from Rochefort. The field through which we passed was sown with corn. Wishing, before I left our beautiful France, to make my farewell to the flowers, and, whilst our family went leisurely forward to the place where we were to embark upon the Charente, I crossed the furrows, and gathered a few blue-bottles and poppies. We soon arrived at the place of embarkation, where we found some of our fellow-passengers, who, like myself, seemed casting a last look to Heaven, whilst they were yet on the French soil. We embarked, however, and left these happy shores. In descending the tortuous course of the Charente, contrary winds so impeded our progress, that we did not reach the *Medusa* till the morrow, having taken twenty-four hours in sailing four leagues. At length we mounted the deck of the *Medusa*, of painful memory. When we got on board, we found our births not provided for us, consequently were obliged to remain indiscriminately together till next day. Our family, which consisted of nine persons, was placed in a birth near the main deck. As the wind was still contrary, we lay at anchor for seventeen days.

On the 17th of June, at four in the morning, we set sail, as did the whole expedition, which consisted of the *Medusa* frigate, the Loire store-ship, the *Argus* brig, and the *Echo* corvette. The wind being very favourable, we soon lost sight of the green fields of l'Aunis. At six in the morning, however, the island of Rhé still appeared above the horizon. We fixed our eyes upon it with regret, to salute for the last time our dear country. Now, imagine the ship born aloft, and surrounded by huge mountains of water, which at one moment tossed it in the air, and at another plunged it into the profound abyss.

The waves, raised by a stormy north-west breeze, came dashing in a horrible manner against the sides of our ship. I know not whether it was a presentiment of the misfortune which menaced us that had made me pass the preceding night in the most cruel inquietude. In my agitation, I sprang upon deck, and contemplated with horror the frigate winging its way upon the waters. The winds pressed against the sails with great violence, strained and whistled among the cordage; and the great hulk of wood seemed to split every time the surge broke upon its sides. On looking a little out to sea I perceived, at no great distance on our right, all the other ships of the expedition, which quieted me much.

Towards ten in the morning the wind changed; immediately an appalling cry was heard, concerning which the passengers, as well as myself, were equally ignorant. The whole crew were in motion. Some climbed the rope ladders, and seemed to perch on the extremities of the yards; others mounted to the highest parts of the mast; these bellowing and pulling certain cordages in cadence; those crying, swearing, whistling, and filling the air with barbarous and unknown sounds. The officer on duty, in his turn, roaring out these words, *starboard! larboard! hoist! luff! tack!* which the helmsman repeated in the same tone. All this hubbub, however, produced its effect: the yards were turned on their pivots, the sails set, the cordage tightened, and the unfortunate sea-boys having received their lesson, descended to the deck. Everything remained tranquil, except that the waves still roared, and the masts continued their creaking. However the sails were swelled, the winds less violent, though favourable, and the mariner, whilst he carolled his song, said we had a noble voyage.

During several days we did indeed enjoy a delightful passage. All the ships of the expedition still kept together; but at length the breeze became changeable, and they all disappeared. The *Echo*, however, still kept in sight, and persisted in accompanying us, as if to guide us on our route. The wind becoming more favourable, we held due south, sailing at the rate of sixty-two leagues a day. The sea was so fine, and our journey so rapid, that I began to think it nearly as agreeable to travel by sea as by land; but my illusion was not of long duration.

On the 28th of June, at six in the morning, we discovered the Peak of Tenerife, towards the south, the summit of whose cone seemed lost among the clouds. We were then distant about two leagues, which we made in less than a quarter of an hour. At ten o'clock we brought to before the town of St Croix. Several officers got leave to go on shore to procure refreshments.

Whilst these gentlemen were away, a certain passenger, member of the self-instituted Philanthropic Society of Cape Verde,[2] suggested that it was very dangerous to remain where we were, adding that he was well acquainted with the country, and had navigated in all these latitudes. M. Le Roy Lachaumareys, Captain of the *Medusa*, believing the pretended knowledge of the intriguing Richefort, gave him the command of the frigate. Various officers of the navy, represented to the captain how shameful it was to put such confidence in a stranger, and that they would never obey a man who had no character as a commander. The captain despised these wise remonstrances; and, using his authority, commanded the pilots, and all the crew, to obey Richefort; saying he was king, since the orders of the king were, that they should obey him. Immediately the impostor, desirous of displaying his great skill in navigation, made them change the route for no purpose but that of showing his skill in manoeuvring a ship. Every instant he changed the tack, went, came, and returned,

---

2: This Society, which was so ill named *Philanthropic*, was composed of sixty individuals of all nations, among whom figured Hébrard, Corréard,[3] Richefort, &c. They had obtained from government a free passage, and authority to go and cultivate the peninsula of Cape Verde; but that new colony afterwards ended like that of Champ-d'Asile.

3: Not that Corréard, the coadjutor of Savigny, mentioned in the Author's preface. *Trans*.

and approached the very reefs, as if to brave them. In short, he beat about so much, that the sailors at length refused to obey him, saying boldly that he was a vile impostor. But it was done. The man had gained the confidence of Captain Lachaumareys, who, ignorant of navigation himself, was doubtless glad to get someone to undertake his duty. But it must be told, and told, too, in the face of all Europe, that this blind and inept confidence was the sole cause of the loss of the *Medusa* frigate, as well as of all the crimes consequent upon it.

Towards three in the afternoon, those officers who had gone on shore in the morning, returned on board loaded with vegetables, fruits, and flowers. They laughed heartily at the manoeuvres that had been going on during their absence, which doubtless did not please the captain, who flattered himself he had already found in his pilot Richefort *a good and able seaman*: such were his words. At four in the afternoon we took a southerly direction. M. Richefort then beaming with exultation for having, as he said, saved the *Medusa* from certain shipwreck, continued to give his pernicious counsels to Captain Lachaumareys, persuading him he had been often employed to explore the shores of Africa, and that he was perfectly well acquainted with the Arguin Bank. The journals of the 29th and 30th afford nothing very remarkable.

The hot winds from the desert of Sahara began to be felt, which told us we approached the tropic; indeed, the sun at noon seemed suspended perpendicularly above our heads, a phenomenon which few among us had ever seen.

On the 1st of July, we recognised Cape Bojador, and then saw the shores of Sahara. Towards ten in the morning, they set about the frivolous ceremony which the sailors have invented for the purpose of exacting something from those passengers who have never crossed the line. During the ceremony, the frigate doubled Cape Barbas, hastening to its destruction. Captain Lachaumareys very good humouredly presided at this species of baptism, whilst his dear Richefort promenaded the forecastle, and looked with indifference upon a shore bristling with dangers. However that may be, all passed on well; nay, it may be even said that the farce was well played off. But the route which we pursued soon made us forget the short-lived happiness we had experienced. Every one began to observe the sudden change which had taken place in the colour of the sea, as we ran upon the bank in shallow water. A general murmur rose among the passengers and officers of the navy;—they were far from partaking in the blind confidence of the captain.

On the 2nd of July, at five in the morning, the captain was persuaded that a large cloud, which was discovered in the direction of Cape Blanco, was that Cape itself. After this pretended discovery, they ought to have steered to the west, for about fifty leagues, to have gained sea room to double with certainty the Arguin Bank; moreover, they ought to have conformed to the instructions which the Minister of Marine had given to the ships which set out for Senegal. The other part of the expedition, from having followed these instructions arrived in safety at their destination. During the preceding night, the *Echo*, which had hitherto accompanied the *Medusa*, made several signals, but being replied to with contempt, abandoned us. Towards ten in the morning, the danger which threatened us was again represented to the Captain, and he was strongly urged, if he wished to avoid the Arguin Bank, to take a westerly course; but the advice was again neglected, and he despised the predictions. One of the officers of the frigate, from having wished to expose the intriguing Richefort, was put under arrest. My father, who had already twice made the voyage to Senegal, and who with various persons was persuaded they were going right upon the bank, also made his observations to the unfortunate pilot. His advice was no better received than those of Messrs Reynaud, Espiau, Maudet, &c. Richefort, in the sweetest tone, replied, "My dear, we know our business; attend to yours, and be quiet. I have already twice passed the Arguin Bank; I have sailed upon the Red Sea, and you see I am not drowned."

What reply could be made to such a preposterous speech? My father, seeing it was impossible to get our route changed, resolved to trust to Providence to free us from our danger, and descended to our cabin, where he sought to dissipate his fears in the oblivion of sleep.

Chapter 3

Aground

At noon, on the 2nd of July, soundings were taken. M. Maudet, ensign of the watch, was convinced we were upon the edge of the Arguin Bank. The Captain said to him, as well as to everyone, that there was no cause of alarm. In the mean while, the wind blowing with great violence, impelled us nearer and nearer to the danger which menaced us. A species of stupor overpowered all our spirits, and every one preserved a mournful silence, as if they were persuaded we would soon touch the bank. The colour of the water entirely changed, a circumstance even remarked by the ladies. About three in the afternoon, being in 19° 30' north latitude, and 19° 45' west longitude, an universal cry was heard upon deck. All declared they saw sand rolling among the ripple of the sea. The Captain in an instant ordered to sound. The line gave eighteen fathoms; but on a second sounding it only gave six.

He at last saw his error, and hesitated no longer on changing the route, but it was too late. A strong concussion told us the frigate had struck. Terror and consternation were instantly depicted on every face. The crew stood motionless; the passengers in utter despair. In the midst of this general panic, cries of vengeance were heard against the principal author of our misfortunes, wishing to throw him overboard; but some generous persons interposed, and endeavoured to calm their spirits, by diverting their attention to the means of our safety. The confusion was already so great, that M. Poinsignon, commandant of a troop, struck my sister Caroline a severe blow, doubtless thinking it was one of his soldiers. At this crisis my father was buried in profound sleep, but he quickly awoke, the cries and the tumult upon deck having informed him of our misfortunes. He poured out a thousand reproaches on those whose ignorance and boasting had been so disastrous to us. However, they set about the means of averting our danger. The officers, with an altered voice, issued their orders, expecting every moment to see the ship go in pieces. They strove to lighten her, but the sea was very rough and the current strong. Much time was lost in doing nothing; they only pursued half measures, and all of them unfortunately failed.

When it was discovered that the danger of the *Medusa* was not so great as was at first supposed, various persons proposed to transport the troops to the island of Arguin, which was conjectured to be not far from the place where we lay aground. Others advised to take us all successively to the coast of the desert of Sahara, by the means of our boats, and with provisions sufficient to form a caravan, to reach the island of Saint Louis, at Senegal. The events which afterwards ensued proved this plan to have been the best, and which would have been crowned with success; unfortunately it was not adopted. M. Schmaltz, the governor, suggested the making of a raft of a sufficient size to carry two hundred men, with provisions: which latter plan was seconded by the two officers of the frigate, and put in execution.

The fatal raft was then begun to be constructed, which would, they said, carry provisions for everyone. Masts, planks, boards, cordage, were thrown overboard. Two officers were charged with the framing of these together. Large barrels were emptied and placed at the angles of the machine, and the workmen were taught to say, that the passengers would be in greater security there, and more at their ease, than in the boats. However, as it was forgotten to erect rails, every one supposed, and with reason, that those who had given the plan of the raft, had had no design of embarking upon it themselves.

When it was completed, the two chief officers of the frigate publicly promised, that all the boats would tow it to the shore of the desert; and, when there, stores of provisions and fire-arms would be given us to form a caravan to take us all to Senegal. Why was not this plan executed? Why were these promises, sworn before the French flag, made in vain? But it is necessary to draw a veil over the past. I will only add, that if these promises had been fulfilled, everyone would have been saved, and that, in spite of the detestable egotism of certain personages, humanity would not now have had to deplore the scenes of horror consequent on the wreck of the *Medusa*!

On the 3rd of July, the efforts were renewed to disengage the frigate, but without success. We then prepared to quit her. The sea became very rough, and the wind blew with great violence. Nothing now was heard but the plaintive and confused cries of a multitude, consisting of more than four hundred persons, who, seeing death before their eyes, deplored their hard fate in bitter lamentations. On the 4th, there was a glimpse of hope. At the hour the tide flowed, the frigate, being considerably lightened by all that had been thrown overboard, was found nearly afloat; and it is very certain, if on that day they had thrown the artillery into the water, the *Medusa* would have been saved; but M. Lachaumareys said, he could not thus sacrifice the King's cannon, as if the frigate did not belong to the King also. However, the sea ebbed, and the ship sinking into the sand deeper than ever, made them relinquish that on which depended our last ray of hope.

On the approach of night, the fury of the winds redoubled, and the sea became very rough. The frigate then received some tremendous concussions, and the water rushed into the hold in the most terrific manner, but the pumps would not work. We had now no alternative but to abandon her for the frail boats, which any single wave would overwhelm. Frightful gulfs environed us; mountains of water raised their liquid summits in the distance. How were we to escape so many dangers? Whither could we go? What hospitable land would receive us on its shores? My thoughts, then reverted to our beloved country. I did not regret Paris, but I could have esteemed myself happy to have been yet in the marshes on the road to Rochefort. Then starting suddenly from my reverie, I exclaimed:

"O terrible condition! that black and boundless sea resembles the eternal night which will engulf us! All those who surround me seem yet tranquil; but that fatal calm will soon be succeeded by the most frightful torments. Fools, what had we to find in Senegal, to make us trust to the most perfidious of elements! Did France not afford every necessary for our happiness? Happy! yes, thrice happy, they who never set foot on a foreign soil! Great God! succour all these unfortunate beings; save our unhappy family!"

My father perceived my distress, but how could he console me? What words could calm my fears, and place me above the apprehension of those dangers to which we were exposed? How, in a word, could I assume a serene appearance, when friends, parents, and all that was most dear to me were, in all human probability, on the very verge of destruction? Alas! my fears were but too well founded. For I soon perceived that, although we were the only ladies, besides the Misses Schmaltz, who formed a part of the Governor's suit, they had the barbarity of intending our family to embark upon the raft, where were only soldiers, sailors, planters of Cape Verde, and some generous officers who had not the honour (if it could be accounted one) of being considered among the ignorant confidents of MM. Schmaltz and Lachaumareys. My father, indignant at a proceeding so indecorous, swore we would not embark upon the raft, and that, if we were not judged worthy of a place in one of the six boats, he would himself, his wife, and children, remain on board the wrecks of the frigate. The tone in which he spoke these words, was that of a man resolute to avenge any insult that might be offered to him. The governor of Senegal, doubtless fearing the world would one day reproach him for his inhumanity, decided we should have a place in one of the boats. This having in some measure quieted our fears concerning our unfortunate situation, I was desirous of taking some repose, but the uproar among the crew was so great I could not obtain it.

Towards midnight, a passenger came to inquire at my father if we were disposed to depart; he replied, we had been forbid to go yet. However, we were soon convinced that a great part of the crew and various passengers were secretly preparing to set off in the boats. A conduct so perfidious could not fail to alarm us, especially as we perceived among those so eager to embark unknown to us, several who had promised, but a little while before, not to go without us.

M. Schmaltz, to prevent that which was going on upon deck, instantly rose to endeavour to quiet their minds; but the soldiers had already assumed a threatening attitude, and, holding cheap the words of their commander, swore they would fire upon whosoever attempted to depart in a clandestine manner. The firmness of these brave men produced the desired effect, and all was restored to order. The governor returned to his cabin; and those who were desirous of departing furtively were confused and covered with shame. The governor, however, was ill at ease; and as he had heard very distinctly certain energetic words which had been addressed to him, he judged it proper to assemble a council. All the officers and passengers being collected, M. Schmaltz there solemnly swore before them not to abandon the raft, and a second time promised, that all the boats would tow it to the shore of the desert, where they would all be formed into a caravan. I confess this conduct of the governor greatly satisfied every member of our family; for we never dreamed he would deceive us, nor act in a manner contrary to what he had promised.

CHAPTER 4

Abandon Ship

About three in the morning, some hours after the meeting of the council, a terrible noise was heard in the powder room; it was the helm which was broken. All who were sleeping were roused by it. On going on deck everyone was more and more convinced that the frigate was lost beyond all recovery. Alas! the wreck was for our family the commencement of a horrible series of misfortunes. The two chief officers then decided with one accord, that all should embark at six in the morning, and abandon the ship to the mercy of the waves. After this decision, followed a scene the most whimsical, and at the same time the most melancholy that can be well conceived. To have a more distinct idea of it, let the reader transport himself in imagination to the midst of the liquid plains of the ocean; then let him picture to himself a multitude of all classes, of every age, tossed about at the mercy of the waves upon a dismasted vessel, foundered, and half submerged; let him not forget these are thinking beings with the certain prospect before them of having reached the goal of their existence.

Separated from the rest of the world by a boundless sea, and having no place of refuge but the wrecks of a grounded vessel, the multitude addressed at first their vows to heaven, and forgot, for a moment, all earthly concerns. Then, suddenly starting from their lethargy, they began to look after their wealth, the merchandise they had in small ventures, utterly regardless of the elements which threatened them. The miser, thinking of the gold contained in his coffers, hastening to put it in a place of safety, either by sewing it into the lining of his clothes, or by cutting out for it a place in the waistband of his trousers. The smuggler was tearing his hair at not being able to save a chest of contraband which he had secretly got on board, and with which he had hoped to have gained two or three hundred per cent. Another, selfish to excess, was throwing over board all his hidden money, and amusing himself by burning all his effects. A generous officer was opening his portmanteau, offering caps, stockings, and shirts, to any who would take them. These had scarcely gathered together their various effects, when they learned that they could not take anything with them; those were searching the cabins and store-rooms to carry away everything that was valuable. Ship-boys were discovering the delicate wines and fine liqueurs, which a wise foresight had placed in reserve. Soldiers and sailors were penetrating even into the spirit-room, broaching casks, staving others, and drinking till they fell exhausted. Soon the tumult of the inebriated made us forget the roaring of the sea which threatened to engulf us. At last the uproar was at its height; the soldiers no longer listened to the voice of their captain. Some knit their brows and muttered oaths; but nothing could be done with those whom wine had rendered furious. Next, piercing cries mixed with doleful groans were heard—this was the signal of departure.

At six o'clock on the morning of the 5th, a great part of the military were embarked upon the raft, which was already covered with a large sheet of foam. The soldiers were expressly prohibited from taking their arms. A young officer of infantry, whose brain seemed to be powerfully affected, put his horse beside the *barricadoes* of the frigate, and then, armed with two pistols, threatened to fire upon any one who refused to go upon the raft. Forty men had scarcely descended when it sunk to the depth of about two feet. To facilitate the embarking of a greater number, they were obliged to throw over several barrels of provisions which had been placed upon it the day before. In this manner did this furious officer get about one hundred and fifty heaped upon that floating tomb; but he did not think of adding one more to the number by descending himself, as he ought to have done, but went peaceably away, and placed himself in one of the best boats. There should have been sixty sailors upon the raft, and there were but about ten. A list had been made out on the 4th, assigning each his proper place; but this wise precaution being disregarded, every one pursued the plan he deemed the best for his own preservation. The precipitation with which they forced one hundred and fifty unfortunate beings upon the raft was such, that they forgot to give them one morsel of biscuit. However, they threw towards them twenty-five pounds in a sack, whilst they were not far from the frigate; but it fell into the sea, and was with difficulty recovered.

During this disaster, the governor of Senegal, who was busied in the care of his own dear self, effeminately descended in an arm-chair into the barge, where were already various large chests, all kinds of provisions, his dearest friends, his daughter and his wife. Afterwards the captain's boat received twenty-seven persons, amongst whom were twenty-five sailors, good rowers. The shallop, commanded by M. Espiau, ensign of the ship, took forty-five passengers, and put off. The boat, called the *Senegal*, took twenty-five; the pinnace thirty-three; and the yawl, the smallest of all the boats, took only ten.

Almost all the officers, the passengers, the mariners and supernumeraries, were already embarked—all, but our weeping family, who still remained upon the boards of the frigate, till some charitable souls would kindly receive us into a boat. Surprised at this abandonment, I instantly felt myself roused, and, calling with all my might to the officers of the boats, besought them to take our unhappy family along with them. Soon after, the barge, in which were the governor of Senegal and all his family, approached the *Medusa*, as if still to take some passengers, for there were but few in it. I made a motion to descend, hoping that the Misses Schmaltz, who had, till that day, taken a great interest in our family, would allow us a place in their boat; but I was mistaken: those ladies, who had embarked in a mysterious incognito, had already forgotten us; and M. Lachaumareys, who was still on the frigate, positively told me they would not embark along with us.

Nevertheless I ought to tell, what we learned afterwards, that that officer who commanded the pinnace had received orders to take us in, but, as he was already a great way from the frigate, we were certain he had abandoned us. My father however hailed him, but he persisted on his way to gain the open sea. A short while afterwards we perceived a small boat among the waves, which seemed desirous to approach the *Medusa*; it was the yawl. When it was sufficiently near, my father implored the sailors who were in it to take us on board, and to carry us to the pinnace, where our family ought to be placed. They refused. He then seized a firelock, which lay by chance upon deck, and swore he would kill every one of them if they refused to take us into the yawl, adding that it was the property of the king, and that he would have advantage from it as well as another.

The sailors murmured, but durst not resist, and received all our family, which consisted of nine persons, *viz*. Four children, our stepmother, my cousin, my sister Caroline, my father, and myself. A small box, filled with valuable papers, which we wished to save, some clothes, two bottles of *ratafia*, which we had endeavoured to preserve amidst our misfortunes, were seized and thrown overboard by the sailors of the yawl, who told us we would find in the pinnace everything which we could wish for our voyage. We had then only the clothes which covered us, never thinking of dressing ourselves in two suits; but the loss which affected us most was that of several MSS. at which my father had been labouring for a long while. Our trunks, our linen, and various chests of merchandise of great value, in a word, everything we possessed, was left in the *Medusa*.

When we boarded the pinnace, the officer who commanded it began excusing himself for having set off without forewarning us, as he had been ordered, and said a thousand things in his justification. But without believing the half of his fine protestations, we felt very happy in having overtaken him; for it is most certain they had had no intention of encumbering themselves with our unfortunate family. I say encumber, for it is evident that four children, one of whom was yet at the breast, were very indifferent beings to people who were actuated by a selfishness without all parallel. When we were seated in the long-boat, my father dismissed the sailors with the yawl, telling them he would ever gratefully remember their services. They speedily departed, but little satisfied with the good action they had done. My father hearing their murmurs and the abuse they poured out against us, said, loud enough for all in the boat to hear:

"We are not surprised sailors are destitute of shame, when their officers blush at being compelled to do a good action."

The commandant of the boat feigned not to understand the reproaches conveyed in these words, and, to divert our minds from brooding over our wrongs, endeavoured to counterfeit the man of gallantry.

CHAPTER 5

The Raft Cast Adrift

All the boats were already far from the *Medusa*, when they were brought to, to form a chain in order to tow the raft. The barge, in which was the governor of Senegal, took the first tow, then all the other boats in succession joined themselves to that. M. Lachaumareys embarked, although there yet remained upon the *Medusa* more than sixty persons. Then the brave and generous M. Espiau, commander of the shallop, quitted the line of boats, and returned to the frigate, with the intention of saving all the wretches who had been abandoned. They all sprung into the shallop; but as it was very much overloaded, seventeen unfortunates preferred remaining on board, rather than expose themselves as well as their companions to certain death. But, alas! the greater part afterwards fell victims to their fears or their devotion. Fifty-two days after they were abandoned, no more than three of them were alive, and these looked more like skeletons than men. They told that their miserable companions had gone afloat upon planks and hen-coops, after having waited in vain forty-two days for the succour which had been promised them, and that all had perished.[4]

The shallop, carrying with difficulty all those she had saved

---

[4]: Two, out of the three wretches who were saved from the wrecks of the *Medusa*, died a few days after their arrival at the colony; and the third, who pretended to know a great many particulars relative to the desertion of the frigate, was assassinated in his bed at Senegal, when he was just upon the eve of setting off for France. The authorities could not discover the murderer, who had taken good care to flee from his victim after having killed him.

from the *Medusa*, slowly rejoined the line of boats which towed the raft. M. Espiau earnestly besought the officers of the other boats to take some of them along with them; but they refused, alleging to the generous officer that he ought to keep them in his own boat, as he had gone for them himself. M. Espiau, finding it impossible to keep them all without exposing them to the utmost peril, steered right for a boat which I will not name.

Immediately a sailor sprung from the shallop into the sea, and endeavoured to reach it by swimming; and when he was about to enter it, an officer who possessed great influence, pushed him back, and, drawing his sabre, threatened to cut off his hands, if he again made the attempt. The poor wretch regained the shallop, which was very near the pinnace, where we were. Various friends of my father supplicated M. Lapérère, the officer of our boat, to receive him on board. My father had his arms already out to catch him, when M. Lapérère instantly let go the rope which attached us to the other boats, and tugged off with all his force. At the same instant every boat imitated our execrable example; and wishing to shun the approach of the shallop, which sought for assistance, stood off from the raft, abandoning in the midst of the ocean, and to the fury of the waves, the miserable mortals whom they had sworn to land on the shores of the desert.

Scarcely had these cowards broken their oath, when we saw the French flag flying upon the raft. The confidence of these unfortunate persons was so great, that when they saw the first boat which had the tow removing from them, they all cried out, the rope is broken! the rope is broken! but when no attention was paid to their observation they instantly perceived the treachery of the wretches who had left them so basely. Then the cries of *Vive le Roi* arose from the raft, as if the poor fellows were calling to their father for assistance; or, as if they had been persuaded that, at that rallying word, the officers of the boats would return, and not abandon their countrymen. The officers repeated the cry of *Vive le Roi*, without a doubt, to insult them; but, more particularly, M. Lachaumareys, who, assuming a martial attitude, waved his hat in the air.

Alas! what availed these false professions? Frenchmen, menaced with the greatest peril, were demanding assistance with the cries of *Vive le Roi*; yet none were found sufficiently generous, nor sufficiently French, to go to aid them. After a silence of some minutes, horrible cries were heard; the air resounded with the groans, the lamentations, the imprecations of these wretched beings, and the echo of the sea frequently repeated, Alas! how cruel you are to abandon us!!!

The raft already appeared to be buried under the waves, and its unfortunate passengers immersed. The fatal machine was drifted by currents far behind the wreck of the Frigate; without cable, anchor, mast, sail, oars; in a word, without the smallest means of enabling them to save themselves. Each wave that struck it, made them stumble in heaps on one another. Their feet getting entangled among the cordage, and between the planks, bereaved them of the faculty of moving. Maddened by these misfortunes, suspended, and adrift upon a merciless ocean, they were soon tortured between the pieces of wood which formed the scaffold on which they floated. The bones of their feet and their legs were bruised and broken, every time the fury of the waves agitated the raft; their flesh covered with contusions and hideous wounds, dissolved, as it were, in the briny waves, whilst the roaring flood around them was coloured with their blood.

As the raft, when it was abandoned, was nearly two leagues from the frigate, it was impossible these unfortunate persons could return to it: they were soon after far out at sea. These victims still appeared above their floating tomb; and, stretching out their supplicating hands towards the boats which fled from them, seemed yet to invoke, for the last time, the names of the wretches who had deceived them. O horrid day! a day of shame and reproach! Alas! that the hearts of those who were so well acquainted with misfortune, should have been so inaccessible to pity!

After witnessing that most inhuman scene, and seeing they were insensible to the cries and lamentations of so many unhappy beings, I felt my heart bursting with sorrow. It seemed to me that the waves would overwhelm all these wretches, and I could not suppress my tears. My father, exasperated to excess, and bursting with rage at seeing so much cowardice and inhumanity among the officers of the boats, began to regret he had not accepted the place which had been assigned for us upon the fatal raft.

"At least," said he, "we would have died with the brave, or we would have returned to the wreck of the *Medusa*; and not have had the disgrace of saving ourselves with cowards."

Although this produced no effect upon the officers, it proved very fatal to us afterwards; for, on our arrival at Senegal, it was reported to the Governor, and very probably was the principal cause of all those evils and vexations which we endured in that colony.

Let us now turn our attention to the several situations of all those who were endeavouring to save themselves in the different boats, as well as to those left upon the wreck of the *Medusa*.

We have already seen, that the frigate was half sunk when it was deserted, presenting nothing but a hulk and wreck. Nevertheless, seventeen still remained upon it, and had food, which, although damaged, enabled them to support themselves for a considerable time; whilst the raft was abandoned to float at the mercy of the waves, upon the vast surface of the ocean. One hundred and fifty wretches were embarked upon it, sunk to the depth of at least three feet on its fore part, and on its poop immersed even to the middle. What victuals they had were soon consumed, or spoiled by the salt water; and perhaps some, as the waves hurried them along, became food for the monsters of the deep.

Two only of all the boats which left the *Medusa*, and these with very few people in them, were provisioned with every necessary; these struck off with security and despatch. But the condition of those who were in the shallop was but little better than those upon the raft; their great number, their scarcity of provisions, their great distance from the shore, gave them the most melancholy anticipations of the future. Their worthy commander, M. Espiau, had no other hope but of reaching the shore as soon as possible. The other boats were less filled with people, but they were scarcely better provisioned; and, as by a species of fatality, the pinnace, in which were our family, was destitute of everything. Our provisions consisted of a barrel of biscuit, and a tierce of water; and, to add to our misfortunes, the biscuit being soaked in the sea, it was almost impossible to swallow one morsel of it. Each passenger in our boat was obliged to sustain his wretched existence with a glass of water, which he could get only once a day.

To tell how this happened, how this boat was so poorly supplied, whilst there were abundance left upon the *Medusa*, is far beyond my power. But it is at least certain, that the greater part of the officers commanding the boats, the Shallop, the pinnace, the Senegal boat, and the yawl, were persuaded, when they quitted the frigate, that they would not abandon the raft, but that all the expedition would sail together to the coast of Sahara; that when there, the boats would be again sent to the *Medusa* to take provisions, arms, and those who were left there; but it appears the chiefs had decided otherwise.

After abandoning the raft, although scattered, all the boats formed a little fleet, and followed the same route. All who were sincere hoped to arrive the same day at the coast of the desert, and that everyone would get on shore; but MM. Schmaltz and Lachaumareys gave orders to take the route for Senegal. This sudden change in the resolutions of the chiefs was like a thunderbolt to the officers commanding the boats. Having nothing on board but what was barely necessary to enable us to allay the cravings of hunger for one day, we were all sensibly affected. The other boats, which, like ourselves, hoped to have got on shore at the nearest point, were a little better provisioned than we were; they had at least a little wine, which supplied the place of other necessaries.

We then demanded some from them, explaining our situation, but none would assist us, not even Captain Lachaumareys, who, drinking to a kept mistress, supported by two sailors, swore he had not one drop on board. We were next desirous of addressing the boat of the Governor of Senegal, where we were persuaded were plenty of provisions of every kind, such as oranges, biscuits, cakes, comfits, plumbs, and even the finest liqueurs; but my father opposed it, so well was he assured we would not obtain anything.

We will now turn to the condition of those on the raft, when the boats left them to themselves.

If all the boats had continued dragging the raft forward, favoured as we were by the breeze from the sea, we would have been able to have conducted them to the shore in less than two days. But an inconceivable fatality caused the generous plan to be abandoned which had been formed.

When the raft had lost sight of the boats, a spirit of sedition began to manifest itself in furious cries. They then began to regard one another with ferocious looks, and to thirst for one another's flesh. Someone had already whispered of having recourse to that monstrous extremity, and of commencing with the fattest and youngest. A proposition so atrocious filled the brave Captain Dupont and his worthy lieutenant M. L'Heureux with horror; and that courage which had so often supported them in the field of glory, now forsook them.

Among the first who fell under the hatchets of the assassins, was a young woman who had been seen devouring the body of her husband. When her turn was come, she sought a little wine as a last favour, then rose, and without uttering one word, threw herself into the sea. Captain Dupont being proscribed for having refused to partake of the sacrilegious viands with which the monsters were feeding on, was saved as by a miracle from the hands of the butchers. Scarcely had they seized him to lead him to the slaughter, when a large pole, which served in place of a mast, fell upon his body; and believing that his legs were broken, they contented themselves by throwing him into the sea. The unfortunate captain plunged, disappeared, and they thought him already in another world.

Providence, however, revived the strength of the unfortunate warrior. He emerged under the beams of the raft, and clinging with all his might, holding his head above water, he remained between two enormous pieces of wood, whilst the rest of his body was hid in the sea. After more than two hours of suffering, Captain Dupont spoke in a low voice to his lieutenant, who by chance was seated near the place of his concealment. The brave

L'Heureux, with eyes glistening with tears, believed he heard the voice, and saw the shade of his captain; and trembling, was about to quit the place of horror; but, O wonderful! he saw a head which seemed to draw its last sigh, he recognised it, he embraced it, alas! it was his dear friend! Dupont was instantly drawn from the water, and M. L'Heureux obtained for his unfortunate comrade again a place upon the raft. Those who had been most inveterate against him, touched at what Providence had done for him in so miraculous a manner, decided with one accord to allow him entire liberty upon the raft.

The sixty unfortunates who had escaped from the first massacre, were soon reduced to fifty, then to forty, and at last to twenty-eight. The least murmur, or the smallest complaint, at the moment of distributing the provisions, was a crime punished with immediate death. In consequence of such a regulation, it may easily be presumed the raft was soon lightened. In the meanwhile the wine diminished sensibly, and the half rations very much displeased a certain chief of the conspiracy. On purpose to avoid being reduced to that extremity, the *executive power* decided it was much wiser to *drown thirteen people*, and to get full rations, than that twenty-eight should have half rations. Merciful Heaven! what shame! After the last catastrophe, the chiefs of the conspiracy, fearing doubtless of being assassinated in their turn, threw all the arms into the sea, and swore an inviolable friendship with the heroes which the hatchet had spared. On the 17th of July, in the morning, Captain Parnajon, commandant of the *Argus* brig, still found fifteen men on the raft. They were immediately taken on board, and conducted to Senegal. Four of the fifteen are yet alive, *viz.* Captain Dupont, residing in the neighbourhood of Maintenon, Lieutenant L'Heureux, since Captain, at Senegal, Savigny, at Rochefort, and Corréard, I know not where.

Chapter 6

Hardships at Sea

On the 5th of July, at ten in the morning, one hour after abandoning the raft, and three after quitting the *Medusa*, M. Lapérère, the officer of our boat, made the first distribution of provisions. Each passenger had a small glass of water and nearly the fourth of a biscuit. Each drank his allowance of water at one draught, but it was found impossible to swallow one morsel of our biscuit, it being so impregnated with sea-water. It happened, however, that some was found not quite so saturated. Of these we eat a small portion, and put back the remainder for a future day. Our voyage would have been sufficiently agreeable, if the beams of the sun had not been so fierce.

On the evening we perceived the shores of the desert; but as the two chiefs (MM. Schmaltz and Lachaumareys) wished to go right for Senegal, notwithstanding we were still one hundred leagues from it, we were not allowed to land. Several officers remonstrated, both on account of our want of provisions and the crowded condition of the boats, for undertaking so dangerous a voyage. Others urged with equal force, that it would be dishonouring the French name, if we were to neglect the unfortunate people on the raft, and insisted we should be set on shore, and whilst we waited there, three boats should return to look after the raft, and three to the wrecks of the frigate, to take up the seventeen who were left there, as well as a sufficient quantity of provisions to enable us to go to Senegal by the way of Barbary. But MM. Schmaltz and Lachaumareys, whose boats were sufficiently well provisioned, scouted the advice of their subalterns, and ordered them to cast anchor till the following morning. They were obliged to obey these orders, and to relinquish their designs. During the night, a certain passenger, who was doubtless no doctor, and who believed in ghosts and witches, was suddenly frightened by the appearance of flames, which he thought he saw in the waters of the sea, a little way from where our boat was anchored. My father, and some others, who were aware that the sea is sometimes phosphorated, confirmed the poor credulous man in his belief, and added several circumstances which fairly turned his brain. They persuaded him the Arabic sorcerers had fired the sea to prevent us from travelling along their deserts.

On the morning of the 6th of July, at five o'clock, all the boats were under way on the route to Senegal. The boats of MM. Schmaltz and Lachaumareys took the lead along the coast, and all the expedition followed. About eight, several sailors in our boat, with threats, demanded to be set on shore; but M. Lapérère, not acceding to their request, the whole were about to revolt and seize the command; but the firmness of this officer quelled the mutineers. In a spring which he made to seize a firelock which a sailor persisted in keeping in his possession, he almost tumbled into the sea.

My father fortunately was near him, and held him by his clothes, but he had instantly to quit him, for fear of losing his hat, which the waves were floating away. A short while after this slight accident, the shallop, which we had lost sight of since the morning, appeared desirous of rejoining us. We plied all hands to avoid her, for we were afraid of one another, and thought that that boat, encumbered with so many people, wished to board us to oblige us to take some of its passengers, as M. Espiau would not suffer them to be abandoned like those upon the raft. That officer hailed us at a distance, offering to take our family on board, adding, he was anxious to take about sixty people to the desert.

The officer of our boat, thinking that this was a pretence, replied, we preferred suffering where we were. It even appeared to us that M. Espiau had hid some of his people under the benches of the shallop. But, alas! in the end we deeply deplored being so suspicious, and of having so outraged the devotion of the most generous officer of the *Medusa*.

Our boat began to leak considerably, but we prevented it as well as we could, by stuffing the largest holes with oakum, which an old sailor had had the precaution to take before quitting the frigate. At noon the heat became so strong—so intolerable, that several of us believed we had reached our last moments. The hot winds of the desert even reached us; and the fine sand with which they were loaded, had completely obscured the clearness of the atmosphere. The sun presented a reddish disk; the whole surface of the ocean became nebulous, and the air which we breathed, depositing a fine sand, an impalpable powder, penetrated to our lungs, already parched with a burning thirst. In this state of torment we remained till four in the afternoon, when a breeze from the north-west brought us some relief.

Notwithstanding the privations we felt, and especially the burning thirst which had become intolerable, the cool air which we now began to breath, made us in part forget our sufferings. The heavens began again to resume the usual serenity of those latitudes, and we hoped to have passed a good night. A second distribution of provisions was made; each received a small glass of water, and about the eighth part of a biscuit. Notwithstanding our meagre fare, everyone seemed content, in the persuasion we would reach Senegal by the morrow. But how vain were all our hopes, and what sufferings had we yet to endure!

At half past seven, the sky was covered with stormy clouds. The serenity we had admired a little while before, entirely disappeared, and gave place to the most gloomy obscurity. The surface of the ocean presented all the signs of a coming tempest. The horizon on the side of the desert had the appearance of a long hideous chain of mountains piled on one another, the summits of which seemed to vomit fire and smoke. Bluish clouds, streaked with a dark copper colour, detached themselves from that shapeless heap, and came and joined with those which floated over our heads. In less than half an hour the ocean seemed confounded with the terrible sky which canopied us. The stars were hid. Suddenly a frightful noise was heard from the west, and all the waves of the sea rushed to founder our frail bark. A fearful silence succeeded to the general consternation. Every tongue was mute; and none durst communicate to his neighbour the horror with which his mind was impressed. At intervals the cries of the children rent our hearts.

At that instant a weeping and agonized mother bared her breast to her dying child, but it yielded nothing to appease the thirst of the little innocent who pressed it in vain. O night of horrors! what pen is capable to paint thy terrible picture! How describe the agonizing fears of a father and mother, at the sight of their children tossed about and expiring of hunger in a small boat, which the winds and waves threatened to engulf at every instant! Having full before our eyes the prospect of inevitable death, we gave ourselves up to our unfortunate condition, and addressed our prayers to Heaven. The winds growled with the utmost fury; the tempestuous waves arose exasperated. In their terrific encounter a mountain of water was precipitated into our boat, carrying away one of the sails, and the greater part of the effects which the sailors had saved from the *Medusa*. Our bark was nearly sunk; the females and the children lay rolling in its bottom, drinking the waters of bitterness; and their cries, mixed with the roaring of the waves and the furious north wind, increased the horrors of the scene.

My unfortunate father then experienced the most excruciating agony of mind. The idea of the loss which the shipwreck had occasioned to him, and the danger which still menaced all he held dearest in the world, plunged him into a deep swoon. The tenderness of his wife and children recovered him; but alas! his recovery was to still more bitterly to deplore the wretched situation of his family. He clasped us to his bosom; he bathed us with his tears, and seemed as if he was regarding us with his last looks of love.

Every soul in the boat were seized with the same perturbation, but it manifested itself in different ways. One part of the sailors remained motionless, in a bewildered state; the other cheered and encouraged one another; the children, locked in the arms of their parents, wept incessantly. Some demanded drink, vomiting the salt water which choked them; others, in short, embraced as for the last time, intertwining their arms, and vowing to die together.

In the meanwhile the sea became rougher and rougher. The whole surface of the ocean seemed a vast plain furrowed with huge blackish waves fringed with white foam. The thunder growled around us, and the lightning discovered to our eyes all that our imagination could conceive most horrible. Our boat, beset on all sides by the winds, and at every instant tossed on the summit of mountains of water, was very nearly sunk in spite of our every effort in baling it, when we discovered a large hole in its poop. It was instantly stuffed with everything we could find;—old clothes, sleeves of shirts, shreds of coats, shawls, useless bonnets, everything was employed, and secured us as far as it was possible. During the space of six hours, we rowed suspended alternately between hope and fear, between life and death. At last towards the middle of the night, Heaven, which had seen our resignation, commanded the floods to be still. Instantly the sea became less rough, the veil which covered the sky became less obscure, the stars again shone out, and the tempest seemed to withdraw. A general exclamation of joy and thankfulness issued at one instant from every mouth. The winds calmed, and each of us sought a little sleep, whilst our good and generous pilot steered our boat on a still very stormy sea.

The day at last, the day so desired, entirely restored the calm; but it brought no other consolation. During the night, the currents, the waves, and the winds had taken us so far out to sea, that, on the dawning of the 7th of July, we saw nothing but sky and water, without knowing whether to direct our course; for our compass had been broken during the tempest. In this hopeless condition, we continued to steer sometimes to the right and sometimes to the left, until the sun arose, and at last showed us the east.

Chapter 7
Thrown Ashore

On the morning of the 7th of July, we again saw the shores of the desert, notwithstanding we were yet a great distance from it. The sailors renewed their murmurings, wishing to get on shore, with the hope of being able to get some wholesome plants, and some more palatable water than that of the sea; but as we were afraid of the Moors, their request was opposed. However, M. Lapérère proposed to take them as near as he could to the first breakers on the coast; and when there, those who wished to go on shore should throw themselves into the sea, and swim to land.

Eleven accepted the proposal; but when we had reached the first waves, none had the courage to brave the mountains of water which rolled between them and the beach. Our sailors then betook themselves to their benches and oars, and promised to be more quiet for the future. A short while after, a third distribution was made since our departure from the *Medusa*; and nothing more remained than four pints of water, and one half dozen biscuits. What steps were we to take in this cruel situation? We were desirous of going on shore, but we had such dangers to encounter. However, we soon came to a decision, when we saw a caravan of Moors on the coast. We then stood a little out to sea.

According to the calculation of our commanding officer, we would arrive at Senegal on the morrow. Deceived by that false account, we preferred suffering one day more, rather than to be taken by the Moors of the desert, or perish among the breakers. We had now no more than a small half glass of water, and the seventh of a biscuit. Exposed as we were to the heat of the sun, which darted its rays perpendicularly on our heads, that ration, though small, would have been a great relief to us; but the distribution was delayed to the morrow. We were then obliged to drink the bitter sea-water, ill as it was calculated to quench our thirst. Must I tell it! thirst had so withered the lungs of our sailors, that they drank water saltier than that of the sea! Our numbers diminished daily, and nothing but the hope of arriving at the colony on the following day sustained our frail existence. My young brothers and sisters wept incessantly for water. The little Laura, aged six years, lay dying at the feet of her mother. Her mournful cries so moved the soul of my unfortunate father, that he was on the eve of opening a vein to quench the thirst which consumed his child; but a wise person opposed his design, observing that all the blood in his body would not prolong the life of his infant one moment.

The freshness of the night-wind procured us some respite. We anchored pretty near to the shore, and, though dying of famine, each got a tranquil sleep. On the morning of the 8th of July at break of day, we took the route for Senegal. A short while after the wind fell, and we had a dead calm. We endeavoured to row, but our strength was exhausted. A fourth and last distribution was made, and, in the twinkling of an eye, our last resources were consumed. We were forty-two people who had to feed upon *six biscuits* and about *four pints* of water, with no hope of a farther supply. Then came the moment for deciding whether we were to perish among the breakers, which defended the approach to the shores of the desert, or to die of famine in continuing our route. The majority preferred the last species of misery.

We continued our progress along the shore, painfully pulling our oars. Upon the beach were distinguished several downs of white sand, and some small trees. We were thus creeping along the coast, observing a mournful silence, when a sailor suddenly exclaimed, Behold the Moors! We did, in fact, see various individuals upon the rising ground, walking at a quick pace, and whom we took to be the Arabs of the desert. As we were very near the shore, we stood farther out to sea, fearing that these pretended Moors, or Arabs, would throw themselves into the sea, swim out, and take us. Some hours after, we observed several people upon an eminence, who seemed to make signals to us. We examined them attentively, and soon recognised them to be our companions in misfortune. We replied to them by attaching a white handkerchief to the top of our mast. Then we resolved to land, at the risk of perishing among the breakers, which were very strong towards the shore, although the sea was calm.

On approaching the beach, we went towards the right, where the waves seemed less agitated, and endeavoured to reach it, with the hope of being able more easily to land. Scarcely had we directed our course to that point, when we perceived a great number of people standing near to a little wood surrounding the sand-hills. We recognised them to be the passengers of that boat, which, like ourselves, were deprived of provisions.

Meanwhile we approached the shore, and already the foaming surge filled us with terror. Each wave that came from the open sea, each billow that swept beneath our boat, made us bound into the air; so we were sometimes thrown from the poop to the prow, and from the prow to the poop. Then, if our pilot had missed the sea, we would have been sunk; the waves would have thrown us aground, and we would have been buried among the breakers. The helm of the boat was again given to the old pilot, who had already so happily steered us through the dangers of the storm. He instantly threw into the sea the mast, the sails, and everything that could impede our proceedings.

When we came to the first landing point, several of our shipwrecked companions, who had reached the shore, ran and hid themselves behind the hills, not to see us perish; others made signs not to approach at that place; some covered their eyes with their hands; others, at last despising the danger, precipitated themselves into the waves to receive us in their arms. We then saw a spectacle that made us shudder. We had already doubled two ranges of breakers; but those which we had still to cross raised their foaming waves to a prodigious height, then sunk with a hollow and monstrous sound, sweeping along a long line of the coast. Our boat sometimes greatly elevated, and sometimes engulfed between the waves, seemed, at the moment, of utter ruin. Bruised, battered, tossed about on all hands, it turned of itself, and refused to obey the kind hand which directed it.

At that instant a huge wave rushed from the open sea, and dashed against the poop; the boat plunged, disappeared, and we were all among the waves. Our sailors, whose strength had returned at the presence of danger, redoubled their efforts, uttering mournful sounds. Our bark groaned, the oars were broken; it was thought aground, but it was stranded; it was upon its side. The last sea rushed upon us with the impetuosity of a torrent. We were up to the neck in water; the bitter sea-froth choked us. The grapnel was thrown out. The sailors threw themselves into the sea; they took the children in their arms; returned, and took us upon their shoulders; and I found myself seated upon the sand on the shore, by the side of my step-mother, my brothers and sisters, almost dead. Everyone was upon the beach except my father and some sailors; but that good man arrived at last, to mingle his tears with those of his family and friends.

Instantly our hearts joined in addressing our prayers and praises to God. I raised my hands to heaven, and remained some time immoveable upon the beach. Every one also hastened to testify his gratitude to our old pilot, who, next to God, justly merited the title of our preserver. M. Dumège, a naval surgeon, gave him an elegant gold watch, the only thing he had saved from the *Medusa*.

Let the reader now recollect all the perils to which we had been exposed in escaping from the wreck of the frigate to the shores of the desert—all that we had suffered during our four days' voyage—and he will perhaps have a just notion of the various sensations we felt on getting on shore on that strange and savage land. Doubtless the joy we experienced at having escaped, as by a miracle, the fury of the floods, was very great; but how much was it lessened by the feelings of our horrible situation! Without water, without provisions, and the majority of us nearly naked, was it to be wondered at that we should be seized with terror on thinking of the obstacles which we had to surmount, the fatigues, the privations, the pains and the sufferings we had to endure, with the dangers we had to encounter in the immense and frightful desert we had to traverse before we could arrive at our destination? Almighty Providence! it was in Thee alone I put my trust.

CHAPTER 8

Encountering the Moors

After we had a little recovered from the fainting and fatigue of our getting on shore, our fellow-sufferers told us they had landed in the forenoon, and had cleared the breakers by the strength of their oars and sails; but they had not all been so lucky as we were. One unfortunate person, too desirous of getting quickly on shore, had his legs broken under the Shallop, and was taken and laid on the beach, and left to the care of Providence. M. Espiau, commander of the shallop, reproached us for having doubted him when he wished to board us to take our family along with him. It was most true he had landed sixty-three people that day. A short while after our refusal, he took the passengers of the yawl, who would infallibly have perished in the stormy night of the 6th and 7th. The boat named the *Senegal*, commanded by M. Maudet, had made the shore at the same time with M. Espiau. The boats of MM. Schmaltz and Lachaumareys were the only ones which continued the route for Senegal, whilst nine-tenths of the Frenchmen entrusted to these gentlemen were butchering each other on the raft, or dying of hunger on the burning sands of Sahara.

About seven in the morning, a caravan was formed to penetrate into the interior, for the purpose of finding some fresh water. We did accordingly find some at a little distance from the sea, by digging among the sand. Every one instantly flocked round the little wells, which furnished enough to quench our thirst. This brackish water was found to be delicious, although it had a sulphurous taste: its colour was that of whey. As all our clothes were wet and in tatters, and as we had nothing to change them, some generous officers offered theirs. My step-mother, my cousin, and my sister, were dressed in them; for myself, I preferred keeping my own. We remained nearly an hour beside our beneficent fountain then took the route for Senegal; that is, a southerly direction, for we did not know exactly where that country lay. It was agreed that the females and children should walk before the caravan, that they might not be left behind. The sailors voluntarily carried the youngest on their shoulders, and every one took the route along the coast. Notwithstanding it was nearly seven o'clock, the sand was quite burning, and we suffered severely, walking without shoes, having lost them whilst landing. As soon as we arrived on the shore, we went to walk on the wet sand, to cool us a little. Thus we travelled during all the night, without encountering anything but shells, which wounded our feet.

On the morning of the 9th, we saw an antelope on the top of a little hill, which instantly disappeared, before we had time to shoot it. The desert seemed to our view one immense plain of sand, on which was seen not one blade of verdure. However, we still found water by digging in the sand. In the forenoon, two officers of marine complained that our family incommoded the progress of the caravan. It is true, the females and the children could not walk so quickly as the men. We walked as fast as it was possible for us, nevertheless, we often fell behind, which obliged them to halt till we came up. These officers, joined with other individuals, considered among themselves whether they would wait for us, or abandon us in the desert. I will be bold to say, however, that but few were of the latter opinion.

My father being informed of what was plotting against us, stepped up to the chiefs of the conspiracy, and reproached them in the bitterest terms for their selfishness and brutality. The dispute waxed hot. Those who were desirous of leaving us drew their swords, and my father put his hand upon a *poignard*, with which he had provided himself on quitting the frigate. At this scene, we threw ourselves in between them, conjuring him rather to remain in the desert with his family, than seek the assistance of those who were, perhaps, less humane than the Moors themselves. Several people took our part, particularly M. Bégnère, captain of infantry, who quieted the dispute by saying to his soldiers:

"My friends, you are Frenchmen, and I have the honour of being your commander; let us never abandon an unfortunate family in the desert, so long as we are able to be of use to them."

This brief, but energetic speech, caused those to blush who wished to leave us. All then joined with the old captain, saying they would not leave us on condition we would walk quicker. M. Bégnère and his soldiers replied, they did not wish to impose conditions on those to whom they were desirous of doing a favour; and the unfortunate family of Picard were again on the road with the whole caravan. Sometime after this dispute, M. Rogéry, member of the Philanthropic Society of Cape Verde, secretly left the caravan, striking into the middle of the desert, without knowing very well what he sought. He wished perhaps to explore the ancient country of the Numidians and Getulians, and to give himself a slave to the great Emperor of Morocco. What would it avail to acquire such celebrity? That intrepid traveller had not time to find that after which he searched; for a few days after he was captured by the Moors, and taken to Senegal, where the governor paid his ransom.

About noon hunger was felt so powerfully among us, that it was agreed upon to go to the small hills of sand which were near the coast, to see if any herbs could be found fit for eating; but we only got poisonous plants, among which were various kinds of euphorbium. Convolvuluses of a bright green carpeted the downs; but on tasting their leaves we found them as bitter as gall. The caravan rested in this place, whilst several officers went farther into the interior.

They came back in about an hour, loaded with wild *purslain*, which they distributed to each of us. Every one instantly devoured his bunch of herbage, without leaving the smallest branch; but as our hunger was far from being satisfied with this small allowance, the soldiers and sailors betook themselves to look for more. They soon brought back a sufficient quantity, which was equally distributed, and devoured upon the spot, so delicious had hunger made that food to us. For myself, I declare I never eat anything with so much appetite in all my life. Water was also found in this place, but it was of an abominable taste. After this truly frugal repast, we continued our route.

The heat was insupportable in the last degree. The sands on which we trod were burning, nevertheless several of us walked on these scorching coals without shoes; and the females had nothing but their hair for a cap. When we reached the sea-shore, we all ran and lay down among the waves. After remaining there some time, we took our route along the wet beach. On our journey we met with several large crabs, which were of considerable service to us. Every now and then we endeavoured to slake our thirst by sucking their crooked claws.

About nine at night we halted between two pretty high sand hills. After a short talk concerning our misfortunes, all seemed desirous of passing the night in this place, notwithstanding we heard on every side the roaring of leopards. We deliberated on the means of securing ourselves, but sleep soon put an end to our fears. Scarcely had we slumbered a few hours when a horrible roaring of wild beasts awoke us, and made us stand on our defence. It was a beautiful moonlight night, and in spite of my fears and the horrible aspect of the place, nature never appeared so sublime to me before. Instantly something was announced that resembled a lion.

This information was listened to with the greatest emotion. Every one being desirous of verifying the truth, fixed upon something he thought to be the object; one believed he saw the long teeth of the king of the forest; another was convinced his mouth was already open to devour us; several, armed with muskets, aimed at the animal, and advancing a few steps, discovered the pretended lion to be nothing more than a shrub fluctuating in the breeze. However, the howlings of ferocious beasts had so frightened us, being yet heard at intervals, that we again sought the sea-shore, on purpose to continue our route towards the south.

Our situation had been thus perilous during the night; nevertheless at break of day we had the satisfaction of finding none missing. About sunrise we held a little to the east to get farther into the interior to find fresh water, and lost much time in a vain search. The country which we now traversed was a little less arid than that which we had passed the preceding day. The hills, the valleys, and a vast plain of sand, were strewed with mimosa or sensitive plants, presenting to our sight a scene we had never before seen in the desert. The country is bounded as it were by a chain of mountains, or high downs of sand, in the direction of north and south, without the slightest trace of cultivation.

Towards ten in the morning some of our companions were desirous of making observations in the interior, and they did not go in vain. They instantly returned, and told us they had seen two Arab tents upon a slight rising ground. We instantly directed our steps thither. We had to pass great downs of sand very slippery, and arrived in a large plain, streaked here and there with verdure; but the turf was so hard and piercing, we could scarcely walk over it without wounding our feet. Our presence in these frightful solitudes put to flight three or four Moorish shepherds, who herded a small flock of sheep and goats in an oasis.[5]

At last we arrived at the tents after which we were searching, and found in them three Mooresses and two little children, who did not seem in the least frightened by our visit. A negro servant, belonging to an officer of marine, interpreted between us; and the good women, who, when they had heard of our misfortunes, offered us millet and water for payment. We bought a little of that grain at the rate of thirty pence a handful; the water was got for three *francs* a glass; it was very good, and none grudged the money it cost. As a glass of water, with a handful of millet, was but a poor dinner for famished people, my father bought two kids, which they would not give him under twenty *piasters*. We immediately killed them, and our Mooresses boiled them in a large kettle. Whilst our repast was preparing, my father, who

---

5: Oasis, a fertile tract of land situated among sand. T.

could not afford the whole of the expense, got others to contribute to it; but an old officer of marine, who was to have been captain of the port of Senegal, was the only person who refused, notwithstanding he had about him nearly *three thousand francs*, which he boasted of in the end. Several soldiers and sailors had seen him count it in round pieces of gold, on coming ashore on the desert, and reproached him for his sordid avarice; but he seemed insensible to their reproaches, nor eat the less of his portion of kid with his companions in misfortune.

When about to resume our journey, we saw several Moors approaching to us armed with lances. Our people instantly seized their arms, and put themselves in readiness to defend us in case of an attack. Two officers, followed by several soldiers and sailors, with our interpreter, advanced to discover their intentions. They instantly returned with the Moors, who said, that far from wishing to do us harm, they had come to offer us their assistance, and to conduct us to Senegal. This offer being accepted of with gratitude by all of us, the Moors, of whom we had been so afraid, became our protectors and friends, verifying the old proverb, *there are good people everywhere*! As the camp of the Moors was at some considerable distance from where we were, we set off altogether to reach it before night. After having walked about two leagues through the burning sands, we found ourselves again upon the shore. Towards night, our conductors made us strike again into the interior, saying we were very near their camp, which is called in their language Berkelet. But the short distance of the Moors was found very long by the females and the children, on account of the downs of sand which we had to ascend and descend every instant, also of prickly shrubs over which we were frequently obliged to walk. Those who were barefooted, felt most severely at this time the want of their shoes. I myself lost among the bushes various shreds of my dress, and my feet and legs were all streaming with blood. At length, after two long hours of walking and suffering, we arrived at the camp of that tribe to which belonged our Arab conductors. We had scarcely got into the camp, when the dogs, the children, and the Moorish women, began to annoy us. Some of them threw sand in our eyes, others amused themselves by snatching at our hair, on pretence of wishing to examine it. This pinched us, that spit upon us; the dogs bit our legs, whilst the old harpies cut the buttons from the officers coats, or endeavoured to take away the lace. Our conductors, however, had pity on us, and chased away the dogs and the curious crowd, who had already made us suffer as much as the thorns which had torn our feet. The chiefs of the camp, our guides, and some good women, at last set about getting us some supper. Water in abundance was given us without payment, and they sold us fish dried in the sun, and some bowlfuls of sour milk, all at a reasonable price. We found a Moor in the camp who had previously known my father at Senegal, and who spoke a little French. As soon as he recognised him, he cried, "*Tiens toi, Picard! ni a pas connaître moi Amet?*"

Hark ye, Picard, know you not Amet? We were all struck with astonishment at these French words coming from the mouth of a Moor. My father recollected having employed long ago a young goldsmith at Senegal, and discovering the Moor Amet to be the same person, shook him by the hand. After that good fellow had been made acquainted with our shipwreck, and to what extremities our unfortunate family had been reduced, he could not refrain from tears; and this perhaps was the first time a Musulman had ever wept over the misfortunes of a Christian. Amet was not satisfied with deploring our hard fate; he was desirous of proving that he was generous and humane, and instantly distributed among us a large quantity of milk and water free of any charge. He also raised for our family a large tent of the skins of camels, cattle and sheep, because his religion would not allow him to lodge with Christians under the same roof.

The place appeared very dark, and the obscurity made us uneasy. Amet and our conductors lighted a large fire to quiet us; and at last, bidding us good night, and retiring to his tent, said, "Sleep in peace; the God of the Christians is also the God of the Musulmen."

We had resolved to quit this truly hospitable place early in the morning; but during the night, some people who had probably too much money, imagined the Moors had taken us to their camp to plunder us. They communicated their fears to others, and pretending that the Moors, who walked up and down among their flocks, and cried from time to time, to keep away the ferocious beasts, had already given the signal for pursuing and murdering us. Instantly a general panic seized all our people, and they wished to set off forthwith. My father, although he well knew the perfidy of the inhabitants of the desert, endeavoured to assure them we had nothing to fear, because the Arabs were too frightened for the people of Senegal, who would not fail to avenge us if we were insulted; but nothing could quiet their apprehensions, and we had to take the route during the middle of the night.

The Moors being soon acquainted with our fears, made us all kinds of protestations; and seeing we persisted in quitting the camp, offered us asses to carry us as far as the Senegal. These beasts of burden were hired at the rate of 12 *francs* a day, for each head, and we took our departure under the guidance of those Moors who had before conducted us to the camp. Amet's wife being unwell, he could not accompany us, but recommended us strongly to our guides. My father was able to hire only two asses for the whole of our family; and as it was numerous, my sister Caroline, my cousin, and myself, were obliged to crawl along, whilst my unfortunate father followed in the suite of the caravan, which in truth went much quicker than we did.

A short distance from the camp, the brave and compassionate Captain Bégnère, seeing we still walked, obliged us to accept of the ass he had hired for himself, saying he would not ride when young ladies, exhausted with fatigue, followed on foot. The King afterwards honourably recompensed this worthy officer, who ceased not to regard our unfortunate family with a care and attention I will never forget.

During the remainder of the night, we travelled in a manner sufficiently agreeable, mounting alternately the ass of Captain Bégnère.

CHAPTER 9

Arrival at Senegal

At five in the morning of the 11th of July we regained the sea-shore. Our asses, fatigued with the long journey among the sands, ran instantly and lay down among the breakers, in spite of our utmost exertions to prevent them. This caused several of us to take a bath we wished not: I was myself held under my ass in the water, and had great difficulty in saving one of my young brothers who was floating away. But, in the end, as this incident had no unfortunate issue, we laughed, and continued our route, some on foot, and some on the capricious asses. Towards ten o'clock, perceiving a ship out at sea, we attached a white handkerchief to the muzzle of a gun, waving it in the air, and soon had the satisfaction of seeing it was noticed.

The ship having approached sufficiently near the coast, the Moors who were with us threw themselves into the sea, and swam to it. It must be said we had very wrongfully supposed that these people had had a design against us, for their devotion could not appear greater than when five of them darted through the waves to endeavour to communicate between us and the ship; notwithstanding, it was still a good quarter of a league distant from where we stood on the beach. In about half an hour we saw these good Moors returning, making float before them three small barrels. Arrived on shore, one of them gave a letter to M. Espiau from M. Parnajon. This gentleman was the captain of the *Argus* brig, sent to seek after the raft, and to give us provisions. This letter announced a small barrel of biscuit, a tierce of wine, a half tierce of brandy, and a Dutch cheese. O fortunate event! We were very desirous of testifying our gratitude to the generous commander of the brig, but he instantly set out and left us. We staved the barrels which held our small stock of provisions, and made a distribution. Each of us had a biscuit, about a glass of wine, a half glass of brandy, and a small morsel of cheese. Each drank his allowance of wine at one gulp; the brandy was not even despised by the ladies. I however preferred quantity to quality, and exchanged my ration of brandy for that of wine.

To describe our joy, whilst taking this repast, is impossible. Exposed to the fierce rays of a vertical sun; exhausted by a long train of suffering; deprived for a long while the use of any kind of spirituous liquors, when our portions of water, wine, and brandy, mingled in our stomachs we became like insane people. Life, which had lately been a great burden, now became precious to us. Foreheads, lowering and sulky, began to unwrinkle; enemies became most brotherly; the avaricious endeavoured to forget their selfishness and cupidity; the children smiled for the first time since our shipwreck; in a word, everyone seemed to be born again from a condition melancholy and dejected. I even believe the sailors sang the praises of their mistresses.

This journey was the most fortunate for us. Some short while after our delicious meal, we saw several Moors approaching, who brought milk and butter, so that we had refreshments in abundance. It is true we paid a little dear for them; the glass of milk cost not less than three francs. After reposing about three hours, our caravan proceeded on its route.

About six in the evening, my father finding himself extremely fatigued, wished to rest himself. We allowed the caravan to move on, whilst my step-mother and myself remained near him, and the rest of the family followed with their asses. We all three soon fell asleep. When we awoke, we were astonished at not seeing our companions. The sun was sinking in the west. We saw several Moors approaching us, mounted on camels; and my father reproached himself for having slept so long. Their appearance gave us great uneasiness, and we wished much to escape from them, but my step-mother and myself fell quite exhausted. The Moors, with long beards, having come quite close to us, one of them alighted and addressed us in the following words.

"Be comforted, ladies; under the costume of an Arab, you see an Englishman who is desirous of serving you. Having heard at Senegal that Frenchmen were thrown ashore on these deserts, I thought my presence might be of some service to them, as I was acquainted with several of the princes of this arid country."

These noble words from the mouth of a man we had at first taken to be a Moor, instantly quieted our fears. Recovering from our fright, we rose and expressed to the philanthropic Englishman the gratitude we felt. Mr Carnet,[6] the name of the generous Briton, told us that our caravan, which he had met, waited for us at about the distance of two leagues. He then gave us some biscuit, which we eat; and we then set off together to join our companions. Mr Carnet wished us to mount his camels, but my stepmother and myself, being unable to persuade ourselves we could sit securely on their hairy haunches, continued to walk on the moist sand, whilst my father, Mr Carnet, and the Moors who accompanied him, proceeded on the camels.

We soon reached a little river, called in the country Marigot des Maringoins. We wished to drink of it, but found it as salt as the sea. Mr Carnet desired us to have patience, and we should find some at the place where our caravan waited. We forded that river knee-deep. At last, having walked about an hour, we rejoined our companions, who had found several wells of fresh water. It was resolved to pass the night in this place, which seemed less arid than any we saw near us. The soldiers, being requested

---

6: In the work of MM. Corréard and Savigny, this gentleman is made mention of in substance as follows. "On the evening of the 11th, they met with more of the natives, and an Irishman, captain of a merchantman, who, of his own accord, had left St Louis with the intention of assisting the sufferers. He spoke the language of the country, and was dressed in the Moorish costume. We are sorry we cannot recollect the name of this foreign officer, which we would have a real pleasure in publishing; but, since time has effaced it from our memories, we will at least publish his zeal and his noble efforts, titles well worthy the gratitude of every feeling heart." pp. 164-165. Paris, 1818, 8vo.—*Trans.*

to go and seek wood to light a fire, for the purpose of frightening the ferocious beasts which were heard roaring around us, refused; but Mr Carnet assured us, that the Moors who were with him knew well how to keep all such intruders from our camp. In truth, during the whole of the night, these good Arabs promenaded round our caravan, uttering cries at intervals like those we had heard in the camp of the generous Amet.

We passed a very good night, and at four in the morning continued our route along the shore. Mr Carnet left us to endeavour to procure some provisions. Till then our asses had been quite docile; but, annoyed with their riders so long upon their backs, they refused to go forward. A fit took possession of them, and all at the same instant threw their riders on the ground, or among the bushes. The Moors, however, who accompanied us, assisted to catch our capricious animals, who had nearly scampered off, and replaced us on the hard backs of these headstrong creatures. At noon the heat became so violent, that even the Moors themselves bore it with difficulty.

We then determined on finding some shade behind the high mounds of sand which appeared in the interior; but how were we to reach them! The sands could not be hotter. We had been obliged to leave our asses on the shore, for they would neither advance nor recede. The greater part of us had neither shoes nor hats; notwithstanding, we were obliged to go forward almost a long league to find a little shade. The heat reflected by the sands of the desert could be compared to nothing but the mouth of an oven at the moment of drawing out the bread; nevertheless, we endured it; but not without cursing those who had been the occasion of all our misfortunes.

Arrived behind the heights for which we searched, we stretched ourselves under the mimosa-gommier, (the acacia of the desert), several broke branches from the *asclepia* (swallow-wort), and made themselves a shade. But whether from want of air, or the heat of the ground on which we were seated, we were nearly all suffocated. I thought my last hour was come. Already my eyes saw nothing but a dark cloud, when a person of the name of Borner, who was to have been a smith at Senegal, gave me a boot containing some muddy water, which he had had the precaution to keep. I seized the elastic vase, and hastened to swallow the liquid in large draughts.

One of my companions, equally tormented with thirst, envious of the pleasure I seemed to feel, and which I felt effectually, drew the foot from the boot, and seized it in his turn, but it availed him nothing. The water which remained was so disgusting, that he could not drink it, and spilled it on the ground. Captain Bégnère, who was present, judging, by the water which fell, how loathsome must that have been which I had drank, offered me some crumbs of biscuit, which he had kept most carefully in his pocket. I chewed that mixture of bread, dust, and tobacco, but I could not swallow it, and gave it all masticated to one of my young brothers, who had fallen from inanition.

We were about to quit this furnace, when we saw our generous Englishman approaching, who brought us provisions. At this sight I felt my strength revive, and ceased to desire death, which I had before called on to release me from my sufferings. Several Moors accompanied Mr Carnet, and everyone was loaded. On their arrival we had water, with rice and dried fish in abundance. Every one drank his allowance of water, but had not ability to eat, although the rice was excellent.

We were all anxious to return to the sea, that we might bathe ourselves, and the caravan put itself on the road to the breakers of Sahara. After an hour's march of great suffering, we regained the shore, as well as our asses, who were lying in the water. We rushed among the waves, and after a bath of half an hour, we reposed ourselves upon the beach. My cousin and I went to stretch ourselves upon a small rising ground, where we were shaded with some old clothes which we had with us. My cousin was clad in an officer's uniform, the lace of which strongly attracted the eyes of Mr Carnet's Moors. Scarcely had we lain down, when one of them, thinking we were asleep, came to endeavour to steal it; but seeing we were awake, contented himself by looking at us very steadfastly.

Such is the slight incident which it has pleased MM. Corréard and Savigny to relate in their account of the shipwreck of the *Medusa* in a totally different manner. Believing doubtless to make it more interesting or amusing, they say, that one of the Moors who were our guides, either through curiosity or a stronger sentiment, approached Miss Picard whilst asleep, and, after having examined her form, raised the covering which concealed her bosom, gazing awhile like one astonished, at length drew nearer, but durst not touch her. Then, after having looked a long while, he replaced the covering; and, returning to his companions, related in a joyous manner what he had seen.

Several Frenchmen having observed the proceedings of the Moor, told M. Picard, who, after the obliging offers of the officers, decided in clothing the rest of the ladies in the military dress on purpose to prevent their being annoyed by the attentions of the inhabitants of the desert. Mighty well! I beg pardon of MM. Corréard and Savigny, but there is not one word of truth in all this. How could these gentlemen see from the raft that which passed during the 12th of July on the shore of the desert of Sahara? And supposing that this was reported to them by some one of our caravan, and inserted in their work, which contains various other inaccuracies, I have to inform them they have been deceived.

About three in the morning, a north-west wind having sprung up and a little refreshed us, our caravan continued its route; our generous Englishman again taking the task of procuring us provisions. At four o'clock the sky became overcast, and we heard thunder in the distance. We all expected a great tempest, which, happily did not take place. Near seven we reached the spot where we were to wait for Mr. Carnet, who came to us with a bullock he had purchased. Then quitting the shore, we went into the interior to seek a place to cook our supper.

We fixed our camp beside a small wood of acacias, near to which were several wells or cisterns of fresh water. Our ox was instantly killed, skinned, cut to pieces, and distributed. A large fire was kindled, and each was occupied in dressing his meal. At this time I caught a smart fever; notwithstanding I could not help laughing at seeing every one seated round a large fire holding his piece of beef on the point of a bayonet, a sabre, or some sharp-pointed stick. The flickering of the flames on the different faces, sunburned and covered with long beards, rendered more visible by the darkness of the night, joined to the noise of the waves and the roaring of ferocious beasts which we heard in the distance, presented a spectacle at once laughable and imposing.

If a David or a Girodet had seen us, said I to myself, we would soon have been represented on canvass in the galleries of the Louvre as real cannibals; and the Parisian youth, who know not what pleasure it is to devour a handful of wild *purslain*, to drink muddy water from a boot, to eat a roast cooked in smoke—who know not, in a word, how comfortable it is to have it in one's power to satisfy one's appetite when hungry in the burning deserts of Africa, would never have believed that, among these half-savages, were several born on the banks of the Seine.

Whilst these thoughts were passing across my mind, sleep overpowered my senses. Being awaked in the middle of the night, I found my portion of beef in the shoes which an old sailor had lent me for walking among the thorns. Although it was a little burned and smelt strongly of the dish in which it was contained, I eat a good part of it, and gave the rest to my friend the sailor. That seaman, seeing I was ill, offered to exchange my meat for some which he had had the address to boil in a small tin-box. I prayed him to give me a little water if he had any, and he instantly went and fetched me some in his hat. My thirst was so great that I drank it out of this nasty cap without the slightest repugnance.

A short while after, every one awoke, and again took the route for arriving at Senegal at an early hour. Towards seven in the morning, having fallen a little behind the caravan, I saw several Moors coming towards me armed with lances. A young sailor boy, aged about twelve years, who sometimes walked with me, stopped and cried in great terror, "Ah! my God, lady, see the Moors are coming, and the caravan is already a great way before us; if they should carry us away?"

I told him to fear nothing, although I was really more frightened than he was. These Arabs of the desert soon came up to us. One of them advanced with a threatening air, and stopping my ass, addressed to me, in his barbarous language, some words which he pronounced with menacing gestures. My little ship-boy having made his escape, I began to weep; for the Moor always prevented my ass going forward, who was perhaps as well content at resting a little. However, from the gestures which he made, I supposed he wished to know whither I was going, and I cried as loud as I could, "*Ndar! Ndar!*" (Senegal! Senegal!) the only African words I then knew.

At this the Moor let go the bridle of my ass, and also assisted me by making him feel the full weight of the pole of his lance, and then ran off to his companions, who were roaring and laughing. I was well content at being freed from my fears; and what with the word *Ndar*, and the famous thump of his spear, which was doubtless intended for my ass, I soon rejoined the caravan. I told my parents of my adventure, who were ignorant of what had detained me; they reprimanded me as they ought, and I promised faithfully never again to quit them.

At nine o'clock we met upon the shore a large flock herded by young Moors. These shepherds sold us milk, and one of them offered to lend my father an ass for a knife which he had seen him take from his pocket. My father having accepted the proposal, the Moor left his companions to accompany us as far as the river Senegal, from which we were yet two good leagues. There happened a circumstance in the forenoon which had like to have proved troublesome, but it turned out pleasantly.

The steersman of the *Medusa* was sleeping upon the sand, when a Moor found means to steal his sabre. The Frenchman awoke, and as soon as he saw the thief escaping with his booty, rose and pursued him with horrid oaths. The Arab, seeing himself followed by a furious European, returned, fell upon his knees, and laid at the feet of the steersman the sabre which he had stolen; who, in his turn, touched with this mark of confidence or repentance, voluntarily gave it to him to keep. During this scene we frequently stopped to see how it would terminate, whilst the caravan continued its route. Suddenly we left the shore. Our companions appearing quite transported with joy, some of us ran forward, and having gained a slight rising ground, discovered the Senegal at no great distance from them.

We hastened our march, and for the first time since our shipwreck, a smiling picture presented itself to our view. The trees always green, with which that noble river is shaded, the humming birds, the red-birds, the parakeets, the promerops, &c. who flitted among their long yielding branches, caused in us emotions difficult to express. We could not satiate our eyes with gazing on the beauties of this place, verdure being so enchanting to the sight, especially after having travelled through the desert. Before reaching the river, we had to descend a little hill covered with thorny bushes. My ass stumbling threw me into the midst of one, and I tore myself in several places, but was easily consoled when I at length found myself on the banks of a river of fresh water. Every one having quenched his thirst, we stretched ourselves under the shade of a small grove, whilst the beneficent Mr Carnet and two of our officers set forward to Senegal to announce our arrival, and to get us boats. In the meanwhile some took a little repose, and others were engaged in dressing the wounds with which they were covered.

At two in the afternoon, we saw a small boat beating against the current of the stream with oars. It soon reached the spot where we were. Two Europeans landed, saluted our caravans, and inquired for my father. One of them said he came on the part of MM. Artigue and Labouré, inhabitants of Senegal, to offer assistance to our family; the other added, that he had not waited for the boats which were getting ready for us at the island of St Louis, knowing too well what would be our need. We were desirous of thanking them, but they instantly ran off to the boat and brought us provisions, which my father's old friends had sent him. They placed before us large baskets containing several loaves, cheese, a bottle of Madeira, a bottle of filtered water, and dresses for my father. Everyone, who, during our journey, had taken any interest in our unfortunate family, and especially the brave Captain Bégnère, had a share of our provisions. We experienced a real satisfaction in partaking with them, and giving them this small mark of our gratitude.

A young aspirant of marine, who had refused us a glass of water in the desert, pressed with hunger, begged of us some bread; he got it, also a small glass of Madeira.

It was four o'clock before the boats of the government arrived, and we all embarked. Biscuit and wine were found in each of them, and all were refreshed.

That in which our family were was commanded by M. Artigue, captain of the port, and one of those who had sent us provisions. My father and he embraced as two old friends who had not seen one another for eight years, and congratulated themselves that they had been permitted to meet once more before they died. We had already made a league upon the river when a young navy clerk (M. Mollien) was suddenly taken ill. We put him ashore, and left him to the care of a negro to conduct him to Senegal when he should recover.

Immediately the town of St Louis presented itself to our view. At the distance its appearance is fine; but in proportion as it is approached the illusion vanishes, and it looks as it really is—dirty, very ill built, poor, and filled with straw huts black with smoke. At six in the evening we arrived at the port of St Louis. It would be in vain for me to paint the various emotions of my mind at that delicious moment. I am bold to say all the colony, if we except MM. Schmaltz and Lachaumareys, were at the port to receive us from our boats. M. Artigue going on shore first to acquaint the English governor of our arrival, met him coming to us on horseback, followed by our generous conductor Mr Carnet, and several superior officers. We went on shore carrying our brothers and sisters in our arms.

My father presented us to the English governor, who had alighted; he appeared to be sensibly affected with our misfortunes, the females and children chiefly exciting his commiseration. And the native inhabitants and Europeans tenderly shook the hands of the unfortunate people; the negro slaves even seemed to deplore our disastrous fate.

The governor placed the most sickly of our companions in an hospital; various inhabitants of the colony received others into their houses; M. Artigue obligingly took charge of our family. Arriving at his house we there found his wife, two ladies and an English lady, who begged to be allowed to assist us. Taking my sister Caroline and myself, she conducted us to her house, and presented us to her husband, who received us in the most affable manner; after which she led us to her dressing-room, where we were combed, cleansed, and dressed by the domestic negresses, and were most obligingly furnished with linen from her own wardrobe, the whiteness of which was strongly contrasted with our sable countenances.

In the midst of my misfortunes my soul had preserved all its strength; but this sudden change of situation affected me so much, that I thought my intellectual faculties were forsaking me. When I had a little recovered from my faintness, our generous hostess conducted us to the saloon, where we found her husband and several English officers sitting at table. These gentlemen invited us to partake of their repast; but we took nothing but tea and some pastry. Among these English was a young Frenchman, who, speaking sufficiently well their language, served to interpret between us. Inviting us to recite to them the story of our shipwreck and all our misfortunes, which we did in few words, they were astonished how females and children had been able to endure so much fatigue and misery.

We were so confused by our agitation, that we scarcely heard the questions which were put to us, having constantly before our eyes the foaming waves, and the immense tract of sand over which we had passed. As they saw we had need of repose, they all retired, and our worthy Englishwoman put us to bed, where we were not long before we fell into a profound sleep.

CHAPTER 10

Our New Habitation

At nine o'clock next morning, after our arrival, we felt quite free from all our fatigues. We arose, and, as soon as we were dressed, went to thank our generous host and hostess, Mr and Mrs Kingsley; then went to see our parents; and afterwards returned to our benefactors, who were waiting breakfast for us. Our conversation was frequently interrupted during our meal, as they were but little acquainted with the French language, and we knew nothing of English. After breakfast we learned that the English governor had not received any orders for giving up the colony to the French; and until that took place, the whole of the French expedition would be obliged to go to the peninsula of Cape Verde, distant from Senegal about fifty leagues.

This information distressed us much, but our affliction was at its height, when my father came and told that the French governor, M. Schmaltz, had ordered him to quit Senegal with all his family, and go and stay at Cape Verde, until farther orders. Mr and Mrs Kingsley, sensibly affected with the misfortunes we had already experienced, assured us they would not part with us, and that they would endeavour to obtain the permission of the English governor. In fact, on the following day, that gentleman informed us by his aid-de-camp, that, having seen the wretched condition in which our family were, he had allowed us to remain at Senegal, and that he had permitted all the officers of the *Medusa* to stay.

This renewed instance of the benevolence of the English governor tranquillized us. We remained comfortably at the house of our benefactors; but a great part of our unhappy companions in misfortune, fearing if they stayed at Senegal they would disobey the French governor, set off for Cape Verde, where hunger and death awaited them. Our family lived nearly twenty days with our benevolent hosts MM. Artigue and Kingsley; but my father, fearing we were too great a burden for the extraordinary expenses which they made each day for us, hired a small apartment, and, on the first of August, we took possession of it, to the great regret of our generous friends, who wished us to stay with them till the surrender of the colony.

When we were settled in our new habitation, my father sent a petition to M. Schmaltz, for the purpose of obtaining provisions from the general magazine of the French administration; but, angry with the reception we had met with from the English, he replied he could not give him anything. Nevertheless, several French officers, who, like ourselves, had remained at Senegal, each day received their rations, or, which was better, were admitted to the table of M. D——, with whom also the governor, his family and staff, messed. It may be remarked here, that this same M. D——, advanced to the governor of the forts, in provisions and money, to the amount of 50,000 *francs*; and, it was the general opinion, found means to charge cent. per cent. on these advances, as a small perquisite for himself; moreover, he received, at the request of the governor, the decoration of the Legion of Honour. But I return to that which concerns myself. My father being unable to obtain anything, either from the governor or M. D——, was obliged to borrow money to enable us to subsist. We were reduced to feed on negroes food, for our means would not allow us to purchase bread at 15 *sous* the pound, and wine at 3 francs the bottle. However, we were content, and perfectly resigned to our fate; when an English officer, Major Peddie, came and visited us precisely at the moment we were at dinner. That gentleman, astonished at seeing an officer of the French administration dining upon a dish of *Kouskou*,[7] said to my father:

7: Vide Note A.

"How, Mr Picard! you being in the employment of your government, and living so meanly!"

Mortified that a stranger should have seen his misery, my father felt his tears flowing; but, instantly collecting himself, said in a calm yet firm tone, "Know, Sir, that I blush not for my poverty, and that you have wronged me by upbraiding me. It is true I have not food like the other Europeans in the colony; but I do not consider myself the more unfortunate. I have requested the man who represents my sovereign in this country, to give me the rations to which I have a right; but he has had the inhumanity to refuse. But what of that? I know how to submit, and my family also."

Major Peddie, at these words, touched with our misfortunes, and vexed, doubtless, at having mortified us, though that certainly was not his intention, bade us good bye, and retired. Early on the morning of next day, we received a visit from M. Dubois, mayor of the town of St Louis in Senegal. That good and virtuous magistrate told us he had come, at the instance of the English governor, to offer us assistance; *viz.* an officer's allowance, which consisted of bread, wine, meat, sugar, coffee, &c. As my father had not been able to procure anything from governor Schmaltz, he thought it his duty to accept that which the English governor had so generously offered. We thanked M. Dubois; and, in a few hours afterwards, we had plenty of provisions sent to us.

If my father had made himself some enemies among the authors of the shipwreck of the *Medusa*, and the abandoning the raft, he was recompensed by real good friends among the old inhabitants of Senegal, who, with himself, deplored the fate of the unfortunate beings who were left in the midst of the ocean. Among the numerous friends my father had, I ought particularly to mention the families of Pellegrin, Darneville, Lamotte, Dubois, Artigue, Feuilletaine, Labouré, Valentin, Debonnet, Boucaline, Waterman, &c.: And in truth all the inhabitants of Senegal, if we except one family, were disposed to befriend us. Even the poor negroes of the interior, after hearing of our misfortunes, came and offered us a small share of their crop. Some gave us beans, others brought us milk, eggs, &c.; in a word, every one offered us some assistance, after they had heard to what misery our shipwreck had reduced us.

About a month after our arrival at Senegal, we went to look at the islands of Babaguey and Safal, situated about two leagues from the town of St Louis. The first of these islands had been given to M. Artigue, who had cultivated it; the other had been given to my father in 1807, and he had planted in it about one hundred thousand cotton plants, when the capture of Senegal by the English in 1809 obliged him to abandon his projects, and return to France.

Those who have seen the countries of Europe, and admired the fine soil of France, need not expect to enjoy the same scene at Senegal. Everywhere nature shows a savage and arid aspect; every where the dregs of a desert and parched soil presents itself to the view; and it is only by care and unremitting toil it can be made to produce anything. All the cotton which my father had planted in the island of Safal had been devoured by the cattle during his absence; he found not a plant. He then proposed to begin again his first operations.

After having walked round the island of Safal, we went to dine with M. Artigue in the island of Babaguey, where we spent the remainder of the day, and in the evening returned to the town of Senegal. Some days after this jaunt, my father endeavoured to find whether the plants with which the island was covered would be useful in making potash. He arranged with a person in Senegal to hire for him some negroes, and a canoe to gather the ashes of the plants after they were burned. A covered gallery which we had in the small house we inhabited, seemed convenient to hold the apparatus of our manufacture. Here we placed our coppers.

We then commenced the making of potash, waiting for the surrender of the colony. The first essay we made gave us hopes. Our ashes produced a potash of fine colour, and we did not doubt of succeeding, when we should have sent a sample of it to France. We made about four barrels, and my father sent a box of it to a friend of his at Paris to analyze. Whilst waiting the reply of the chemist, he hired three negroes to begin the cultivation of his island of Safal. He went himself to direct their operations, but he fell ill of fatigue. Fortunately his illness was not of long continuance, and in the month of December he was perfectly recovered. At this period an English expedition went from Senegal into the interior of Africa, commanded by Major Peddie,[8] the gentleman who had given so great assistance to the unfortunates of the *Medusa*. That worthy philanthropic Englishman died soon after his departure; we sincerely lamented him.

On the 1st of January 1817, the colony of Senegal was surrendered to the French. The English left it, some for Great Britain, others for Sierra Leone and the Cape of Good Hope; and France entered into all her possessions on the west coast of Africa. We remained yet a month in our first house; at last we procured one much larger. My father then commenced his functions of attorney, and we at last began to receive provisions from the French government. The house in which we lived was very large; but the employment which my father followed was very incompatible with the tranquillity we desired. To remove us from the noise and tumultuous conversations of the people who perpetually came to the office, we had a small hut of reeds constructed for us in the midst of our garden, which was very large. Here my sister, my cousin, and myself, passed the greater part of the day. From that time we began to see a little of the world, and to return unavoidable visits.

Every Sunday the family went to the island of Safal, where we very agreeably spent the day; for that day seemed as short in the country, as the six other days of the week were long and listless at Senegal. That country was so little calculated for people of our age, that we continually teased our father to return with us to France. But as he had great expectations from the manufacture of potash, he made us stay, as we would be of great service to him in the end, for superintending the works of that manufacture.

8:Vide Note B.

It is now time to give a brief description of Senegal and its environs, to enable the reader better to appreciate that which I have to say in the sequel.

Travellers who have written about Africa, have given too magnificent a picture of that country known by the name of Senegal. Apparently, after the fatigues of a long and tedious journey, they have been charmed with the first fresh spot where they could repose. That first impression has all the force of reality to the superficial observer; but if he remain any time, the illusion vanishes, and Senegal appears what it really is—a parched and barren country, destitute of the most necessary vegetables for the nourishment and preservation of the health of man.

The town of St Louis, which is also called Senegal, because it is the head-quarters of the French establishments on that coast, is built upon a small island or a bank of sand, formed in the midst of the river Senegal, at about two leagues from its mouth. It is two thousand *toises* in length, and three hundred in breadth. The native inhabitants of the country call it *Ndar*, and *Ba-Fing*, or Black River, the river which waters it. The last name corresponds to that of Niger, which ancient geographers have given to that river.

The population of St Louis is about ten thousand souls, five hundred of whom are Europeans, two thousand negroes or free mulattoes, and nearly seven thousand five hundred slaves. There are about one hundred and fifty houses in St Louis inhabited by Europeans; the remainder consists of simple squares, or huts of straw, which a slight flame would cause to vanish in a moment, as well as all the houses of brick which are near them. The streets are spacious, but not paved. The greater part are so completely filled with sand, which the winds and hurricanes bring from the deserts of Sahara, that it is nearly impossible to walk along them when the winds are blowing. That fine and burning sand so impregnates the air, that it is inhaled, and swallowed with the food; in short, it penetrates everything. The narrow and little frequented streets are often blocked up. Some of the houses are fine enough; they have but one story. Some have covered galleries; but in general the roofs are in the Oriental fashion, in the form of a terrace.

The gardens of Senegal, though their plants have been much praised, are nevertheless few in number, and in very bad condition. The whole of their cultivation is limited to some bad cabbages, devoured by the insects, a plot of bitter radishes, and two or three beds of salad, withered before it is fit for use; but these vegetables, it must be said, are very exquisite, because there are none better. The governor's garden, however, is stocked with various plants, such as cucumbers, melons, carrots, Indian pinks, some plants of barren pineapple, and some marigolds. There are also in the garden three date trees, a small vine arbour, and some young American and Indian plants. But these do not thrive, as much on account of the poverty of the soil, as the hot winds of the desert, which wither them. Some, nevertheless, are vigorous, from being sheltered by walls, and frequently watered.

Five or six trees, somewhat bushy (island fig-trees), are planted here and there in the streets, where may be seen also four or five *baobabs*, the leaves of which are devoured by the negroes before they are fully blown,[9] and a palm of the species of Ronn, which serves as a signal-post for ships at sea.

A league and a half from the island of St Louis, is situated the island of Babaguey. It is almost entirely cultivated, but the soil is so arid that it will scarcely grow anything but cotton. There is a military station on this island, and a signal-post. MM. Artigue and Gansfort each have a small dwelling here. The house, built in the European manner, which is there seen, serves to hold the soldiers, and to accommodate the officers of Senegal on their parties of pleasure.

The island of Safal is situated to the east of Babaguey, and is separated from it by an arm of the river. This was the asylum which we chose in the end to withdraw from misery, as will be seen in the sequel.

To the east of the island of Safal, is situated the large island of Bokos, the fertility of which is very superior to the three

---

9: The negroes use the leaves of the Baobab as gluten, prepare their Kouskou, (a kind of pulp).

preceding. Here are seen large fields of millet, maize, cotton, and indigo, of the best quality. The negroes have established large villages here, the inhabitants of which live in happy ease.

To the north of these islands, and to the east of Senegal, is the island of Sor, where resides a kind of Black Prince, called by the French Jean Bart. The general aspect of this island is arid, but there are places susceptible of being made into large plantations. M. Valentin, merchant at St Louis, has already planted several thousand feet of cotton, which is in a thriving condition. But that island being very much exposed to the incursions of the Moors of the desert, it would perhaps be imprudent to live in it.

A multitude of other islands, formed by the encroachments of the river upon the mainland, border on those of which I have already spoken, several leagues distant to the north and east. They are principally covered with marshes, which it would be difficult to drain. In these islands grows the patriarch of vegetables described by the celebrated Adanson, under the name of *baobab*,[10] the circumference of which is often found to be above one hundred feet.

Several other islands, more or less extended than the preceding, rise above the river near to St Louis, as far as Podor; the greater part of which are not inhabited, although their soil is as fertile as those near Senegal. This indifference of the negroes in cultivating these islands, is explained by the influence which the Moors of the desert of Sahara are permitted to have over all the country bordering upon Senegal, the inhabitants of which they carry off to sell to the slave merchants of the island of St Louis. It is not to be doubted, that the abolition of the slave trade, and the acquisition which the French have made in the country of Dagama, will soon destroy the preponderance of the barbarians of the desert upon the banks of the Senegal; and that things being placed on their former footing, the negroes established in the French colonies will be permitted to enjoy in peace the fields which they have planted.

10: Vide Note C.

Among all the islands, Tolde, which is about two leagues in circumference, seems to be the most convenient for a military and agricultural station. The fertility of its soil, and its being situated between the two principal points where the gum trade is carried on, gives it the triple advantage of being able to maintain the garrison which is placed upon it, of protecting the trade and navigation of the river, and of preventing the Moors from driving away the negroes from their peaceful habitations. Plantations have already been made in the island of Tolde, of coffee, sugar-canes, indigo, and cotton, which have perfectly succeeded. M. Richard, agricultural botanist to the government, has placed there a general nursery for the French establishments.

Three leagues from the island of Tolde, farther up the river, is the village of Dagama, situated upon the left bank of the river, and at the extremity of the kingdom of Brak, or of Walo. In that village, the French have already planted several batteries, where begin their agricultural establishments, which end about six leagues from the island of St Louis. A large portion of that ground has been given to the French planters, who have planted cotton upon it of the best kind, which promises to be a branch of lucrative commerce to France. Here is placed the plantation of M. Boucaline, as being the largest and best cultivated, the king having given him a premium of encouragement of 10,000 *franks*. A little distant from the plantation of Boucaline are the grounds of the royal grant, covered with more than ten thousand feet of cotton. This beautiful plantation, established by the care of M. Roger, now governor of Senegal, is at present directed by M. Rougemont with a zeal above all praise.

Near to the village of Dagama, up the river, is the island of Morfil, which is not less than fifty leagues from east to west, and about eight or ten in breadth. The negroes of the republic of Peules cultivate great quantities of millet, maize, indigo, cotton, and tobacco. The country of the Peules negroes extends about one hundred and twenty leagues, by thirty in breadth. It is a portion of the ancient empire of the negro Wolofs, which, in former times, comprehended all the countries situated between the rivers Senegal and Gambia. The country of the Peules is watered by a branch of the Senegal, which they call Morfil; and, like Lower Egypt, owes its extreme fertility to its annual overflowing. The surprising abundance of their harvests, which are twice a year, makes it considered as the granary of Senegal. Here are to be seen immense fields finely cultivated, extensive forests producing the rarest and finest kinds of trees, and a prodigious diversity of plants and shrubs fit for dying and medicine.

To the east of the Peules is the country of Galam,[11] or Kayaga, situated two hundred leagues from the island of St Louis. The French have an establishment in the village of Baquel. This country, from its being a little elevated, enjoys at all times a temperature sufficiently cool and healthful. Its soil is considered susceptible of every species of cultivation: the mines of gold and silver, which border upon it, promise one day to rival the richest in the possession of Spain in the New World. This conjecture is sufficiently justified by the reports sent to Europe by the agents of the African and Indian Companies, and particularly by M. de Buffon, who, in a MS. deposited in the archives of the colonies, thus expresses himself:

> It is certain that there are found in the sand of the rivers (in the country of Galam) various precious stones, such as rubies, topazes, sapphires, and perhaps some diamonds; and there are in the mountains veins of gold and silver.

Two productions, not less estimable perhaps than gold and silver, are indigenous to this fine country, and increase in the most prodigious manner there; *viz.* the Lotus, or bread-tree, of the ancients, spoken of by Pliny, and the Shea, or butter-tree,[12] of which the English traveller Mungo Park has given a description.

11: Vide Note D.
12: Vide Note E.

Chapter 11
Hard Times

We were happy enough, at least content, at Senegal, until the sickness of my stepmother broke in upon the repose we enjoyed. Towards the middle of July 1817, she fell dangerously ill; all the symptoms of a malignant fever appeared in her; and in spite of all the assistance of art and the care we bestowed upon her, she died in the beginning of November of the same year. Her loss plunged us all into the deepest affliction. My father was inconsolable. From that melancholy period, there was no happiness for our unfortunate family: chagrin, sickness, enemies, all seemed to conspire against us.

A short while after her death my father received a letter from the chemist at Paris, informing him that the sample of potash which he had sent to France was nothing but marine salt, and some particles of potash and saltpetre. This news, although disagreeable, did not affect us, because we had still greater misfortunes to deplore.

About the end of the year, my father finding his employment would scarcely enable him to support his numerous family, turned his attention to commerce, hoping thus to do some good, as he intended to send me to look after the family, and to take charge of the new improvements in the island, which had become very dear to him from the time he had deposited in it the mortal remains of his wife and his youngest child. For the better success of his project, he went into co-partnery with a certain personage in the colony; but instead of benefiting his speculations, as he had flattered himself, it proved nothing but loss. Besides he was cheated in an unworthy manner by the people in whom he had placed his confidence; and as he was prohibited by the French authorities from trafficking, he could not plead his own defence, nor get an account of the merchandise of which they had defrauded him. Sometime after he had sustained this loss, he bought a large boat, which he refitted at a considerable expense. He made the purchase in the hope of being able to traffic with the Portuguese of the island of Cape Verde, but in vain; the governor of the colony prohibited him from all communication with these islands. Such were the first misfortunes which we experienced at Senegal, and which were only the precursors of still greater to come.

Besides all these, my father had much trouble and vexation to endure in the employment he followed. The bad state of the affairs of the colony, the poverty of the greater part of its inhabitants, occasioned to him all sorts of contradictions and disagreements. Debts were not paid, the ready money sales did not go off; processes multiplied in a frightful manner; every day creditors came to the office soliciting actions against their debtors; in a word, he was in a state of perpetual torment either with his own personal matters, or with those of others. However, as he hoped soon to be at the head of the agricultural establishment projected at Senegal, he supported his difficulties with great courage.

In the expedition which was to have taken place in 1815, the Count Trigant de Beaumont, whom the king had appointed governor of Senegal, had promised my father to reinstate him in the rank of captain of infantry, which he had held before the Revolution, and after that to appoint him to the command of the counting-house of Galam, dependent upon the government of Senegal. In 1816, my father again left Paris with that hope, for the employment of attorney did not suit his disposition, which was peaceable and honest. He had the first gift of the documents concerning the countries where they were to found the agricultural establishments in Africa, and had proposed plans which were accepted of at the time by the President of the Council of State, and by the Minister of Marine, for the colonization of Senegal; but the unfortunate events of 1815 having overturned everything, another governor was nominated for that colony in place of Count Trigant de Beaumont. All his plans and proposed projects were instantly altered for the purpose of giving them the appearance of novelty; and my father found himself in a situation to apply these lines of Virgil to himself:

Hos ego versiculos feci, tulit alter honores.
These lines I made, another has the praise.

At first the new governor (M. Schmaltz) was almost disposed to employ my father in the direction of the Agricultural Establishment of Senegal; but he allowed himself to be circumvented by certain people, to whom my father had perhaps spoken too much truth. He thought no more of him, and we were set up as a mark of every kind of obloquy.

Finding then that he could no longer reckon upon the promises which had been made to him on the subject of the plans which he had proposed for the colony of Senegal, my father turned his attention to the island of Safal, which seemed to promise a little fortune for himself and family. He doubled the number of his labouring negroes, and appointed a black overseer for superintending his work.

In the beginning of 1818, we believed our cotton crop would make us amends for the loss which we had sustained at various times. All our plants were in the most thriving condition, and promised an abundant harvest. We had also sown maize, millet, and some country beans, which looked equally well.

At this period, M. Schmaltz was recalled to France. M. Flauriau succeeded him; but the nomination of the new governor did not alleviate our condition. Every Sunday my father went to visit his plantation, and to give directions for the labours of the week. He had built a large hut for the overseer, upon the top of a little hill, which was almost exactly in the centre of the island. It was at a little distance from the small house which he had raised as a tomb, to receive the remains of his wife and child, whom he had at first buried in a place to the south of the cotton field. He surrounded the monument of his sorrow with a kind of evergreen bean tree, which soon crept over the grave, and entirely concealed it from the view. This little grove of verdure attracted, by the freshness of its foliage, a multitude of birds, and served them for a retreat. My father never left this place but he was more tranquil, and less affected with his misfortunes.

Towards the middle of April, seeing his plants had produced less cotton than he expected, and that the hot winds and grasshoppers had made great havoc in his plantations, my father decided to leave upon it but one old negro, for superintending the day-labourers, whom he had reduced to four. In the mean time, we learned that some merchants, settled at Senegal, had written to France against my father. They complained that he had not employed sufficient severity against some unfortunate persons who had not been able to pay their debts; and they exclaimed against some miserable speculations which he had made in the country of Fouta Toro, for procuring grain necessary for the support of his negroes.

The expedition to Galam making preparations for its departure,[13] my father, in spite of the insinuations of some merchants of the colony, was desirous also of trying his fortune. He associated himself with a person who was to make the voyage; he bought European goods, and refitted his boat, which again occasioned him loss. Towards the middle of August 1818, the expedition set off. A month after its departure, my cousin, whom the country had considerably affected, returned to France, to our great regret. My sister and myself found ourselves the only society to enable us to support our sorrows; however, as we hoped to return to France in a few years, we overcame our disappointment. We had already in some degree recovered our tranquillity,

---

13: The voyage from Senegal to the country of Galam is made but once a year, because it is necessary to take advantage of the overflowing of the river, either in coming or going. The merchant boats which are destined to make the voyage, look like a fleet, and depart in the middle of August, under escort of a king's ship, commissioned to pay the *droits* and customs to the Negro princes of the interior, with whom that colony is connected.

in spite of all our misfortunes and the solitude in which we lived, when my father received a letter from the governor of the colony, announcing to him, that, by the decision of the Minister of Marine, a new attorney had come to Senegal, and enjoining him at the same time to place the papers of the office in the hands of his successor.

Such a circumstance could not fail to affect us much; for the few resources we possessed made us anticipate an event almost as horrible as the shipwreck, which exposed our family to all the horrors of want in the boundless deserts of Sahara. My father, however, having nothing with which he could reproach himself, courageously supported this new misfortune, hoping sooner or later to be able to unmask those who had urged his ruin. He wrote a letter to his Excellency the Minister of Marine, in which he detailed the affairs of the office of the colony, the regularity of the accounts, the unfortunate condition to which his numerous family were reduced by the loss of his employment, and concluded with these words:

> Broken without being heard, at the end of twenty-nine years of faithful service, but too proud to make me afraid of a disgrace which cannot but be honourable to me, especially as it has its source in those philanthropic principles which I manifested in the abandoning of the raft of the *Medusa*, I resign myself in silence to my destiny.

This letter, full of energy, although a little too firm, failed not to affect the feeling heart of the Minister of Marine, who wrote to the governor of Senegal to give my father some employment in the administration of the colony. But that order had either remained too long in the office of the minister, or the governor of Senegal had judged it proper not to communicate the good news to us, as we did not hear of the order of the minister till after the death of my father, nearly fifteen months after its date.

When my father had rendered his accounts, and installed his successor into the colony's office, he told me it would be quite necessary to think of returning into his island of Safal, to cultivate it ourselves. He persuaded me that our plantation suffered solely from the want of our personal care, and that the happiness and tranquillity of a country life would soon make us forget our enemies and our sufferings. It was then decided that I should set off on the morrow, with two of my brothers, to go and cultivate the cotton at the plantation. We took our little shallop, and two negro sailors, and, by daybreak, were upon the river, leaving at Senegal my father, my sister Caroline, and the youngest of our brothers and sisters.

CHAPTER 12

The Plantation at Safal

For the space of two months I endured, as did my little brothers, the beams of a burning sun, the irritations of insects and thorns, and the want of that food to which we had been accustomed. I suffered during all the day from a severe headache; but I collected from the ground which belonged to us the cotton, on which were founded all our hopes. At night my two young brothers and myself retired into the cottage, which we used in the island; the working negroes brought the cotton we had collected during the day; after which I set about preparing supper. The children, accompanied by the old negro Etienne (the keeper of the plantation), went and picked up some branches of dry wood.

We lighted a large fire in the middle of the hut, and I kneaded the cakes of millet flour which were to be our supper, as well as what was to supply us next day. My paste being prepared, I laid each cake upon the fire which the children had lighted. Often, and especially when we were very hungry, I placed them on a shovel of iron which I set upon the fire. This quick mode of proceeding procured us millet-bread in less than half an hour; but it must be confessed that this species of wafers or cakes, though well enough prepared and baked, was far from having the taste of those we eat at Paris. However, to make them more palatable, I added butter when I had it, or we ate them with some sour milk. With the first dish was served up at the same time the dessert, which stood in place of dainties, of roast meat and salad;

it generally consisted of boiled beans, or roasted pistachio nuts. On festival days, being those when my father came to see us, we forgot our bad fare in eating the sweet bread he brought with him from Senegal.

In the month of December 1818, having gone one morning with my brothers to take a walk among the woods behind our cottage, I found a tree covered with blossoms as white as snow, and which had a delicious smell. We gathered a great quantity of them, which we carried home; but these flowers, as we afterwards found by sad experience, contained a deleterious poison. Their strong and pungent odour caused violent pains in the head, forerunners of a malignant fever, which brought us within two steps of the grave. Two days after my young brothers were seized; fortunately my father arrived on the following day, and removed them to Senegal.

Now then I was alone with my old negro Etienne in the island of Safal, far from my family, isolated in the midst of a desert island, in which the birds, the wolves, and the tigers, composed the sole population. I gave free course to my tears and sorrows. The civilized world, said I to myself, is far from me, an immense river separates me from my friends. Alas! what comfort can I find in this frightful solitude? What can I do upon this wretched earth? But although I had said I was unfortunate, was I not necessary to my unhappy father? Had I not promised to assist him in the education of his children, whom cruel death had deprived of their mother? Yes! yes! I was too sensible my life was yet necessary.

Engaged in these melancholy reflections, I fell into a depression of mind which it would be difficult to describe. Next morning the tumult of my thoughts led me to the banks of the river, where the preceding evening I had seen the canoe carry away my father and my young brothers. There I fixed my humid eyes upon the expanse of water without seeing anything but a horrible immensity; then, as recovered from my sorrow, I turned to the neighbouring fields to greet the flowers and plants which the sun was just beginning to gild. They were my friends, my companions; they alone could yet alleviate my melancholy, and render my loneliness supportable. At last the star of day arising above the horizon, admonished me to resume my labours.

Having returned to the cottage, I went to the harvest with Etienne. For the space of two days, I continued at my accustomed occupation, but on the morning of the third, on returning from the plantation to the house, I felt myself suddenly seized with a violent pain in my head. As soon as I reached home I lay down. On the morning I found myself unable to rise out of bed; a burning fever had manifested itself during the night, and even deprived me of the hope of being able to return to Senegal.

I was incapable of doing anything. The good Etienne, touched with my condition, took his fowling-piece, and went into the neighbouring woods, to endeavour to shoot me some game. An old vulture was the only produce of the chase. He brought it to me, and, in spite of the repugnance I expressed for that species of bird, he persisted in boiling some of it for me. In about an hour afterwards, he presented me with a bowl of that African broth; but I found it so bitter, I could not swallow it. I felt myself getting worse, and every moment seemed to be the last of life. At last, about noon, having collected all my remaining strength, I wrote to my father the distressed state I was in; Etienne took the charge of carrying my letter, and left me alone in the midst of our island.

At night I experienced a great increase of fever; my strength abandoned me entirely; I was unable to shut the door of the house in which I lay. I was far from my family; no human being dwelt in the island; no person witnessed my sufferings; I fell into a state of utter unconsciousness, and I knew not what I did during the remainder of the night. On the following morning, having recovered from my insensibility, I heard some person near me utter sorrowful cries; it was my good sister Caroline. I opened my eyes, and, to my astonishment, found myself at Senegal, surrounded by my afflicted family. I felt as if I had returned from the other world.

My father had set off on the instant he received my letter,

with Etienne to the island, and, finding me delirious, took me to Senegal without my being conscious of it. Recovering by degrees from my confusion, I was desirous of seeing my brothers, who had been attacked the same way as myself. Our house looked like an hospital. Here a dying child wished them to take away the monster he imagined he saw before his bed; there another demanded something to drink, then, refusing to take the medicines which were offered to him, filled the house with his groans; at a distance my feeble voice was heard asking something to quench the thirst which consumed me.

However, the unremitting care we received, as well as the generous medicine of M. Quincey, with the tender concern of my father and my sister Caroline, soon placed us out of danger. I then understood that the flowers I had had the imprudence to collect in the wood of Safal, had been the principal cause of my illness, as well as that of my brothers. In the meanwhile, my father built two new huts in the island, with the intention of going and living there with all his family. But, as his affairs kept him yet some days at Senegal, he was prevented from returning to Safal with the children to continue the collecting of cotton. On the morrow, we all three set off.

When we had arrived upon the Marigot, in the island of Babaguey, we hailed the keeper of our island to come and take us over in his canoe. In the mean time I amused myself in looking at our habitation, which seemed to be very much embellished since my departure, as it had been augmented with two new cottages. I discovered the country to be much greener since I last saw it; in a word, all nature seemed smiling and beautiful. At last Etienne, to whom we had been calling for a quarter of an hour, arrived with his canoe, into which we stepped, and soon were again in the island of Safal.

Arrived at my cottage, I began to examine all the changes my father had made during my illness. The small cottage situated to the west, I chose as my sleeping apartment. It was well made with straw and reeds yet green, and the window, whence was seen the cotton-field, was of the greatest advantage to me. I began to clean the floor of our apartments, which was nothing else than sand, among which were various roots and blades of grass. After that I went to visit the little poultry yard, where I found two ducks and some hens placed there a short while before. I was very glad of these little arrangements; and returned to the principal cottage to prepare breakfast. After this we betook ourselves to the business of cotton gathering.

Eight days had already elapsed since our return to the island of Safal, when one morning we perceived our shallop upon the river, which we always knew by a signal placed upon the masthead. It was my father, who brought twelve negroes with him, which he had hired at Senegal, for assisting him in the cultivation of his island. The men were instantly set to break up the soil; the women and children assisted us in gathering cotton. My father then dismissed the negroes, who worked by the day, as he had to come and go to Senegal, where the urgency of his business yet required his presence.

I remained a long while without seeing him; but, at the end of eight days, I was agreeably surprised at finding our boat in the little bay of Babaguey. I ran with the family negroes to disembark our effects, and I soon had the pleasure of holding my sister Caroline in my arms. My father came on shore afterwards with the youngest children, and all the family found themselves united under the roof of the African Cottage, in the island of Safal.

"You see, my child," said my father to me on entering our huts, "you see all our riches! we have neither moveables nor house at Senegal; everything we can claim as our own is here."

I embraced my father, and my brothers and sisters, and then went to unload our boat. Our house was soon filled. It served at once for a cellar, granary, store-house, a parlour, and bed-chamber. However, we found a place for everything. Next day we began to fit them up more commodiously. My sister and myself lived in the small house to the west; my father took up his residence in that towards the east; and the large hut in the centre was the place where the children slept. Round about the last we suspended some boards by cords, to hold our dishes and various kitchen utensils. A table, two benches, some chairs, a large couch, some old barrels, a mill to grind the cotton, implements of husbandry, constituted the furniture of that cottage. Nevertheless, in spite of its humbleness, the sun came and gilded our roofs of straw and reeds. My father fitted up his cottage as a study. Here were boards suspended by small cords, upon which his books and papers were arranged with the greatest order;—there a fir board, supported by four feet, driven into the ground, served as a desk; at a distance stood his gun, his pistols, his sword, his clarinet, and some mathematical instruments. A chair, a small couch, a pitcher, and a cup, formed his little furniture.

Our cottage was situated on the top of a little hill of gentle ascent. Forests of mangrove-trees, gum-trees, tamarind-trees, sheltered us on the west, the north, and the east. To the south was situated the plantation which we called South-field. This field was already covered with about three hundred thousand feet of cotton, a third of which had nearly begun to be productive. Upon the banks of the river, and to the west of the cotton field, was situated our garden; finally, to the south of the plain, were our fields of maize, beans, and millet.

Our little republic, to which my father gave laws, was governed in the following manner:—We usually rose about daybreak, and met altogether in the large cottage. After having embraced our father, we fell upon our knees to return thanks to the Supreme Being for the gift of another day. That finished, my father led the negroes to their work, during which my sister and myself arranged the family affairs, and prepared breakfast, when, about eight o'clock, he returned to the cottage. Breakfast being over, each took his little bag, and went and gathered cotton.

About noon, as the heat became insupportable, all returned to the cottage, and worked at different employments. I was principally charged with the education of my young brothers and sisters, and the young negroes of the family. Round my little hut were suspended various pictures for study, upon which I taught them to read according to the method of mutual assistance. A bed of sand, smoothed upon a small bench, served the younger ones to trace and understand the letters of the alphabet: the others wrote upon slates. We bestowed nearly two hours upon each exercise, and then my scholars amused themselves at different games. At three o'clock, all returned to the cotton field, and remained till five.

Dinner, which we usually had at six, was followed by a little family conversation, in which the children were interrogated concerning what they had been taught during the day. When I was well pleased with them, I promised them a story, or a fable, in the evening. Sometimes after dinner, we went to take a short walk on the banks of the river; then returned to the cottage, where Etienne had had the care of lighting a large fire, the heat of which forced the mosquitoes and gnats to yield their place to the little circle which our family made round the hearth. Then my sister Caroline and myself related some fables to the children, or read them a lesson from the Evangelists or the Bible; whilst my father smoked his pipe, amusing himself by contemplating all his family around him. The hour of going to bed being arrived, we made a common prayer, after which all retired to their separate huts to sleep.

Thus did our days glide away amid the occupations of the fields and the recreations of the family. On Sundays, our labours were suspended. Sometimes to spend the day more agreeably, and avoid the molestations of the hunters, who often came to our island, we went to the island of Bokos, situated to the east of Safal. On reaching it, we seated ourselves under a large baobab, which was more than thirty feet in circumference.

After having finished our humble repast under the umbrage of that wonderful tree, my father would go and amuse himself with the chase; my sister Caroline and myself went to search for rare plants, to assist our studies in botany; whilst the children hunted butterflies and other insects. Charles, the eldest of the boys, swam like a fish; and, when my father shot a duck or *aigrette* upon the water, he would instantly throw himself in, and fetch the game. At other times he would climb to the top of the trees to rob the birds, or bury himself in the midst of bushes to gather the fruits of the country, then ran, all breathless and delighted, to present us with his discovery. We would remain in the island till nearly four in the afternoon, then return to our boat, and our negroes rowed us to our island.

During the time of the greatest heats, for we could not long endure the rays of the sun, we passed a part of the Sunday under a very bushy tamarind-tree, which stood at a little distance from our cottage. Thus, in the good old times, did the lords, barons, and marquises gather themselves under the old elms of the village, to discuss the concerns of their vassals; in like manner did my father collect us under the tamarind-tree to regulate the affairs of his republic, and also to enjoy the landscapes which our island afforded. We sometimes took our meals there, and on those occasions the ground served us at once for table, table-cloth, and seat. The children gambolled on the grass, and played a thousand tricks to amuse us. We now began to discover that every condition of life had its own peculiar enjoyments. If the labours of the week seemed long and laborious, the Sabbath recompensed us by our country recreations. We lived thus for some time in the greatest tranquillity. Shut up in a desert island, from all society, we ventured to think we had discovered the condition of real happiness.

Every Wednesday we sent two negroes to the village of Gandiolle, to purchase provisions, such as butter, milk, eggs, &c. One day, however, my father resolved to purchase a cow and thirty fowls, that we might have in our island all the little necessaries used by a family. Our poultry yard being thus augmented, we looked upon ourselves as great as the richest princes in Africa; and in truth, since we had a cottage, milk, butter, eggs, maize, millet, cotton, tranquillity and health, what more was necessary for our comfort?

Chapter 13

Financial Ruin

Whilst we were thus enjoying in peace our little good fortune, my father received a letter, desiring him to return to Senegal in all possible speed. He went, and left me at the head of our establishment, but a great misfortune happened, which we could not prevent;—six of our labouring negroes, whom he had hired, deserted during the night, and took our small boat with them. I was extremely distressed, and instantly made Etienne swim the river, and go and beg of the President at Babaguey to take him to my father, who was still at Senegal, to tell him the melancholy news. That good negro was soon on the other side of the water, and went to M. Lerouge (the name of the president), who gave him his canoe. At night, we saw him returning without my father, who went into the country to search for the fugitive negroes.

He spent three whole days in the countries of Gandiolle and Touby, which lie in the neighbourhood of our island, but all his labour was in vain. The deserting negroes had already gained the forests of the interior; and my father, exhausted with fatigue, returned to Safal. I confess, though I was deeply distressed at the desertion of these slaves, who were so necessary to us for realizing our agricultural projects, my heart could not blame these unfortunate creatures, who only sought to recover that freedom from which they had been torn.

At this date, that is about the 1st of March 1819, we learned that M. Schmaltz had returned from France, and was in the Bay of St Louis; and that the Minister of Marine had approved of all the projects relative to the agricultural establishment at Senegal. This news revived my father's hopes. As this establishment had been originally proposed by him, he flattered himself they would do him justice in the end. In this expectation, he went to meet with governor Schmaltz, who had to pass our house on the morrow; but he would not speak with him.

On the following day, my father wrote to him from the hotel at St Louis; four days after which, we were assured that the governor was very far from wishing us well, and still farther from doing justice to my father. However, some of his friends encouraged him to make fresh endeavours, and persuaded him he would obtain a premium of encouragement for having first set the example of cultivating cotton at Senegal; they assured him also that funds had been sent to M. Schmaltz for that purpose. Vain hope! every claim was rejected, we had not even the satisfaction of knowing whether the premium which my father sought was due to him or not; we got no reply. My father wishing to make a last attempt to ward off the misery which menaced us, went to supplicate the governor to allow us either money to purchase food, or rations. This last petition was not more successful than the former. We were abandoned to our unhappy fate, whilst more than twenty persons, who had never done any service to the government, received gratis rations every day from the magazines of the colony.

"Very well!" said my father to me, when he found he was refused that assistance which M. Schmaltz had ordered to the other unfortunate persons in the colony, "let the governor be happy if he can, I will not envy his felicity. Behold, my child, behold this roof of thatch which covers us; see these hurdles of reeds which moulder into dust, this bed of rashes, my body already impaired by years, and my children weeping around me for bread! You see a perfect picture of poverty! Nevertheless, there are yet beings upon the earth more unfortunate than we are!"

"Alas!" said I to him, "our misery is great; but I can support it, and even greater, without complaining, if I saw you exposed to less harassing cares. All your children are young, and of a good constitution; we can endure misfortune, and even habituate ourselves to it; but we have cause to fear that the want of wholesome and sufficient food will make you fall, and then we shall be deprived of the only stay we have upon earth."

"O! my dear child," cried my father, "you have penetrated into the secrets of my soul, you know all my fears, and I will no longer endeavour to conceal the sorrow which has weighed for a long time upon my heart. However, my death may perhaps be a blessing to my family; my bitter enemies will then doubtless cease to persecute you."

"My father," replied I, "break not my heart; how can you, forgetting your children, their tender affection, the assistance which you ought to give them, and which they have a right to expect from you, wish us to believe your death will be a benefit to us?"

He was moved with these words, and his tears flowed in abundance; then, pressing me to his bosom, he cried:

"No, no, my dear children, I will not die, but will live to procure for you an existence more comfortable than that you have experienced since we came to Senegal. From this moment I break every tie which binds me to the government of this colony; I will go and procure for you a new abode in the interior of the country of the negroes; yes, my dear children, we will find more humanity among the savage hordes that live in our neighbourhood, than among the greater part of those Europeans who compose the administration of the colony."

In fact, some time after, my father obtained from the negro prince of the province of Cayor, a grant on his estates, and we were to take possession of it after the rainy season; but Heaven had decided otherwise.

From this time, my father, always indignant at the manner in which the governor had acted towards us, resolved to retire altogether to his island, and to have as little intercourse with the Europeans of the colony as he could. Nevertheless, he received with pleasure the friends who from time to time came to visit us, and who sometimes carried him to St Louis, where they disputed among themselves the pleasure of entertaining him, and of making him forget his misfortunes by the favours which they heaped upon him; but the mortifications he had experienced in that town made him always impatient till he returned to his island. One day as he returned from Senegal, after having spent two days at the house of his friends, they lent him a negro mason to build an oven for us; for till then we had always baked our bread upon the embers. With this oven we were no longer obliged to eat our millet-bread with the cinders which so plenteously stuck to it.

One morning, as he was preparing to take the negroes to their labour, he perceived his dog did not follow him as usual. He called, but in vain. Then he thought his faithful companion had crossed the river to Babaguey, as he used to do sometimes. Arrived at the cotton-field, my father remarked large foot-prints upon the sand, which seemed to be those of a tiger, and beside them several drops of blood, and doubted not that his poor Sultan had been devoured. He immediately returned to the cottage to acquaint us with the fate of his dog, which we greatly regretted. From that day the children were prohibited from going any distance from home; my sister and myself durst no more walk among the woods as we used to do.

Four days after the loss of the faithful Sultan, as we were going to bed, we heard behind our cottage mewings like those of a cat, but much louder. My father instantly rose, and, in spite of our entreaties and fears, went out armed with his sword and gun, in the hope of meeting with the animal whose frightful cries had filled us with dread; but the ferocious beast, having heard a noise near the little hill where it was, made a leap over his head, and disappeared in the woods. He returned, a little frightened at the boldness and agility of the creature, and gave up the pursuit till the following night.

On the evening of the following day, he caused some negroes to come from the island of Babaguey, whom he joined with his own, and putting himself at their head, he thought he would soon return with the skin of the tiger. But the carnivorous animal did not appear during all that night; he contented himself with uttering dismal howlings in the midst of the woods. My father being called to Senegal by some of his friends, left us on the morrow. Before going, he strictly enjoined us to keep fast the doors of the house, and to secure ourselves against ferocious beasts. At night we barricaded every avenue to our cottage, and shut up the dog with us, which a friend of my father had brought to him from the town to supply the place of that which we had lost. But my sister and myself were but ill at ease; for our huts being already decayed, we were afraid the tiger would get in, and devour the successor of poor Sultan. However, Etienne came and quieted our fears a little, by saying he would make the round of the huts during the night. We then lay down, having left our lamp burning.

Towards the middle of the night, I was awoke by a hollow noise which issued from the extremity of our large chamber. I listened attentively; and the noise increasing, I heard our dog growling and also a kind of roaring like that of a lion. Seized with the greatest terror, I awoke my sister Caroline, who, as well as myself, thought a ferocious beast had got into the cottage. In an instant our dog raised the most terrible barking; the other animal replied by a hollow, but hideous growl. All this uproar passed in my father's chamber. Our minds were paralyzed; the children awoke, and came and precipitated themselves into our arms; but none durst call Etienne to our assistance. At last my sister and myself decided we should go and see what occasioned all this noise. Caroline took the lamp in one hand, and a stick in the other, and I armed myself with a long lance.

Arrived at the middle of the large cottage, we discovered at the end of my father's study our dog, who had seized a large animal covered with yellowish hair. The fears which perplexed us left us no doubt but that it was either a lion or at least a tiger. We durst neither advance nor retreat, and our weapons fell from our hands. In a moment these two furious creatures darted into the hut where we were; the air was rent with their cries; our legs bent under us; we fell upon the floor in a faint; the lamp was extinguished, and we believed we were devoured. Etienne at length awoke, knocked at the door, then burst it open, ran up to us, lighted the lamp, and showed us our mistake. The supposed lion was nothing else than a large dog from the island of Babaguey, fighting with ours. Etienne separated them with a stick; and the furious animal, which had frightened us so much, escaped through the same hole by which he had entered our house. We stopped up the opening and retired to bed, but were not able to sleep. My father having arrived next morning from Senegal, we recounted to him the fright we had during the night, and he instantly set about repairing the walls of our cottage.

It was now the beginning of May; our cotton harvest was completely finished, but it was not so productive as we had hoped. The rains had not been abundant the preceding year, which caused the deficiency in our crop. We now became more economical than ever, to be able to pass the bad season which had set in. We now lived entirely on the food of the negroes; we also put on clothing more suitable to our situation than that we had hitherto worn. A piece of coarse cotton, wrought by the negroes, served to make us dresses, and clothes for the children; my father was habited in coarse blue silk. On purpose to ameliorate our condition, he sent on Sundays to Senegal a negro to purchase two or three loaves of white bread. It was, in our melancholy condition, the finest repast we could procure.

One Sunday evening, as all the family were seated round a large fire eating some small loaves which had been brought from Senegal, a negro from the main land gave my father a letter; it was from M. Renaud, Surgeon-Major at Bakal in Galam, announcing to us, to complete the sum of our misfortunes, that the merchandize he had sent to Galam the preceding year had been entirely consumed by fire.

"Now," cried my unhappy father, "my ruin is complete! Nothing more wretched can touch us. You see, my dear children, that Fortune has not ceased persecuting us. We have nothing more to expect from her, since the only resource which remained has been destroyed."

This new misfortune, which we little expected, plunged all our family in the deepest distress.

"What misfortunes! what mortifications!" cried I; "it is time to quit this land of wretchedness! Leave it then, return to France; there only we will be able to forget all our misfortunes. And you, cruel enemies of my father, whom we have to reproach for all the misery we have experienced in these lands, may you, in punishment for all the evil you have done us, be tortured with the keenest remorse!"

It cost all the philosophy of my father to quiet our minds after the fatal event. He comforted us by saying, that Heaven alone was just, and that it was our duty to rely upon it. Some days after, our friends from Senegal came to pay us a visit, and testified for us the greatest sorrow. They agreed among themselves to engage all the Europeans in the colony in a voluntary subscription in our behalf; but my father opposed it by saying, he could not receive assistance from those who were so truly his friends. The generous M. Dard, director of the French school, was not the last nor least who took an interest in us. As soon as he heard of the unfortunate news, he cordially offered my father all the money he had, and even endeavoured to get provisions for us from the government stores, but he failed. After the visit of my father's friends, we were not so unhappy, and yet enjoyed some tranquillity in our humble cottage. He bought a barrel of wine, and two of flour, to support us during the rainy season or winter, a period so fatal to Europeans who inhabit the torrid zone.

Chapter 14

Great Loss

It was yet but about the beginning of June 1819, and already the humid winds of the south announced the approach of the bad season, or winter. The whirlwinds of the north no longer brought the hot sands of the desert; but instead of them came the south-east, bringing clouds of locusts, mosquitoes, and gnats. We could no longer spend our twilights at the cottage, it was so filled with these insects. We fled every morning to escape their stings, and did not return home till overcome with sleep. One night, on entering the hut, after a long day's work at the cotton-field, we perceived an animal stealing among the bushes at a soft slow pace; but having heard us, it leaped a very high hedge, and disappeared. From its agility, we discovered it to be a tiger-cat, which had been prowling about our poultry-yard, in the hope of catching some chickens, of which these animals are very fond.

The same night, my sister and myself were awoke with a hollow noise which we heard near our bed. Our thoughts instantly returned to the tiger-cat; we believed that it was it we heard, and, springing up, we awoke my father. Being all three armed, we began by looking under my bed, as the noise seemed to proceed from the bottom of a large hole, deep underground. We were then convinced it was caused by a serpent, but found it impossible to get at it. The song of this reptile so frightened us that we could sleep no longer; however, we soon became accustomed to its invisible music, for at short intervals we heard it all the night. Sometime after the discovery of the den of this reptile songster, my sister, going to feed five or six pigeons which she had in a little hut, perceived a large serpent, who seemed to have a wing on each side of his mouth. She instantly called my father, who quickly ran to her with his gun, but the wings which the creature seemed to have, had already disappeared.

As his belly was prodigiously swelled, my father made the negroes open it, and, to our great surprise, found four of the pigeons of our dove-cote. The serpent was nearly nine feet in length, and about nine inches in circumference in the middle. After it was skinned, we gave it to the negroes, who regaled themselves upon it. This was not the one, however, which we had heard during the night, for in the evening on which it was killed, we heard the whistlings of its companions. We then resolved to look for a more comfortable place to plant our cottage, and to abandon the rising ground to the serpents, and the woods to the tigers. We chose a spot on the south side of our island, pretty near to the banks of the river.

When this new ground was prepared, my father surrounded it with a hurdle of reeds, and then transported our cottage thither. This manner of removing from one place to another is very expeditious; in less than three days we were fairly seated in our new abode. However, as we had not time to carry away our poultry, we left them upon the hill till the place we had appropriated for them was completed. It was fenced on all sides, and covered with a large net, to prevent the birds of prey taking away our little chickens, and we had no fear in leaving them during the night.

On the evening of the next day, my sister, accompanied with the children, went to feed the various inhabitants of the poultry-yard; but on approaching it she saw the frame of reeds half fallen, the net rent, and feathers scattered here and there upon the road. Having reached the site of our former cottage, heaps of worried ducks and chickens were the only objects which presented themselves. She instantly sent one of the children to acquaint us with the disaster, and my father and myself hastened to the scene of carnage, but it was too late to take any precautions,—all our poultry were destroyed! Two hens and a duck only had escaped the massacre, by having squatted in the bottom of an old barrel. We counted the dead which were left in the yard, and found that the ferocious beasts had eat the half; about two hundred eggs of ducks and hens, nearly hatched, were destroyed at the same time.

This was a great loss to us, especially as we counted as much upon our poultry-yard as upon our plantation. We were obliged to resign ourselves to our fate; for to what purpose would sorrow serve? The evil was done, and it only remained for us to guard against the recurrence of a like misfortune. The poultry-yard was instantly transported to our new habitation, and we took care to surround it with thorns, to keep off the wolves, the foxes, and the tigers. Our two hens and the duck were placed in it till we could purchase others.

Our new cottage was, as I have already said, situated on the banks of the river. A small wood of mangrove trees and acacias grew to the left, presenting a scene sufficiently agreeable. But the marshy wood sent forth such clouds of mosquitoes, that, from the first day, we were so persecuted, as scarcely to be able to inhabit our cottage during the night. We were forced to betake ourselves to our canoe, and sail up and down the river; but we were not more sheltered from the stings of the insects than upon land. Sometimes, after a long course, we would return to the hut, where, in spite of the heat, we would envelop ourselves in thick woollen blankets, to pass the night; then, after being half suffocated, we would fill the house full of smoke, or go and plunge ourselves in the river.

I am bold to say, we were the most miserable creatures that ever existed on the face of the earth. The thought of passing all the bad season in this state of torture, made us regret a hundred times we had not perished in the shipwreck. How, thought I, how is it possible to endure the want of sleep, the stings of myriads of insects, the putrid exhalations of marshes, the heat of the climate, the smoke of our huts, the chagrin which consumes us, and the want of the most necessary articles of life, without being overcome! My father, however, to prevent us seeing the melancholy which weighed upon him, assumed a serene air, when his soul was a prey to the most horrible anguish; but through this pretended placidity it was easy to see the various sentiments by which his heart was affected. Often would that good man say to us:

"My children, I am not unhappy, but I suffer to see you buried in the deserts. If I could gather a sufficient fund to convey you to France, I would at least have the satisfaction of thinking you there enjoyed life, and that your youth did not pass in these solitudes far from human society."

"How, my father," replied I to him, "how can you think we could be happy in France, when we knew you were in misery in Africa! O, afflict us not. You know, and we have said so a hundred times, that our sole desire is to remain near you, to assist you to bring up our young brothers and sisters, and to endeavour by our care to make them worthy of all your tenderness."

The good man would then fold us in his arms; and the tears which trickled down his cheeks, for a while soothed his sufferings.

Often, to divert our thoughts from the misery we endured, would we read some of the works of our best authors. My father was usually on these occasions the reader, whilst Caroline and myself listened. Sometimes we would amuse ourselves with shooting the bow, and chasing the wild ducks and fowls which went about our house. In this manner we endeavoured to dissipate in part our ennui during the day. As our cottage was situated close to the banks of the river, we amused ourselves in fishing, whilst the heat and the mosquitoes would permit us. Caroline and our young brothers were chiefly charged with fishing for crabs, and they always caught sufficient to afford supper to all the family. But sometimes we had to forego this evening's repast, for the mosquitoes at that hour were in such prodigious numbers, that it was impossible to remain more than an instant in one place, unless we were enveloped in our coverings of wool. But the children not having so much sense, would not allow themselves to be thus suffocated; they could not rest in any place, and every instant their doleful groans forced our tears of pity. O cruel remembrance! thou makest me yet weep as I write these lines.

Towards the beginning of July, the rains showed us it was seed time. We began by sowing the cotton, then the fields of millet, maize, and beans. Early in the morning, the family went to work; some digged, others sowed, till the fierceness of the sun forced us to retire to the cottage, where we expected a plate of couscous, of fish, and a little rest. At three o'clock, we all returned to the fields, and did not leave off working till the approach of night; then we all went home, and each occupied himself in fishing or hunting. Whilst we were thus busied in providing our supper, and provisions for the morrow, we sometimes would receive a visit from the sportsmen who were returning to Senegal. Some would feel for our misery, but many made us weep with their vulgar affronts. On these occasions, Caroline and myself would fly from these disgusting beings as from the wild beasts who prowled about us. Sometimes, to make us forget the insults and mortifications we experienced from the negro merchants who live at Senegal, and whom curiosity brought to our island, my father would say to us:

"Wherefore, my dears, are you distressed with the impertinences of these beings? Only think that, in spite of your wretchedness, you are a hundred times better than them, who are nothing more than vile traffickers in human flesh, sons of soldiers, without manners, rich sailors, or freebooters, without education and without country."

One day, a French negro merchant, whom I will not name, having crossed the Senegal to the station of Babaguey, and seeing our cottage in the distance, inquired to whom it belonged. He was told it was the father of a family whom misfortune had forced to seek a refuge in that island. I wish I could see them, said the merchant, it will be very *drôle*. In fact, a short while after, we had a visit from this *curieux*, who, after he had said all manner of impertinences to us, went to hunt in our plantation, where he killed the only duck which we had left, and which he had the audacity to carry away in spite of our entreaties. Fortunately for the insolent thief, my father was absent, else he would have avenged the death of the duck, which even the tigers had spared in the massacre of our poultry-yard.

Since the commencement of winter, we had had but little rain, when one night we were roused by a loud peal of thunder. A horrible tempest swept over us, and the hurricane bent the trees of the fields. The lightning tore up the ground, the sound of the thunder redoubled, and torrents of water were precipitated upon our cottage. The winds roared with the utmost fury, our roofs were swept away, our huts were blown down, and all the waters of heaven rushed in upon us. A flood penetrated our habitation; all our family drenched, confounded, sought refuge under the wrecks of our walls of straw and reeds. All our effects were floating, and hurried off by the floods which surrounded us. The whole heavens were in a blaze; the thunderbolt burst, fell, and burned the main-mast of the French brig *Nantaise*, which was anchored at a little distance from our island.

After this horrible detonation, calm was insensibly restored, whilst the hissing of serpents and howlings of the wild beasts were the only sounds heard around us. The insects and reptiles, creeping out of the earth, dispersed themselves through all the places of our cottage which water had not covered. Large beetles went buzzing on all sides, and attached themselves to our clothes, whilst the millipedes, lizards, and crabs of an immense size, crawled over the wrecks of our huts. At last, about ten o'clock, nature resumed her tranquillity, the thunder ceased to be heard, the winds instantly fell, and the air remained calm and dull.

After the tempest had ceased, we endeavoured to mend our huts a little, but we could not effect it; and were obliged to remain all day under the wrecks of our cottage. Such, however, was the manner in which we spent nearly all our days and nights. In reading this recital, the reader has but a feeble idea of the privations, the sufferings, and the evils, to which the unfortunate Picard family were exposed during their stay in the island of Safal.

About this time, my father was obliged to go to Senegal. During his absence, the children discovered that the negroes who remained with us had formed a scheme of deserting during the night. Caroline and myself were much embarrassed and undecided what course to pursue, to prevent their escape; at last, having well considered the matter, we thought, as Etienne would be in the plot, we had no other means of preventing their escape but by each of us arming ourselves with a pistol, and thus passing the night in watching them. We bound our canoe firmly with a chain, and seated ourselves, the better to observe their motions.

About nine in the evening, the two negroes came to the banks of the river, but having discovered us, they feigned to fish, really holding in their hands a small line; but on coming nearer to them, I saw they had no hooks. I desired them to go to bed, and return on the morrow to fish. One of them came close to our canoe, and threw himself into it, thinking he could instantly put off; but when he found it chained, he left it quite ashamed, and went and lay down with his comrade. I set off to look for Etienne, whom we suspected to have been in the plot, and told him of the design of the two negroes, and prayed him to assist us in watching them during the night. He instantly rose, and taking my father's gun, bade us sleep in quiet, whilst he alone would be sufficient to overcome them; however, they made no farther attempt that night, hoping, doubtless, to be more fortunate another time.

Next day I wrote to my father, to return to Safal before night, for that we were on the eve of losing the remainder of our negroes. He returned in the evening, resolving never again to quit our cottage. He interrogated the negroes concerning their design of desertion, and asked them what excuse they had to plead.

"We are comfortable here," replied one of them, "but we are not in our native country; our parents and friends are far from us. We have been deprived of our liberty, and we have made, and will make still farther efforts, for its recovery." He added, addressing himself to my father, "If thou, Picard, my master, wert arrested when cultivating thy fields, and carried far, far from thy family, wouldst thou not endeavour to rejoin them, and recover thy liberty?"

My father promptly replied, "I would!"

"Very well," continued Nakamou, "I am in the same situation as thyself, I am the father of a numerous family; I have yet a mother, some uncles; I love my wife, my children; and dost thou think it wonderful I should wish to rejoin them?"

My unfortunate father, melted to tears with this speech, resolved to send them to the person from whom he had hired them, for fear he should lose them. If he had thought like the colonists, he would have put them in irons, and treated them like rebels; but he was too kind-hearted to resort to such measures. Some days after, the person to whom the negroes were sent, brought us two others; but they were so indolent, we found it impossible to make them work.

Chapter 15
Further Family Deaths

We however continued sowing; and more than twenty-four thousand feet of cotton had already been added to the plantation, when our labours were stopped by war suddenly breaking out between the colony and the Moors. We learned that a part of their troops were in the island of Bokos, situated but a short distance from our own. It was said that the Arab merchants and the Marabouts, (priests of the Musulmen), who usually travel to Senegal on affairs of commerce, had been arrested by the French soldiers. In the fear that the Moors would come to our island and make us prisoners, we resolved to go to the head-quarters of the colony, and stay there till the war had ceased.

My father caused all his effects to be transported to the house of the resident at Babaguey, after which we left our cottage and the island of Safal. Whilst Etienne slowly rowed the canoe which contained our family, I ran my eye over the places we were leaving, as if wishing them an eternal *adieu*. In contemplating our poor cottage, which we had built with such difficulty, I could not suppress my tears. All our plantations, thought I, will be ravaged during our absence; our home will be burned; and we will lose in an instant that which cost us two years of pain and fatigue. I was diverted from these reflections by our canoe striking against the shore of Babaguey.

We landed there, and instantly set off to the residence of M. Lerouge; but he was already at Senegal. We found his house filled with soldiers, which the governor had sent to defend that position against the Moors. My father then borrowed a little shallop to take us to Senegal. Whilst the boat was preparing, we eat a morsel of millet-bread I had had the precaution to make before we left Safal; at last, at six in the evening, we embarked for St Louis, leaving our negroes at Babaguey. My father promised to Etienne to go and rejoin him to continue the work, if it was possible, as soon as we were in safety.

It was very late before we reached Senegal. As we had no lodgings, a friend of my father, (M. Thomas) admitted us, his worthy wife loading us with kindness. During our stay in the island of Safal, my father had made various trips to Senegal; but as my sister and myself had not quitted it for a long time, we found ourselves in another world. The isolated manner in which we had lived, and the misfortunes we had endured, contributed in no small degree to give us a savage and embarrassed appearance. Caroline especially had become so timid, she could not be persuaded to appear in company. It is true the nakedness to which we were reduced, a good deal caused the repugnance we felt at seeing company. Having no cap but our hair, no clothes but a half-worn robe of coarse silk, without stockings and shoes, we felt very distressed in appearing thus habited before a society among whom we had formerly held a certain rank. The good lady Thomas seeing our embarrassment, kindly dispensed with our appearance at table, as they had strangers in the house. She caused supper to be brought to our chamber, under the pretext that we were indisposed. In this manner we escaped the curious and imprudent regards of various young people, who had not yet been tutored by the hand of misfortune. We learned that we were known at Senegal by different names, some calling us *The Hermits of the Isle of Safal*, others *The Exiles in Africa*.

On the morrow, my father hired an apartment in the house of one of his old friends (M. Valentin.) After breakfast we thanked our hosts, and went to our new lodging. It consisted of a large chamber, the windows of which were under ground, filled with broken panes; thus, in the first night, we had such a quantity of mosquitoes, that we thought we were yet in the island of Safal.

On the following day, my father was desirous of returning to his plantation. We in vain represented to him the dangers to which he exposed himself; nothing would divert him from his design. He promised, however, to go to Safal only during the day, and to sleep at the house of the resident at Babaguey. He told us that it was not the war with the Moors alone which caused him to bring us to Senegal, but also the state of suffering in which the whole family was. It is true our strength was considerably diminished; the youngest of my brothers had been for several days attacked with a strong fever; and we were all slightly seized with the same disease. My father, taking our oldest brother with him, left us for the isle of Safal, promising to come and see us every Sunday. I went with him to the court-gate, conjuring him, above all things, not to expose himself, and to take care of his health, which was so precious to us. That worthy man embraced me, and bade me fear nothing on that head, for he too well felt how necessary his life was to his children, to expose it imprudently.

"For my health," added he, "I hope to preserve it long, unless Heaven has decided otherwise."

With these words he bid *adieu*, and went away; I returned to the house and gave free vent to my tears. I know not what presentiment then seized me, for I felt as if I had seen my father for the last time; and it was only at the end of the third day, on receiving a letter written with his own hand, that I could divest myself of these gloomy ideas. He told us he was very well, and that all was quiet at Safal. On the same day I wrote to inform him of the condition of our young brother, who was a little better during the evening; I sent him at the same time some loaves of new bread and three bottles of wine which a generous person had had the goodness to give us. On the following Sunday we sat waiting his arrival, but a frightful tempest that raged during all the day, deprived us of that pleasure; we, however, received accounts from him every two days, which were always satisfactory.

About the 1st of August 1819, the best friend of my father, M. Dard, who, from the commencement of our misfortunes, had not withheld his helping hand from us, came to announce his approaching departure for France, and to bid us farewell. We congratulated him on the happiness of leaving so melancholy a place as Senegal. After we had talked some time about our unfortunate situation, and of the little hope we had of ever getting out of it, that sensible man, feeling his tears beginning to flow, took leave of us, promising to visit my father in passing Babaguey.

Some days after, our young sister became dangerously ill; the fever attacked me also; and in less than forty-eight hours all our family were seized with the same disease. Caroline, however, had still sufficient strength to take care of us; and, but for her assistance, we would all perhaps have become a prey to the malady which oppressed us. That good sister durst not acquaint my father with the deplorable condition in which we all were; but alas! she was soon obliged to tell him the melancholy news. I know not what passed during two days after my sister had written my father, having been seized with delirium. When the fit had somewhat abated, and I had recovered my senses a little, I began to recognise the people who were about me, and I saw my father weeping near my bed. His presence revived the little strength I had still left. I wished to speak, but my ideas were so confused that I could only articulate a few unconnected words. I then learned, that after my father was acquainted with our dangerous condition, he had hastened to Senegal with my oldest brother, who also had been attacked.

My father seemed to be no better than we were; but to quiet our fears, he told us that he attributed his indisposition to a cold he had caught from sleeping on a bank of sand at Safal. We soon perceived that his disease was more of the mind than of the body. I often observed him thoughtful, with a wild and disquieted look. This good man, who had resisted with such courage all his indignities and misfortunes, wept like a child at the sight of his dying family.

Meanwhile the sickness increased every day in our family; my young sister was worst. Dr Quincey saw her, and prescribed every remedy he thought necessary to soothe her sufferings. During the middle of the night she complained of a great pain in her abdomen, but, after taking the medicine ordered her, she fell quiet, and we believed she was asleep. Caroline, who watched us during the night in spite of her weakness, took advantage of this supposed slumber to take a little repose. A short while after, wishing to see if little Laura still slept, she raised the quilt which covered her, and uttered a piercing shriek. I awoke, and heard her say in a tremulous voice, Alas! Laura is dead. Our weeping soon awoke our unhappy father. He rose, and, seeing the face of the dead child, cried in wild despair:

"It is then all over; my cruel enemies have gained their victory! They have taken from me the bread which I earned with the sweat of my brow to support my children; they have sacrificed my family to their implacable hate; let them now come and enjoy the fruit of their malice with a sight of the victim they have immolated! let them come to satiate their fury with the scene of misery in which they have plunged us! O cruel S——, thy barbarous heart cannot be that of a Frenchman!"

On uttering these words, he rushed out, and seated himself under a gallery which was at the door of the house in which we lived. He there remained a long while buried in profound meditation, during which time we could not get him to utter one word. At last, about six o'clock in the morning the physician came, and was surprised on hearing of the death of Laura; then went to my father, who seemed to be insensible to everything around him, and inquired at him concerning his health.

"I am very well," replied he, "and I am going to return to Safal; for I always find myself best there."

The Doctor told him his own condition, as well as that of his family, would not allow him to leave Senegal; but he was inflexible. Seeing nothing would induce him to remain at St Louis, I arose, weak as I was, and went to search for a negro and a canoe to carry us to Safal. In the meanwhile a friend of ours took the charge of burying the body of my sister; but my father wished to inter it beside the others in his island, and determined to take it thither along with us. Not to have, however, such a melancholy sight before our eyes during our journey, I hired a second canoe to carry the corpse of poor Laura; and attaching it to the one in which we were, we took our young brothers in our arms and set off.

Having arrived opposite the house possessed by M. Thomas, my father felt himself greatly indisposed. I profited by the circumstance, by getting him to go to the house of his friend; hoping we would persuade him against returning to Safal. He consented without difficulty; but we had scarcely entered the house, when he was again taken very ill. We instantly called a physician, who found in him the seeds of a most malignant fever. We laid him down, and all the family wept around his bed, whilst the canoe which carried the remains of our young sister proceeded to Safal. M. Thomas undertook to procure us a house more healthy than that we had quitted; but the condition of my father was such, that he found it impossible to walk, and we had to put him in a litter to take him to our new habitation. All the worthy people of Senegal could not contain their indignation against governor S——, whose inhuman conduct towards our family had been the principal cause of all our misfortunes. They went to his house, and boldly told him it was a shame for the Chief of the colony thus to allow an unfortunate family entirely to perish. M. S——, either touched with these reproaches, or at last being moved by more friendly feelings towards us, caused provisions secretly to be sent to our house.

We received them under the persuasion they had been sent by some friend of my father; but having at last learned they had come from the governor, my father bid me return them to him. I did not know what to do, for a part of the provisions had already been consumed; and, besides, the distressed condition to which we were reduced, made me flatter myself with the thought, that the governor wished at last to make amends for the wrongs he had done us. But alas! his assistance was too late; the fatal moment was fast approaching when my father had to bend under the pressure of his intolerable sufferings.

CHAPTER 16

Return to France

The day after we had taken possession of our new abode, my father sent me to the Isle of Babaguey, to bring back the things which were left at the house of the Resident. As I found myself considerably better during the last few days, I hired a canoe and went, leaving the sick to the care of Caroline. I soon reached the place of my destination, and finished my business. I was upon the point of returning to Senegal, when a wish came into my head of seeing Safal. Having made two negroes take me to the other side of the river, I walked along the side of the plantation, then visited our cottage, which I found just as we had left it. At last I bent my steps towards the tomb of my step-mother, in which were deposited the remains of my little sister. I seated myself under the shrubs which shaded the place of their repose, and remained a long while wrapt in the most melancholy reflections.

All the misfortunes we had experienced since our ship-wreck, came across my mind, and I asked myself, how I had been able to endure them? I thought that, at this instant, a secret voice said to me, you will yet have greater to deplore. Terrified by this melancholy presentiment, I strove to rise, but my strength failing me, I fell on my knees upon the grave. After having addressed my prayers to the Eternal, I felt a little more tranquil; and, quitting this melancholy spot, old Etienne led me back to Babaguey, where my canoe waited for me. The heat was excessive; however, I endured it, rather than wait for the coolness of evening to return to my father. On my arrival at St Louis, I found him in a violent passion at a certain personage of the colony, who, without any regard to his condition, had said the most humiliating things to him. This scene had contributed, in no small degree, to aggravate his illness; for, on the evening of the same day, the fever returned, and a horrible delirium darkened all his faculties. We spent a terrible night, expecting every moment to be his last.

The following day found little change in his condition, except a small glimmering of reason at intervals. In one of these moments, when we hoped he would recover his health, M. Dard, whom we thought already far from Senegal, entered our house. My father instantly recognised him, and, making him sit near to his bed, took his hand, and said:

"My last hour is come; Heaven, to whose decrees I humbly submit, will soon remove me from this world; but one consolation remains with me,—the thought you will not abandon my children. I recommend to you my oldest daughter; you are dear to her, doubt not; would she were your wife, and that you were to her, as you have always been to me, a sincere friend!"

On saying these words, he took my hands and pressed them to his burning lips. Tears suffocated my voice, but I pressed him tenderly in my arms; and as he saw I was extremely affected with his situation, he quickly said to me:

"My daughter, I have need of rest."

I instantly quitted him, and was joined by M. Dard, when we retired to another room, where we found Caroline and the good Mad. Thomas. This worthy friend seeing the deplorable condition to which we were reduced, endeavoured to console us, and to give us hope, saying, that having heard of my father's illness on board the brig Vigilant, in which he had embarked at the port of St Louis, he had obtained leave to come on shore, and to go and offer us some assistance; after which he left us, promising to return on the morrow.

Towards the middle of the night of the 15th August 1819, it struck me that my father wished to speak with me. I drew near to him, and seeing him pale and his eyes wild, I turned away my head to conceal the tears which I could not suppress; but having perceived my distress, he said to me in a mournful voice:

"Why are you so much afflicted, my child? My last hour approaches, I cannot escape it; then summon all the strength of your soul to bear it with courage. My conscience is pure, I have nothing with which to reproach myself; I will die in peace if you promise to protect the children whom I will soon leave. Tell also to feeling hearts the long train of uninterrupted misfortunes which have assailed me; tell the abandoned condition in which we have lived; and tell at last, that in dying, I forgave my enemies all the evils they had made me as well as my family endure!"

At these words I fell upon his bed, and cried yes, dear father, I promise to do all you require of me. I was yet speaking when Caroline entered the chamber, and throwing herself upon his bed, tenderly embraced him, whilst he held me by the hand. We gazed on one another in profound silence, which was only interrupted by our sighs. During this heart-rending scene, my father again said to me:

"My good Charlotte, I thank you for all the care you have bestowed on me; I die, but I leave you to the protection of friends who will not abandon you. Never forget the obligations you already owe M. Dard. Heaven assist you. Farewell, I go before you to a better world."

These words, pronounced with difficulty, were the last he uttered. He instantly became much convulsed. All the physicians of the colony were called, but the medicines they prescribed produced no effect. In this condition he remained more than six hours, during which time we stood suspended between hope and despair. O horrible night! night of sorrow and desolation! who can describe all which the unfortunate family of Picard suffered during thy terrible reign! But the fatal period approached; the physician who prescribed it went out; I followed, and, still seeking for some illusion in the misfortune which menaced us, I tremblingly interrogated him. The worthy man would not dissemble; he took me by the hand and said, my dear lady, the moment is arrived when you have need to arm yourself with courage; it is all over with M. Picard; you must submit to the will of God. These words were a thunderbolt to me. I instantly returned, bathed in tears; but alas! my father was no more.

Such an irreparable misfortune plunged us into a condition worse than death. Without ceasing, I besought them to put a period to my deplorable life. The friends about me used every endeavour to calm me, but my soul was in the depth of affliction, and their consolations reached it not.

"O God!" cried I, "how is it possible thou canst yet let me live? Ought not the misery I feel to make me follow my father to the grave?"

It was necessary to employ force to keep me from that plan of horror and dismay. Madame Thomas took us to her house, whilst our friends prepared the funeral of my unhappy father. I remained insensible for a long while; and, when somewhat recovered, my first care was to pray the people with whom we lived to carry the body of my father to the Isle of Safal to be deposited, agreeably to his request, near the remains of his wife. Our friends accompanied it. Some hours after the departure of the funeral procession, Governor S——, doubtless reproaching himself with the helpless condition in which we had been left for so long a time, gave orders to take care of the remainder of our unfortunate family. He himself came to the house of M. Thomas. His presence made such an impression on me, that I swooned away. We did not, however, refuse the assistance he offered us, convinced, as we were, that it was less to the governor of Senegal we were indebted than to the French government, whose intentions he was only fulfilling.

Several days passed before I could moderate my sorrow; but at last our friends represented to me the duties I owed to the orphans who were left with us, and to whom I had promised to hold the place of mother. Then rousing myself from my lethargy, and recollecting the obligations I had to fulfil, I bestowed all my affections on the innocent beings whom my father had confided to me in his dying moments. Nevertheless I was not at rest; the desire of seeing the place where reposed the mortal remains of my worthy father tormented me. They wished to dissuade me; but when they saw I had been frequently weeping in private, they no longer withheld me. I went alone to Safal, leaving Caroline to take charge of the children, two of whom were still in a dangerous condition.

What changes did I find at our cottage! The person from whom we had hired our negroes had secretly removed them; rank weeds sprung up everywhere; the cotton withered for want of cultivation; the fields of millet, maize, and beans had been devoured by the herds of cattle from the colony; our house was half plundered; the books and papers of my father taken away. Old Etienne still remained; I found him cultivating cotton. As soon as he saw me he drew near; and having inquired if he wished to remain at the plantation, he replied:

"I could stay here all my life; my good master is no more, but he is still here; I wish to work for the support of his children."

I promised in my turn to take care of him during my stay in Africa. At last I bent my steps towards my father's grave. The shrubs which surrounded it were covered with the most beautiful verdure; their thorny branches hung over it as if to shield it from the rays of the sun. The silence which reigned around this solitary place was only interrupted by the songs of the birds, and the rustling of the foliage, agitated by a faint breeze. At the sight of this sacred retreat, I suddenly felt myself penetrated by a religious sentiment, and falling on my knees upon the grass, and resting my head upon the humid stone, remained a long while in deep meditation. Then starting up, I cried:

"Dear *manes* of the best of fathers! I come not hither to disturb your repose; but I come to ask of Him who is omnipotent, resignation to his august decrees. I come to promise also to the worthy author of my existence, to give all my care to the orphans whom he has left on earth. I also promise to make known to feeling hearts all the misfortunes he experienced before being driven to the tomb."

After a short prayer, I arose and returned to the cottage. To consecrate a monument to the memory of my father, I took two cocoa-nuts, which he had planted some time previous to his death, and replanted them beside the grave; I then gave my orders to Etienne, and returned to the family at Senegal.

Next day M. Dard came to see us at the house of M. Thomas. This worthy friend of my father, told us he would not abandon in Senegal the orphans whom he had promised to assist. I come, added he, to return to the governor the leave he had given me to pass six months in France, and I charge myself with providing for all your wants till I can convey you again to Paris. Such generous devotion affected me to tears; I thanked our worthy benefactor, and he went into Mad. Thomas's room. When he had gone, Mad. Thomas took me aside, and said, that M. Dard's intention was not only to adopt the wrecks of our family, but he wished also to offer me his hand as soon as our grief had subsided. This confidence, I own, displeased me not; for it was delightful for me to think that so excellent a man, who had already given us such substantial assistance in our distress, did not think himself degraded by uniting his fate with that of a poor orphan. I recollected what my father had said to me during one of our greatest misfortunes.

"M. Dard," said that worthy man, "is an estimable youth, whose attachment for us has never diminished in spite of our wretchedness; and I am certain he prefers virtue in a wife above all other riches."

Some days after, our benefactor came to tell us he had disembarked all his effects, and that he had resumed his functions as director of the French school at Senegal. We talked a long while together concerning my father's affairs, and he then left us. However, as one of my brothers was very ill, he returned in the evening to see how he was. He found us in tears; for the innocent creature had expired in my arms. M. Dard and M. Thomas instantly buried him, for his body had already become putrid. We took great care to conceal his death from his brother, who, having a mind superior to his age, would doubtless have been greatly affected. Nevertheless, on the following day, poor

Charles inquired where his brother Gustavus was; M. Dard, who was sitting near his bed, told him he was at school; but he discovered the cheat, and cried, weeping, that he wished a hat to go to school, and see if Gustavus was really living. M. Dard had the kindness to go and purchase him one to quiet him, which, when he saw, he was satisfied, and waited till the morrow to go and see if his brother was at school. This young victim to misery dragged out his melancholy existence during two months; and about the end of October we had the misfortune of losing him also.

This last blow plunged me into a gloomy melancholy. I was indifferent to everything. I had seen, in three months, nearly all my relations die. A young orphan (Alphonso Fleury), our cousin, aged five years, to whom my father was tutor, and whom he had always considered as his own child, my sister Caroline, and myself, were all that remained of the unfortunate Picard family, who, on setting out for Africa, consisted of nine. We, too, had nearly followed our dear parents to the grave. Our friends, however, by their great care and attention, got us by degrees to recover our composure, and chased from our thoughts the cruel recollections which afflicted us. We recovered our tranquillity, and dared at last to cherish the hope of seeing more fortunate days. That hope was not delusive. Our benefactor, M. Dard, since then having become my husband, gathered together the wrecks of our wretched family, and has proved himself worthy of being a father to us. My sister Caroline afterwards married M. Richard, agricultural botanist, attached to the agricultural establishment of the colony.

Leaving Senegal with my husband and the young Alphonso Fleury, my cousin, on board his Majesty's ship *Ménagere*, on the 18th November 1820, we safely arrived at L'Orient on the 31st December following. A few days after our landing, we went to Paris, where we remained two months. At last we reached my husband's native place, at Bligny-sous-Beaune, in the department of the Côte d'Or, where I have had the happiness of finding new relations whose tender friendship consoles me in part for the loss of those of whom cruel death deprived me in Africa.

Appendix

The following is the substance, abridged from MM. Corréard and Savigny, of what took place on the raft during thirteen days before the sufferers were taken up by the *Argus* brig.

After the boats had disappeared, the consternation became extreme. All the horrors of thirst and famine passed before our imaginations; besides, we had to contend with a treacherous element, which already covered the half of our bodies. The deep stupor of the soldiers and sailors instantly changed to despair. All saw their inevitable destruction, and expressed by their moans the dark thoughts which brooded in their minds. Our words were at first unavailing to quiet their fears, which we participated with them, but which a greater strength of mind enabled us to dissemble. At last, an unmoved countenance, and our proffered consolations, quieted them by degrees, but could not entirely dissipate the terror with which they were seized.

When tranquillity was a little restored, we began to search about the raft for the charts, the compass, and the anchor, which we presumed had been placed upon it, after what we had been told at the time of quitting the frigate.[14] These things, of the first importance,

---

14: M. Corréard, fearing that on the event of their being separated from the boats by any unforeseen accident, called from the raft to an officer on board the frigate, "Are we in a condition to take the route?—have we instruments and charts?" got the following reply: "Yes, yes, I have provided for you every necessary." M. Corréard again called to him, "Who was to be their commander?" when the same officer said, "'Tis I; I will be with you in an instant;" but he instantly went and seated himself in one of the boats!—*Trans*.

had not been placed upon our machine. Above all, the want of a compass the most alarmed us, and we gave vent to our rage and vengeance. M. Corréard then remembered he had seen one in the hands of one of the principal workmen under his command; he spoke to the man, who replied, "Yes, yes, I have it with me."

This information transported us with joy, and we believed that our safety depended upon this futile resource: it was about the size of a crown-piece, and very incorrect. Those who have not been in situations in which their existence was exposed to extreme peril, can have but a faint knowledge of the price one attaches then to the simplest objects—with what avidity one seizes the slightest means capable of mitigating the rigour of that fate against which they contend. The compass was given to the commander of the raft, but an accident deprived us of it forever: it fell, and disappeared between the pieces of wood which formed our machine. We had kept it but a few hours, and, after its loss, had nothing now to guide us but the rising and setting of the sun.

We had all gone afloat without taking any food. Hunger beginning to be imperiously felt, we mixed our paste of sea-biscuit[15] with a little wine, and distributed it thus prepared. Such was our first meal, and the best we had, during our stay upon the raft.

An order, according to our numbers, was established for the distribution of our miserable provisions. The ration of wine was fixed at three quarters a-day.[16] We will speak no more of the biscuit, it having been entirely consumed at the first distribution. The day passed away sufficiently tranquil. We talked of the means by which we would save ourselves; we spoke of it as a certain circumstance, which reanimated our courage; and we sustained that of the soldiers, by cherishing in them the hope of being able, in a short while, to revenge themselves on those who had so basely abandoned us. This hope of vengeance, it must be avowed, equally animated us all; and we poured out a thousand imprecations against those who had left us a prey to so much misery and danger.

15: The biscuit had fallen into the sea, and was with difficulty recovered.—*Trans.*
16: The original French is *trois quarts*, which certainly cannot mean *three quarts*. In all probability it is three pints.—*Trans.*

The officer who commanded the raft being unable to move, M. Savigny took upon himself the duty of erecting the mast. He caused them to cut in two one of the poles of the frigate's masts, and fixed it with the rope which had served to tow us, and of which we made stays and shrouds. It was placed on the anterior third of the raft. We put up for a sail the main-top-gallant, which trimmed very well, but was of very little use, except when the wind served from behind; and to keep the raft in this course, we were obliged to trim the sail as if the breeze blew athwart us.

In the evening, our hearts and our prayers, by a feeling natural to the unfortunate, were turned towards Heaven. Surrounded by inevitable dangers, we addressed that invisible Being who has established, and who maintains the order of the universe. Our vows were fervent, and we experienced from our prayers the cheering influence of hope. It is necessary to have been in similar situations, before one can rightly imagine what a charm it is to the heart of the sufferer the sublime idea of a God protecting the unfortunate!

One consoling thought still soothed our imaginations. We persuaded ourselves that the little division had gone to the isle of Arguin, and that after it had set a part of its people on shore, the rest would return to our assistance: we endeavoured to impress this idea on our soldiers and sailors, which quieted them. The night came without our hope being realized; the wind freshened, and the sea was considerably swelled. What a horrible night! The thought of seeing the boats on the morrow, a little consoled our men, the greater part of whom, being unaccustomed with the sea, fell on one another at each movement of the raft. M. Savigny, seconded by some people who still preserved their presence of mind amidst the disorder, stretched cords across the raft, by which the men held, and were better able to resist the swell of the sea: some were even obliged to fasten themselves.

In the middle of the night the weather was very rough; huge waves burst upon us, sometimes overturning us with great violence. The cries of the men, mingled with the roaring of the flood, whilst the terrible sea raised us at every instant from the raft, and threatened to sweep us away. This scene was rendered still more terrible, by the horrors inspired by the darkness of the night. Suddenly we believed we saw fires in the distance at intervals. We had had the precaution to hang at the top of the mast, the gun-powder and pistols which we had brought from the frigate. We made signals by burning a large quantity of cartridges; we even fired some pistols, but it seems the fire we saw, was nothing but an error of vision, or, perhaps, nothing more than the sparkling of the waves.

We struggled with death during the whole of the night, holding firmly by the ropes which were made very secure. Tossed by the waves from the back to the front, and from the front to the back, and sometimes precipitated into the sea; floating between life and death, mourning our misfortunes, certain of perishing; we disputed, nevertheless, the remainder of our existence, with that cruel element which threatened to engulf us. Such was our condition till day-break. At every instant were heard the lamentable cries of the soldiers and sailors; they prepared for death, bidding farewell to one another, imploring the protection of heaven, and addressing fervent prayers to God. Every one made vows to him, in spite of the certainty of never being able to accomplish them. Frightful situation! How is it possible to have any idea of it, which will not fall far short of the reality!

Towards seven in the morning the sea fell a little, the wind blew with less fury; but what a scene presented itself to our view! Ten or twelve unfortunates, having their inferior extremities fixed in the openings between the pieces of the raft, had perished by being unable to disengage themselves; several others were swept away by the violence of the sea. At the hour of repast, we took the numbers anew; we had lost twenty men. We will not affirm that this was the exact number; for we perceived some soldiers who, to have more than their share, took rations for two, and even three; we were so huddled together, that we found it absolutely impossible to prevent this abuse.

In the midst of these horrors a touching scene of filial piety drew our tears. Two young men raised and recognised their father, who had fallen, and was lying insensible among the feet of the people. They believed him at first dead, and their despair was expressed in the most afflicting manner. It was perceived, however, that he still breathed, and every assistance was rendered for his recovery in our power. He slowly revived, and was restored to life, and to the prayers of his sons, who supported him closely, folded in their arms. Whilst our hearts were softened by this affecting episode in our melancholy adventures, we had soon to witness the sad spectacle of a dark contrast. Two ship-boys and a baker feared not to seek death, and threw themselves into the sea, after having bid farewell to their companions in misfortune. Already the minds of our people were singularly altered; some believed they saw land, others ships which were coming to save us; all talked aloud of their fallacious visions.

We lamented the loss of our unfortunate companions. At this moment we were far from anticipating the still more terrible scene which took place on the following night; far from that, we enjoyed a positive satisfaction, so well were we persuaded that the boats would return to our assistance. The day was fine, and the most perfect tranquillity reigned all the while on our raft. The evening came, and no boats appeared. Despondency began again to seize our men, and then a spirit of insubordination manifested itself in cries of rage. The voice of the officers was entirely disregarded. Night fell rapidly in, the sky was obscured by dark clouds; the wind which, during the whole of the day, had blown rather violently, became furious and swelled the sea, which in an instant became very rough.

The preceding night had been frightful, but this was still more so. Mountains of water covered us at every instant, and burst with fury into the midst of us. Very fortunately we had the wind from behind, and the strength of the sea was a little broken by the rapidity with which we were driven before it. We were impelled towards the land. The men, from the violence of the sea, were hurried from the back to the front; we were obliged to keep to the centre, the firmest part of the raft, and those who could not get there almost all perished. Before and behind the waves dashed impetuously, and swept away the men in spite of all their resistance. At the centre the pressure was such, that some unfortunates were suffocate by the weight of their comrades, who fell upon them at every instant. The officers kept by the foot of the little mast, and were obliged every moment to call to those around them to go to the one or the other side to avoid the wave; for the sea coming nearly athwart us, gave our raft nearly a perpendicular position, to counteract which they were forced to throw themselves upon the side raised by the sea.

The soldiers and sailors, frightened by the presence of almost inevitable danger, doubted not that they had reached their last hour. Firmly believing they were lost, they resolved to soothe their last moments by drinking till they lost their reason. We had no power to oppose this disorder. They seized a cask which was in the centre of the raft, made a hole in the end of it, and, with small tin cups, took each a pretty large quantity; but they were obliged to cease, for the sea-water rushed into the hole they had made. The fumes of the wine failed not to disorder their brains, already weakened by the presence of danger and want of food. Thus excited, these men became deaf to the voice of reason. They wished to involve, in one common ruin, all their companions in misfortune. They avowedly expressed their intention of freeing themselves from their officers, who, they said, wished to oppose their design; and then to destroy the raft, by cutting the ropes which united its different parts. Immediately after, they resolved to put their plans in execution. One of them advanced upon the side of the raft with a boarding-axe, and began to cut the cords. This was the signal of revolt. We stepped forward to prevent these insane mortals, and he who was armed with the hatchet, with which he even threatened an officer, fell the first victim; a stroke of a sabre terminated his existence.

This man was an Asiatic, and a soldier in a colonial regiment. Of a colossal stature, short hair, a nose extremely large, an enormous mouth, dark complexion, he made a most hideous appearance. At first he had placed himself in the middle of the raft, and, at each blow of his fist, knocked down every one who opposed him; he inspired the greatest terror, and none durst approach him. Had there been six such, our destruction would have been certain.

Some men, anxious to prolong their existence, armed and united themselves with those who wished to preserve the raft; among this number were some subaltern officers and many passengers. The rebels drew their sabres, and those who had none armed themselves with knives. They advanced in a determined manner upon us; we stood on our defence; the attack commenced. Animated by despair, one of them aimed a stroke at an officer; the rebel instantly fell, pierced with wounds. This firmness awed them for an instant, but diminished nothing of their rage. They ceased to advance, and withdrew, presenting to us a front bristling with sabres and bayonets, to the back part of the raft to execute their plan. One of them feigned to rest himself on the small railings on the sides of the raft, and with a knife began cutting the cords. Being told by a servant, one of us sprung upon him. A soldier, wishing to defend him, struck at the officer with his knife, which only pierced his coat; the officer wheeled round, seized his adversary, and threw both him and his comrade into the sea.

There had been as yet but partial affairs: the combat became general. Someone cried to lower the sail; a crowd of infuriated mortals threw themselves in an instant upon the halyards, the shrouds, and cut them. The fall of the mast almost broke the thigh of a captain of infantry, who fell insensible. He was seized by the soldiers, who threw him into the sea. We saved him, and placed him on a barrel, whence he was taken by the rebels, who wished to put out his eyes with a penknife. Exasperated by so much brutality, we no longer restrained ourselves, but rushed in upon them, and charged them with fury. Sword in hand we traversed the line which the soldiers formed, and many paid with their lives the errors of their revolt. Various passengers, during these cruel moments, evinced the greatest courage and coolness.

M. Corréard fell into a sort of swoon; but hearing at every instant the cries, *To arms! with us, comrades; we are lost!* joined with the groans and imprecations of the wounded and dying, was soon roused from his lethargy. All this horrible tumult speedily made him comprehend how necessary it was to be upon his guard. Armed with his sabre, he gathered together some of his workmen on the front of the raft, and there charged them to hurt no one, unless they were attacked. He almost always remained with them; and several times they had to defend themselves against the rebels, who, swimming round to the point of the raft, placed M. Corréard and his little troop between two dangers, and made their position very difficult to defend. At every instant he was opposed to men armed with knives, sabres, and bayonets. Many had carbines which they wielded as clubs. Every effort was made to stop them, by holding them off at the point of their swords; but, in spite of the repugnance they experienced in fighting with their wretched countrymen, they were compelled to use their arms without mercy. Many of the mutineers attacked with fury, and they were obliged to repel them in the same manner. Some of the labourers received severe wounds in this action. Their commander could show a great number received in the different engagements. At last their united efforts prevailed in dispersing this mass who had attacked them with such fury.

During this combat, M. Corréard was told by one of his workmen who remained faithful, that one of their comrades, named Dominique, had gone over to the rebels, and that they had seized and thrown him into the sea. Immediately forgetting the fault and treason of this man, he threw himself in at the place whence the voice of the wretch was heard calling for assistance, seized him by the hair, and had the good fortune to restore him on board. Dominique had got several sabre wounds in a charge, one of which had laid open his head. In spite of the darkness we found out the wound, which seemed very large. One of the workmen gave his handkerchief to bind and stop the blood. Our care recovered the wretch; but, when he had collected strength, the ungrateful Dominique, forgetting at once his duty and the signal service which we had rendered him, went and rejoined the rebels. So much baseness and insanity did not go unrevenged; and soon after he found, in a fresh assault, that death from which he was not worthy to be saved, but which he might in all probability have avoided, if, true to honour and gratitude, he had remained among us.

Just at the moment we finished dressing the wounds of Dominique, another voice was heard. It was that of the unfortunate female who was with us on the raft, and whom the infuriated beings had thrown into the sea, as well as her husband, who had defended her with courage. M. Corréard, in despair at seeing two unfortunates perish; whose pitiful cries, especially the woman's, pierced his heart, seized a large rope which he found on the front of the raft, which he fastened round his middle, and throwing himself a second time into the sea, was again so fortunate as to save the woman, who invoked, with all her might, the assistance of our Lady of Land. Her husband was rescued at the same time by the head workman, Lavilette. We laid these unfortunates upon the dead bodies, supporting their backs with a barrel. In a short while they recovered their senses. The first thing the woman did was to acquaint herself with the name of the person who saved her, and to express to him her liveliest gratitude. Finding, doubtless, that her words but ill expressed her feelings, she recollected she had in her pocket a little snuff, and instantly offered it to him,—it was all she possessed. Touched with the gift, but unable to use it, M. Corréard gave it to a poor sailor, which served him for three or four days. But it is impossible for us to describe a still more affecting scene,—the joy this unfortunate couple testified, when they had sufficiently recovered their senses, at finding they were both saved.

The rebels being repulsed, as it has been stated above, left us a little repose. The moon lighted with her melancholy rays this disastrous raft, this narrow space, on which were found united so many torturing anxieties, so many cruel misfortunes, a madness so insensate, a courage so heroic, and the most generous—the most amiable sentiments of nature and humanity.

The man and wife, who had been but a little before stabbed with swords and bayonets, and thrown both together into a stormy sea, could scarcely credit their senses when they found themselves in one another's arms. The woman was a native of the Upper Alps, which place she had left twenty-four years before, and during which time she had followed the French armies in the campaigns in Italy, and other places, as a sutler.

"Therefore preserve my life," said she to M. Corréard, "you see I am an useful woman. Ah! if you knew how often I have ventured upon the field of battle, and braved death to carry assistance to our gallant men. Whether they had money or not, I always let them have my goods. Sometimes a battle would deprive me of my poor debtors, but after the victory, others would pay me double or triple for what they had consumed before the engagement. Thus I came in for a share of their victories."

Unfortunate woman! she little knew what a horrible fate awaited her among us! They felt, they expressed so vividly that happiness which they alas so shortly enjoyed, that it would have drawn tears from the most obdurate heart. But in that horrible moment, when we scarcely breathed from the most furious attack,—when we were obliged to be continually on our guard, not only against the violence of the men, but a most boisterous sea, few among us had time to attend to scenes of conjugal affection.

After this second check, the rage of the soldiers was suddenly appeased, and gave place to the most abject cowardice. Several threw themselves at our feet, and implored our pardon, which was instantly granted. Thinking that order was re-established, we returned to our station on the centre of the raft, only taking the precaution of keeping our arms. We, however, had soon to prove the impossibility of counting on the permanence of any honest sentiment in the hearts of these beings.

It was nearly midnight; and after an hour of apparent tranquillity, the soldiers rose afresh. Their mind was entirely gone; they ran upon us in despair with knives and sabres in their hands. As they yet had all their physical strength, and besides were armed, we were obliged again to stand on our defence. Their revolt became still more dangerous, as, in their delirium, they were entirely deaf to the voice of reason. They attacked us, we charged them in our turn, and immediately the raft was strewed with their dead bodies. Those of our adversaries who had no weapons endeavoured to tear us with their sharp teeth. Many of us were cruelly bitten. M. Savigny was torn on the legs and the shoulder; he also received a wound on the right arm, which deprived him of the use of his fourth and little finger for a long while. Many others were wounded; and many cuts were found in our clothes from knives and sabres.

One of our workmen was also seized by four of the rebels, who wished to throw him into the sea. One of them had laid hold of his right leg, and had bit most unmercifully the tendon above the heel; others were striking him with great slashes of their sabres, and with the butt end of their guns, when his cries made us hasten to his assistance. In this affair, the brave Lavilette, ex-sergeant of the foot artillery of the Old Guard, behaved with a courage worthy of the greatest praise. He rushed upon the infuriated beings in the manner of M. Corréard, and soon snatched the workman from the danger which menaced him. Some short while after, in a fresh attack of the rebels, sub-lieutenant Lozach fell into their hands. In their delirium, they had taken him for Lieutenant Danglas,[17] of whom we have formerly spoken, and who had abandoned the raft at the moment when we were quitting the frigate. The troop, to a man, eagerly sought this officer, who had seen little service, and whom they reproached for having used them ill during the time they garrisoned the Isle of Rhé. We believed this officer lost, but hearing his voice, we soon found it still possible to save him. Immediately MM. Clairet, Savigny, L'Heureux, Lavilette, Coudin, Corréard, and some workmen, formed themselves into small platoons, and rushed upon the insurgents with great impetuos-

---

17: Danglas had gone upon the raft at first, on which his post had been assigned; "but when he saw the danger which he ran upon this frightful machine, he instantly quitted it on pretence of having forgot something on board, and never returned."—*Trans.*

ity, overturning everyone in their way, and retook M. Lozach, and placed him on the centre of the raft.

The preservation of this officer cost us infinite difficulty. Every moment the soldiers demanded he should be delivered to them, designating him always by the name of Danglas. We endeavoured to make them comprehend their mistake, and told them that they themselves had seen the person for whom they sought return on board the frigate. They were insensible to everything we said; everything before them was Danglas; they saw him perpetually, and furiously and unceasingly demanded his head. It was only by force of arms we succeeded in repressing their rage, and quieting their dreadful cries of death.

Horrible night! thou shrouded with thy gloomy veil these frightful combats, over which presided the cruel demon of despair.

We had also to tremble for the life of M. Coudin. Wounded and fatigued by the attacks which he had sustained with us, and in which he had shown a courage superior to everything, he was resting himself on a barrel, holding in his arms a young sailor boy of twelve years of age, to whom he had attached himself. The mutineers seized him with his barrel, and threw him into the sea with the boy, whom he still held fast. In spite of his burden, he had the presence of mind to lay hold of the raft, and to save himself from this extreme peril.

We cannot yet comprehend how a handful of men should have been able to resist such a number so monstrously insane. We are sure we were not more than twenty to combat all these madmen. Let it not, however, be imagined, that in the midst of all these dangers we had preserved our reason entire. Fear, anxiety, and the most cruel privations, had greatly changed our intellectual faculties. But being somewhat less insane than the unfortunate soldiers, we energetically opposed their determination of cutting the cords of the raft. Permit us now to make some observations concerning the different sensations with which we were affected.

During the first day, M. Griffon entirely lost his senses. He threw himself into the sea, but M. Savigny saved him with his own hands. His words were vague and unconnected. A second time he threw himself in, but, by a sort of instinct, kept hold of the cross pieces of the raft, and was again saved.

The following is what M. Savigny experienced in the beginning of the night. His eyes closed in spite of himself, and he felt a general drowsiness. In this condition the most delightful visions flitted across his imagination. He saw around him a country covered with the most beautiful plantations, and found himself in the midst of objects delightful to his senses. Nevertheless, he reasoned concerning his condition, and felt that courage alone could withdraw him from this species of non-existence. He demanded some wine from the master-gunner, who got it for him, and he recovered a little from this state of stupor. If the unfortunates who were assailed with these primary symptoms had not strength to withstand them, their death was certain. Some became furious; others threw themselves into the sea, bidding farewell to their comrades with the utmost coolness. Some said—"Fear nothing; I am going to get you assistance, and will return in a short while."

In the midst of this general madness, some wretches were seen rushing upon their companions, sword in hand, demanding *a wing of a chicken and some bread* to appease the hunger which consumed them; others asked for their hammocks to go, they said, *between the decks of the frigate to take a little repose*. Many believed they were still on the deck of the *Medusa*, surrounded by the same objects they there saw daily. Some saw ships, and called to them for assistance, or a fine harbour, in the distance of which was an elegant city. M. Corréard thought he was travelling through the beautiful fields of Italy.

An officer said to him—"I recollect we have been abandoned by the boats; but fear nothing. I am going to write to the governor, and in a few hours we shall be saved."

M. Corréard replied in the same tone, and as if he had been in his ordinary condition.—"Have you a pigeon to carry your orders with such celerity?"

The cries and the confusion soon roused us from this languor; but when tranquillity was somewhat restored, we again fell into the same drowsy condition. On the morrow, we felt as if we had awoke from a painful dream, and asked at our companions, if, during their sleep, they had not seen combats, and heard cries of despair. Some replied, that the same visions had continually tormented them, and that they were exhausted with fatigue. Everyone believed he was deceived by the illusions of a horrible dream.

After these different combats, overcome with toil, with want of food and sleep, we laid ourselves down and reposed till the morrow dawned, and showed us the horror of the scene. A great number in their delirium had thrown themselves into the sea. We found that sixty or sixty-five had perished during the night. A fourth part at least, we supposed, had drowned themselves in despair. We only lost two of our own numbers, neither of whom were officers. The deepest dejection was painted on every face; each, having recovered himself, could now feel the horrors of his situation; and some of us, shedding tears of despair, bitterly deplored the rigour of our fate.

A new misfortune was now revealed to us. During the tumult, the rebels had thrown into the sea two barrels of wine, and the only two casks of water which we had upon the raft. Two casks of wine had been consumed the day before, and only one was left. We were more than sixty in number, and we were obliged to put ourselves on half rations.

At break of day, the sea calmed, which permitted us again to erect our mast. When it was replaced, we made a distribution of wine. The unhappy soldiers murmured and blamed us for privations which we equally endured with them. They fell exhausted. We had taken nothing for forty-eight hours, and we had been obliged to struggle continually against a strong sea. We could, like them, hardly support ourselves; courage alone made us still act. We resolved to employ every possible means to catch fish, and, collecting all the hooks and eyes from the soldiers, made fish-hooks of them, but all was of no avail. The currents carried our lines under the raft, where they got entangled. We bent a bayonet to catch sharks; one bit at it, and straightened it, and we abandoned our project. Something was absolutely necessary to sustain our miserable existence, and we tremble with horror at being obliged to tell that of which we made use. We feel our pen fall from our hands: a mortal cold congeals all our members, and our hair bristles erect on our foreheads. Readers! we implore you, feel not indignant towards men already overloaded with misery. Pity their condition, and shed a tear of sorrow for their deplorable fate.

The wretches, whom death had spared during the disastrous night we have described, seized upon the dead bodies with which the raft was covered, cutting them up by slices, which some even instantly devoured. Many nevertheless refrained. Almost all the officers were of this number. Seeing that this monstrous food had revived the strength of those who had used it, it was proposed to dry it, to make it a little more palatable. Those who had firmness to abstain from it, took an additional quantity of wine. We endeavoured to eat shoulder-belts and *cartouche*-boxes, and contrived to swallow some small bits of them. Some eat linen: others the leathers of the hats, on which was a little grease, or rather dirt. We had recourse to many expedients to prolong our miserable existence, to recount which would only disgust the heart of humanity.

The day was calm and beautiful. A ray of hope beamed for a moment to quiet our agitation. We still expected to see the boats or some ships, and addressed our prayers to the Eternal, on whom we placed our trust. The half of our men were extremely feeble, and bore upon their faces the stamp of approaching dissolution. The evening arrived, and we found no help. The darkness of the third night augmented our fears, but the wind was still, and the sea less agitated. The sun of the fourth morning since our departure shone upon our disaster, and showed us ten or twelve of our companions stretched lifeless upon the raft. This sight struck us most forcibly, as it told us we would be soon extended in the same manner in the same place. We gave their bodies to the sea for a grave, reserving only one to feed those who, but the day before, had held his trembling hands, and sworn to him eternal friendship. This day was beautiful. Our souls, anxious for more delightful sensations, were in harmony with the aspect of the heavens, and got again a new ray of hope. Towards four in the afternoon, an unlooked for event happened which gave us some consolation. A shoal of flying fish passed under our raft, and as there were an infinite number of openings between the pieces which composed it, the fish were entangled in great quantities. We threw ourselves upon them, and captured a considerable number. We took about two hundred and put them in an empty barrel; we opened them as we caught them, and took out what is called their milt. This food seemed delicious; but one man would have required a thousand.[18] Our first emotion was to give to God renewed thanks for this unhoped for favour.

An ounce of gunpowder having been found in the morning, was dried in the sun during the day, which was very fine; a steel, gun-flints, and tinder made also a part of the same parcel. After a good deal of difficulty we set fire to some fragments of dry linen. We made a large opening in the side of an empty cask, and placed at the bottom of it several wet things, and upon this kind of scaffolding we set our fire; all of which we placed on a barrel that the sea-water might not extinguish it. We cooked some fish and eat them with extreme avidity; but our hunger was such, and our portion so small, that we added to it some of the sacrilegious viands, which the cooking rendered less revolting. This some of the officers touched for the first time. From this day we continued to eat it; but we could no longer dress it, the means of making a fire having been entirely lost; the barrel having caught fire we extinguished it without being able to preserve anything to rekindle it on the morrow. The powder and tinder were entirely done. This meal gave us all additional strength to support our fatigues. The night was tolerable, and would have been happy, had it not been signalized by a new massacre.

18: These fish are very small, the largest not equal in size to a small herring.

Some Spaniards, Italians, and negroes, had formed a plot to throw us all into the sea. The negroes had told them that they were very near the shore, and that, when there, they would enable them to traverse Africa without danger. We had to take to our arms again, the sailors, who had remained faithful to us, pointing out to us the conspirators. The first signal for battle was given by a Spaniard, who, placing himself behind the mast, holding fast by it, made the sign of the Cross with one hand, invoking the name of God, and with the other held a knife. The sailors seized him and threw him into the sea. An Italian, servant to an officer of the troops, who was in the plot, seeing all was discovered, armed himself with the only boarding axe left on the raft, made his retreat to the front, enveloped himself in a piece of drapery he wore across his breast, and of his own accord threw himself into the sea. The rebels rushed forward to avenge their comrades; a terrible conflict again commenced; both sides fought with desperate fury; and soon the fatal raft was strewed with dead bodies and blood, which should have been shed by other hands, and in another cause. In this tumult we heard them again demanding, with horrid rage, the head of Lieut. Danglas! In this assault the unfortunate sutler was a second time thrown into the sea. M. Coudin, assisted by some workmen, saved her, to prolong for a little while her torments and her existence.

In this terrible night Lavillette failed not to give proofs of the rarest intrepidity. It was to him and some of these who have survived the sequel of our misfortunes, that we owed our safety. At last, after unheard of efforts, the rebels were once more repulsed, and quiet restored. Having escaped this new danger, we endeavoured to get some repose. The day at length dawned upon us for the fifth time. We were now no more than thirty in number. We had lost four or five of our faithful sailors, and those who survived were in the most deplorable condition. The sea-water had almost entirely excoriated the skin of our lower extremities; we were covered with contusions or wounds, which, irritated by the salt water, extorted from us the most piercing cries. About twenty of us only were capable of standing upright or walking.

Almost all our fish was exhausted; we had but four days' supply of wine: in four days, said we, nothing will be left, and death will be inevitable. Thus came the seventh day of our abandonment. In the course of the day two soldiers had glided behind the only barrel of wine that was left; pierced it, and were drinking by means of a reed. We had sworn that those who used such means should be punished with death; which law was instantly put in execution, and the two transgressors were thrown into the sea.

This same day saw the close of the life of a child named Leon, aged twelve years. He died like a lamp which ceases to burn for want of aliment. All spoke in favour of this young and amiable creature, who merited a better fate. His angelic form, his musical voice, the interest of an age so tender, increased still more by the courage he had shown, and the services he had performed, for he had already made in the preceding year a campaign in the East Indies, inspired us all with the greatest pity for this young victim, devoted to so horrible and premature a death. Our old soldiers and all our people in general did everything they could to prolong his existence, but all was in vain. Neither the wine which they gave him without regret, nor all the means they employed, could arrest his melancholy doom, and he expired, in the arms of M. Coudin, who had not ceased to give him the most unwearied attention. Whilst he had strength to move, he ran incessantly from one side to the other, loudly calling for his unhappy mother, for water and food. He trod indiscriminately on the feet and legs of his companions in misfortune, who, in their turn, uttered sorrowful cries, but these were very rarely accompanied with menaces; they pardoned all which the poor boy had made them suffer. He was not in his senses, consequently could not be expected to behave as if he had had the use of his reason.

There now remained but twenty-seven of us. Fifteen of that number seemed able to live yet some days; the rest, covered with large wounds, had almost entirely lost the use of their reason. They still, however, shared in the distributions, and would, before they died, consume thirty or forty bottles of wine, which to us were inestimable. We deliberated, that by putting the sick on half allowance was but putting them to death by halves; but after a counsel, at which presided the most dreadful despair, it was decided they should be thrown into the sea. This means, however repugnant, however horrible it appeared to us, procured the survivors six days' wine. But after the decision was made, who durst execute it? The habit of seeing death ready to devour us; the certainty of our infallible destruction without this monstrous expedient; all, in short, had hardened our hearts to every feeling but that of self-preservation. Three sailors and a soldier took charge of this cruel business. We looked aside and shed tears of blood at the fate of these unfortunates. Among them were the wretched Sutler and her husband. Both had been grievously wounded in the different combats. The woman had a thigh broken between the beams of the raft, and a stroke of a sabre had made a deep wound in the head of her husband. Everything announced their approaching end. We console ourselves with the belief that our cruel resolution shortened but a brief space the term of their existence. Ye who shudder at the cry of outraged humanity, recollect, that it was other men, fellow-countrymen, comrades, who had placed us in this awful situation!

This horrible expedient saved the fifteen who remained; for when we were found by the *Argus* brig, we had very little wine left, and it was the sixth day after the cruel sacrifice we have described. The victims, we repeat, had not more than forty-eight hours to live, and by keeping them on the raft, we would have been absolutely destitute of the means of existence two days before we were found. Weak as we were, we considered it as a certain thing, that it would have been impossible for us to have lived only twenty-four hours more without taking some food. After this catastrophe, we threw our arms into the sea; they inspired us with a horror we could not overcome. We only kept one sabre, in case we had to cut some cordage or some piece of wood.

A new event, for everything was an *event* to wretches to whom the world was reduced to the narrow space of a few *toises*, and for whom the winds and waves contended in their fury as they floated above the abyss; an event happened which diverted our minds from the horrors of our situation. All on a sudden a white butterfly, of a species common in France, came fluttering above our heads, and settled on our sail. The first thought this little creature suggested was, that it was the harbinger of approaching land, and we clung to the hope with a delirium of joy. It was the ninth day we had been upon the raft; the torments of hunger consumed our entrails; and the soldiers and sailors already devoured with haggard eyes this wretched prey, and seemed ready to dispute about it. Others looking upon it as a messenger from Heaven, declared that they took it under their protection, and would suffer none to do it harm. It is certain we could not be far from land, for the butterflies continued to come on the following days, and flutter about our sail. We had also on the same day another indication not less positive, by a Goéland which flew around our raft. This second visitor left us not a doubt that we were fast approaching the African soil, and we persuaded ourselves we would be speedily thrown upon the coast by the force of the currents.

This same day a new care employed us. Seeing we were reduced to so small a number, we collected all the little strength we had left, detached some planks on the front of the raft, and, with some pretty long pieces of wood, raised on the centre a kind of platform, on which we reposed. All the effects we could collect were placed upon it, and rendered to make it less hard; which also prevented the sea from passing with such facility through the spaces between the different planks, but the waves came across, and sometimes covered us completely.

On this new theatre we resolved to meet death in a manner becoming Frenchmen, and with perfect resignation. Our time was almost wholly spent in speaking of our unhappy country. All our wishes, our last prayers, were for the prosperity of France. Thus passed the last days of our abode upon the raft.

Soon after our abandonment, we bore with comparative ease the immersions during the nights, which are very cold in these countries; but latterly, every time the waves washed over us, we felt a most painful sensation, and we uttered plaintive cries. We employed every means to avoid it. Some supported their heads on pieces of wood, and made with what they could find a sort of little parapet to screen them from the force of the waves; others sheltered themselves behind two empty casks. But these means were very insufficient; it was only when the sea was calm that it did not break over us.

An ardent thirst, redoubled in the day by the beams of a burning sun, consumed us. An officer of the army found by chance a small lemon, and it may be easily imagined how valuable such a fruit would be to him. His comrades, in spite of the most urgent entreaties, could not get a bit of it from him. Signs of rage were already manifested, and had he not partly listened to the solicitations of those around him, they would have taken it by force, and he would have perished the victim of his selfishness. We also disputed about thirty cloves of garlic which were found in the bottom of a sack. These disputes were for the most part accompanied with violent menaces, and if they had been prolonged, we might perhaps have come to the last extremities.

There was found also two small phials, in which was a spirituous liquid for cleaning the teeth. He who possessed them kept them with care, and gave with reluctance one or two drops in the palm of the hand. This liquor which, we think, was a tincture of *guiacum*, cinnamon, cloves, and other aromatic substances, produced on our tongues an agreeable feeling, and for a short while removed the thirst which destroyed us. Some of us found some small pieces of powder, which made, when put into the mouth, a kind of coolness. One plan generally employed was to put into a hat a quantity of sea-water, with which we washed our faces for a while, repeating it at intervals. We also bathed our hair, and held our hands in the water.[19] Misfortune made us ingenious, and each thought of a thousand means to alleviate his sufferings.

19: People in a similar situation as that described here, have found great benefit by soaking their clothes in the sea, and then dressing themselves with them. This means was not resorted to by the sufferers on the fatal raft. Mungo Park when much afflicted by thirst in the desert, found great relief by keeping a pebble in his mouth.—*Trans*.

Emaciated by the most cruel privations, the least agreeable feeling was to us a happiness supreme. Thus we sought with avidity a small empty phial which one of us possessed, and in which had once been some essence of roses; and every one as he got hold of it respired with delight the odour it exhaled, which imparted to his senses the most soothing impressions. Many of us kept our ration of wine in a small tin cup, and sucked it out with a quill. This manner of taking it was of great benefit to us, and allayed our thirst much better than if we had gulped it of at once.

Three days passed in inexpressible anguish. So much did we despise life, that many of us feared not to bathe in sight of the sharks which surrounded our raft; others placed themselves naked upon the front of our machine, which was under water. These expedients diminished a little the ardour of their thirst. A species of mollusc, known to seamen by the name of *gatère*, was sometimes driven in great numbers on our raft; and when their long arms rested on our naked bodies, they occasioned us the most cruel sufferings. Will it be believed, that amidst these terrible scenes, struggling with inevitable death, some of us uttered pleasantries which made us yet smile, in spite of the horrors of our situation?

One, besides others, said jestingly, "*If the brig is sent to search for us, pray God it has the eyes of Argus,*" in allusion to the name of the vessel we presumed would be sent to our assistance. This consolatory idea never left us an instant, and we spoke of it frequently.

On the 16th, reckoning we were very near land, eight of the most determined among us resolved to endeavour to gain the coast. A second raft, of smaller dimensions, was formed for transporting them thither; but it was found insufficient, and they at length determined to await death in their present situation. Meanwhile night came on, and its sombre veil revived in our minds the most afflicting thoughts. We were convinced there were not above a dozen or fifteen bottles of wine in our barrel. We began to have an invincible disgust at the flesh which had till then scarcely supported us; and we may say, that the sight of it inspired us with feelings of horror, doubtless produced by the idea of our approaching destruction. On the morning of the 17th, the sun appeared free from clouds. After having addressed our prayers to the Eternal, we divided among us a part of our wine. Each, with delight, was taking his small portion, when a captain of infantry, casting his eyes on the horizon, perceived a ship, and announced it to us by an exclamation of joy. We knew it to be a brig, but it was at a great distance; we could only distinguish the masts. The sight of this vessel revived in us emotions difficult to describe. Each believed his deliverance sure, and we gave a thousand thanks to God. Fears, however, mingled with our hopes. We straightened some hoops of casks, to the ends of which we fixed handkerchiefs of different colours. A man, with our united assistance, mounted to the top of the mast, and waved these little flags. For more than half an hour, we were tossed between hope and fear. Some thought the vessel grew larger, and others were convinced its course was from us. These last were the only ones whose eyes were not blinded by hope, for the ship disappeared.

From the delirium of joy, we passed to that of despondency and sorrow. We envied the fate of those whom we had seen perish at our sides; and we said to ourselves, "When we shall be in want of everything, and when our strength begins to forsake us, we will wrap ourselves up as well as we can, we will stretch ourselves on this platform, the witness of the most cruel sufferings, and there await death with resignation."

At length, to calm our despair, we sought for consolation in the arms of sleep. The day before, we had been scorched by the beams of a burning sun; today, to avoid the fierceness of his rays, we made a tent with the main-sail of the frigate. As soon as it was finished, we laid ourselves under it; thus all that was passing without was hid from our eyes. We proposed then to write upon a plank an abridgement of our adventures, and to add our names at the bottom of the recital, and fix it to the upper part of the mast, in the hope it would reach the government and our families.

After having passed two hours, a prey to the most cruel reflections, the master gunner of the frigate, wishing to go to the front of the raft, went out from below the tent. Scarcely had he put out his head, when he turned to us, uttering a piercing cry. Joy was painted upon his face; his hands were stretched towards the sea; he breathed with difficulty. All he was able to say was: *"Saved! See the brig upon us!"* and in fact it was not more than half a league distant, having every sail set, and steering right upon us.

We rushed from our tent; even those whom enormous wounds in their inferior extremities had confined for many days, dragged themselves to the back of the raft, to enjoy a sight of the ship which had come to save us from certain death. We embraced one another with a transport which looked much like madness, and tears of joy trickled down our cheeks, withered by the most cruel privations. Each seized handkerchiefs, or some pieces of linen, to make signals to the brig, which was rapidly approaching us. Some fell on their knees, and fervently returned thanks to Providence for this miraculous preservation of their lives. Our joy redoubled when we saw at the top of the foremast a large white flag, and we cried, "It is then to Frenchmen we will owe our deliverance."

We instantly recognised the brig to be the *Argus*; it was then about two gun-shots from us. We were terribly impatient to see her reef her sails, which at last she did, and fresh cries of joy arose from our raft. The *Argus* came and lay-to on our starboard, about half a pistol-shot from us. The crew, ranged upon the deck and on the shrouds, announced to us, by the waving of their hands and hats, the pleasure they felt at coming to the assistance of their unfortunate countrymen. In a short time we were all transported on board the brig, where we found the lieutenant of the frigate, and some others who had been wrecked with us. Compassion was painted on every face; and pity drew tears from every eye which beheld us.

We found some excellent broth on board the brig, which they had prepared, and when they had perceived us they added to it some wine, and thus restored our nearly exhausted strength. They bestowed on us the most generous care and attention; our wounds were dressed, and on the morrow many of our sick began to revive. Some, however, still suffered much, for they were placed between decks, very near the kitchen, which augmented the almost insupportable heat of these latitudes. This want of space arose from the small size of the vessel. The number of the shipwrecked was indeed very considerable. Those who did not belong to the navy were laid upon cables, wrapped in flags, and placed under the fire of the kitchen. Here they had almost perished during the course of the night, fire having broken out between decks about ten in the evening; but timely assistance being rendered, we were saved for the second time. We had scarcely escaped when some of us became again delirious. An officer of infantry wished to throw himself into the sea, to look for his pocket-book, and would have done it had he not been prevented. Others were seized in a manner not less frenzied.

The commander and officers of the brig watched over us, and kindly anticipated our wants. They snatched us from death, by saving us from our raft; their unremitting care revived within us the spark of life. The surgeon of the ship, M. Renaud, distinguished himself for his indefatigable zeal. He was obliged to spend the whole of the day in dressing our wounds; and during the two days we were on the brig, he bestowed on us all the aid of his art, with an attention and gentleness which merit our eternal gratitude.

In truth, it was time we should find an end of our sufferings; they had lasted thirteen days, in the most cruel manner. The strongest among us might have lived forty-eight hours, or so, longer. M. Corréard felt that he must die in the course of the day; he had, however, a presentiment we would be saved. He said, that a series of events so unheard of would not be buried in oblivion; that Providence would at least preserve some of us to tell to the world the melancholy story of our misfortunes.

Such is the faithful history of those who were left upon the memorable raft. Of one hundred and fifty, fifteen only were saved. Five of that number never recovered their fatigue, and died at St Louis. Those who yet live are covered with scars; and the cruel sufferings to which they have been exposed, have materially shaken their constitution.—*Naufrage de la Frégate la Meduse*; par A. Corréard et J. B. H. Savigny. Second Edition. Paris, 8vo. 1818.

Notes

NOTE A

In preparing their corn for food, the natives use a large wooden mortar called a *paloon*, in which they bruise the seed until it parts with the outer covering, or husk, which is then separated from the clean corn, by exposing it to the wind, nearly in the same manner as wheat is cleaned from the chaff in England. The corn thus freed from the husk, is returned to the mortar, and beaten into meal; which is dressed variously in different countries; but the most common preparation of it among the nations of the Gambia, is a sort of pudding, which they call couscous.

It is made by first moistening the flour with water, and then stirring and shaking it about in a large calabash, or gourd, till it adheres together in small granules, resembling sago. It is then put into an earthen pot, whose bottom is perforated with a number of holes; and this pot being placed upon another, the two vessels are glued together, either with a paste of meal and water, or cow-dung, and placed upon the fire. In the lower vessel is commonly some animal food and water, the steam or vapour of which ascends through the perforations in the bottom of the upper vessel, and softens and prepares the couscous, which is very much esteemed throughout all the countries that I visited.

I am informed, that the same manner of preparing flour

is very generally used on the Barbary coast, and that the dish so prepared is there so called by the same name. It is therefore probable, that the Negroes borrowed the practise from the Moors.

For gratifying a taste for variety, another sort of pudding, called *realing*, is sometimes prepared from the meal of corn; and they have also adopted two or three different modes of dressing their rice. Of vegetable food, therefore, the natives have no want; and although the common class of people are but sparingly supplied with animal food, yet this article is not wholly withheld from them.—*Park's Travels*, in 1795, 1796, and 1797, pp. 10, 11. Lond. 1799, 4to.

Note B

I cannot withhold the following notice of the worthy Major's death, extracted from a work lately published, entitled *Travels, in Western Africa*, in the years 1818, 1819, 1820 and 1821, by Major William Gray. Lond. 1825, 8vo.

On that day (24th December) Major Peddie was attacked with a violent fever, from which he experienced little relief until the morning of the 1st of January 1817, when, thinking himself better, he left his bed, but was soon obliged to resume it, and in a few hours breathed his last.

This was a sad commencement of the new year, and the melancholy event cast a heavy gloom on the minds of every individual connected with the expedition. It made so deep an impression on some, that it was with much difficulty they could be prevailed on not to abandon the enterprise. Never was a man more sincerely beloved, nor more truly regretted, by all who knew him. His remains were deposited, amidst the heartfelt regrets of his friends and companions, on the following day, in the court-yard of Mr Beatman, under the shade of two orange-trees; and an appropriate epitaph, written by Captain Campbell, and carved on a slab of native mahogany, was placed on his grave.

Note C

When we had reached the other side of the river, they drew the *piroque* on land. This is the only way that the people of the country have to secure their little boats, which the surge would instantly fill, when they cannot cast anchor at a sufficient distance from the shore.

This manoeuvre did not occupy a long time, and I bent my steps to the village of Sor. I was kindly welcomed as usual; and I requested them to point out to me the best place for hunting; for I had that day left my interpreter, because I had gained a sufficient knowledge of the language of the country to understand all that the negroes said to me, and to make myself understood by them. They led me in a direction whence I had seen a troop of antelopes scamper off; but I thought no more of the chase after I had seen a tree, the enormous dimensions of which completely riveted my attention. It was a calabash tree, otherwise called the monkey-bread tree, which the Woloffs call *goui* in their language. Its height was nothing extraordinary, being but about sixty feet; but its trunk was of prodigious dimensions. I spanned it thirteen times with my arms stretched out, but it was more; and, for greater exactness, I at last measured it with twine, and found its circumference to be sixty-five feet, its diameter consequently nearly twenty-two feet. I believe there has never been anything seen equal to it in any country; and, I am persuaded that, had our ancient travellers known it, they would not have failed to have included it among the wonders of the world. It is also very astonishing that this tree has been totally neglected by those who have given us the history of Senegal, especially as there are but few common to the country.

The trunk of the one which I saw was twenty-two feet in diameter, about eight or twelve feet in height, with many branches, some of which stretched out horizontally, and touched the ground with their tops. These were very large, some being about forty-five or fifty-five feet in length. Each branch would have made one of the largest trees in Europe; and the *tout ensemble* of the monkey-bread tree looked less like a single tree than a forest. This was not all. The negro who conducted me took me to a second, which was sixty-three feet in circumference, that is twenty-one feet in diameter, and appeared to be about one hundred and ten feet in length, without counting the root which was concealed under the waters of a neighbouring river, the depth of which I had no means of ascertaining. The same negro told me of a third which was not far from the place where we were, and added that, without leaving the island, I would see a great many more which were not much inferior in size.

It was night before we reached Cogné. Our route was bordered with gum-trees, the yellow flowers of which, arranged in circular bunches, spread a delicious perfume. We also saw some *rates*. The bark of this tree yields a yellow dye; its leaf is without indentation, and of a beautiful green; it is not very high; the wood is white, and the bark is easily reduced to powder. This was the first time that I saw the baobab, that enormous tree which has been described by Adanson, and which bears his name. I measured one, and found it to be forty feet in circumference. Stripped at this time of its foliage, it resembled an immense wooden tower.

This majestic mass is the only monument of antiquity to be met with in Africa. I am astonished that the negroes have not paid to this tree the same honours that the Druids did to the oak; for to them the baobab is perhaps the most valuable of vegetables. Its leaves are used for leaven, its bark furnishes indestructible cordage; and the bees form their hives in the cavities of its trunk. The negroes, too, often shelter themselves from storms in its time-worn caverns. The baobab is indisputably the monarch of African trees, p. 41.—*Travels in the interior of Africa, to the Sources of the Senegal and Gambia*, by G. Mollien. Lond. 1820, 4to.

Mollien was one of the shipwrecked in the *Medusa*, and who got to the shores of the desert in the boats.—*Trans*.

Note D

The kingdom of Kajaaga, in which I was now arrived, is called by the French Gallam; but the name that I have adopted is universally used by the natives.—*Park's Travels*, c. v. p. 1.

Note E

About eight o'clock, we passed a large town called Kabba, situated in the midst of a beautiful and highly cultivated country; bearing a greater resemblance to the centre of England, than what I should have supposed had been the middle of Africa. The people were everywhere employed in collecting the fruit of the Shea-trees, from which they prepare the vegetable butter, mentioned in a former part of this work. These trees grow in great abundance all over this part of Bambaraa. They are not planted by the natives, but are found growing naturally in the woods; and, in clearing wood-land for cultivation, every tree is cut down but the Shea. The tree itself very much resembles the American oak; and the fruit, from the kernel of which, being first dried in the sun, the butter is prepared by boiling the kernel in water, has somewhat the appearance of a Spanish olive. The kernel is enveloped in a sweet pulp, under a thin green rind; and the butter produced from it, besides the advantage of its keeping the whole year without salt; is whiter, firmer, and, to my palate, of a richer flavour, than the best butter I ever tasted made from cows' milk. The growth and preparation of this commodity seem to be among the first objects of African industry in this and the neighbouring states; and it constitutes a main article of their inland commerce.—*Park's Travels*, pp. 202, 203.

ALSO FROM LEONAUR
AVAILABLE IN SOFTCOVER OR HARDCOVER WITH DUST JACKET

CAPTAIN OF THE 95th (Rifles) by *Jonathan Leach*—An officer of Wellington's Sharpshooters during the Peninsular, South of France and Waterloo Campaigns of the Napoleonic Wars.

BUGLER AND OFFICER OF THE RIFLES by *William Green & Harry Smith* With the 95th (Rifles) during the Peninsular & Waterloo Campaigns of the Napoleonic Wars

BAYONETS, BUGLES AND BONNETS by *James 'Thomas' Todd*—Experiences of hard soldiering with the 71st Foot - the Highland Light Infantry - through many battles of the Napoleonic wars including the Peninsular & Waterloo Campaigns

THE ADVENTURES OF A LIGHT DRAGOON by *George Farmer & G.R. Gleig*—A cavalryman during the Peninsular & Waterloo Campaigns, in captivity & at the siege of Bhurtpore, India

THE COMPLEAT RIFLEMAN HARRIS by *Benjamin Harris as told to & transcribed by Captain Henry Curling*—The adventures of a soldier of the 95th (Rifles) during the Peninsular Campaign of the Napoleonic Wars

WITH WELLINGTON'S LIGHT CAVALRY by *William Tomkinson*—The Experiences of an officer of the 16th Light Dragoons in the Peninsular and Waterloo campaigns of the Napoleonic Wars.

SURTEES OF THE RIFLES by *William Surtees*—A Soldier of the 95th (Rifles) in the Peninsular campaign of the Napoleonic Wars.

ENSIGN BELL IN THE PENINSULAR WAR by *George Bell*—The Experiences of a young British Soldier of the 34th Regiment 'The Cumberland Gentlemen' in the Napoleonic wars.

WITH THE LIGHT DIVISION by *John H. Cooke*—The Experiences of an Officer of the 43rd Light Infantry in the Peninsula and South of France During the Napoleonic Wars

NAPOLEON'S IMPERIAL GUARD: FROM MARENGO TO WATERLOO by *J. T. Headley*—This is the story of Napoleon's Imperial Guard from the bearskin caps of the grenadiers to the flamboyance of their mounted chasseurs, their principal characters and the men who commanded them.

BATTLES & SIEGES OF THE PENINSULAR WAR by *W. H. Fitchett*—Corunna, Busaco, Albuera, Ciudad Rodrigo, Badajos, Salamanca, San Sebastian & Others

AVAILABLE ONLINE AT
www.leonaur.com
AND OTHER GOOD BOOK STORES

NAP-1

ALSO FROM LEONAUR
AVAILABLE IN SOFTCOVER OR HARDCOVER WITH DUST JACKET

WELLINGTON AND THE PYRENEES CAMPAIGN VOLUME I: FROM VITORIA TO THE BIDASSOA *by F. C. Beatson*—The final phase of the campaign in the Iberian Peninsula.

WELLINGTON AND THE INVASION OF FRANCE VOLUME II: THE BIDASSOA TO THE BATTLE OF THE NIVELLE *by F. C. Beatson*—The second of Beatson's series on the fall of Revolutionary France published by Leonaur, the reader is once again taken into the centre of Wellington's strategic and tactical genius.

WELLINGTON AND THE FALL OF FRANCE VOLUME III: THE GAVES AND THE BATTLE OF ORTHEZ *by F. C. Beatson*—This final chapter of F. C. Beatson's brilliant trilogy shows the 'captain of the age' at his most inspired and makes all three books essential additions to any Peninsular War library.

NAVAL BATTLES OF THE NAPOLEONIC WARS *by W. H. Fitchett*—Cape St. Vincent, the Nile, Cadiz, Copenhagen, Trafalgar & Others

SERGEANT GUILLEMARD: THE MAN WHO SHOT NELSON? *by Robert Guillemard*—A Soldier of the Infantry of the French Army of Napoleon on Campaign Throughout Europe

WITH THE GUARDS ACROSS THE PYRENEES by *Robert Batty*—The Experiences of a British Officer of Wellington's Army During the Battles for the Fall of Napoleonic France, 1813.

A STAFF OFFICER IN THE PENINSULA *by E. W. Buckham*—An Officer of the British Staff Corps Cavalry During the Peninsula Campaign of the Napoleonic Wars

THE LEIPZIG CAMPAIGN: 1813—NAPOLEON AND THE "BATTLE OF THE NATIONS" *by F. N. Maude*—Colonel Maude's analysis of Napoleon's campaign of 1813.

BUGEAUD: A PACK WITH A BATON by *Thomas Robert Bugeaud*—The Early Campaigns of a Soldier of Napoleon's Army Who Would Become a Marshal of France.

TWO LEONAUR ORIGINALS

SERGEANT NICOL by *Daniel Nicol*—The Experiences of a Gordon Highlander During the Napoleonic Wars in Egypt, the Peninsula and France.

WATERLOO RECOLLECTIONS by *Frederick Llewellyn*—Rare First Hand Accounts, Letters, Reports and Retellings from the Campaign of 1815.

ALSO FROM LEONAUR
AVAILABLE IN SOFTCOVER OR HARDCOVER WITH DUST JACKET

WAR BEYOND THE DRAGON PAGODA by *J. J. Snodgrass*—A Personal Narrative of the First Anglo-Burmese War 1824 - 1826.

ALL FOR A SHILLING A DAY by *Donald F. Featherstone*—The story of H.M. 16th, the Queen's Lancers During the first Sikh War 1845-1846.

AT THEM WITH THE BAYONET by *Donald F. Featherstone*—The first Anglo-Sikh War 1845-1846.

A LEONAUR ORIGINAL

THE HERO OF ALIWAL by *James Humphries*—The days when young Harry Smith wore the green jacket of the 95th-Wellington's famous riflemen-campaigning in Spain against Napoleon's French with his beautiful young bride Juana have long gone. Now, Sir Harry Smith is in his fifties approaching the end of a long career. His position in the Cape colony ends with an appointment as Deputy Adjutant-General to the army in India. There he joins the staff of Sir Hugh Gough to experience an Indian battlefield in the Gwalior War of 1843 as the power of the Marathas is finally crushed. Smith has little time for his superior's 'bull at a gate' style of battlefield tactics, but independent command is denied him. Little does he realise that the greatest opportunity of his military life is close at hand.

THE GURKHA WAR by *H. T. Prinsep*—The Anglo-Nepalese Conflict in North East India 1814-1816.

SOUND ADVANCE! by *Joseph Anderson*—Experiences of an officer of HM 50th regiment in Australia, Burma & the Gwalior war.

THE CAMPAIGN OF THE INDUS by *Thomas Holdsworth*—Experiences of a British Officer of the 2nd (Queen's Royal) Regiment in the Campaign to Place Shah Shuja on the Throne of Afghanistan 1838 - 1840.

WITH THE MADRAS EUROPEAN REGIMENT IN BURMA by *John Butler*—The Experiences of an Officer of the Honourable East India Company's Army During the First Anglo-Burmese War 1824 - 1826.

BESIEGED IN LUCKNOW by *Martin Richard Gubbins*—The Experiences of the Defender of 'Gubbins Post' before & during the sige of the residency at Lucknow, Indian Mutiny, 1857.

THE STORY OF THE GUIDES by *G.J. Younghusband*—The Exploits of the famous Indian Army Regiment from the northwest frontier 1847 - 1900.

AVAILABLE ONLINE AT
www.leonaur.com
AND OTHER GOOD BOOK STORES

ALSO FROM LEONAUR
AVAILABLE IN SOFTCOVER OR HARDCOVER WITH DUST JACKET

DOING OUR 'BIT' *by Ian Hay*—Two Classic Accounts of the Men of Kitchener's 'New Army' During the Great War including *The First 100,000* & *All In It.*

AN EYE IN THE STORM by *Arthur Ruhl*—An American War Correspondent's Experiences of the First World War from the Western Front to Gallipoli and Beyond.

STAND & FALL by *Joe Cassells*—A Soldier's Recollections of the 'Contemptible Little Army' and the Retreat from Mons to the Marne, 1914.

RIFLEMAN MACGILL'S WAR by *Patrick MacGill*—A Soldier of the London Irish During the Great War in Europe including *The Amateur Army, The Red Horizon* & *The Great Push.*

WITH THE GUNS by *C. A. Rose & Hugh Dalton*—Two First Hand Accounts of British Gunners at War in Europe During World War 1- Three Years in France with the Guns and With the British Guns in Italy.

EAGLES OVER THE TRENCHES by *James R. McConnell & William B. Perry*—Two First Hand Accounts of the American Escadrille at War in the Air During World War 1-Flying For France: With the American Escadrille at Verdun and Our Pilots in the Air.

THE BUSH WAR DOCTOR by *Robert V. Dolbey*—The Experiences of a British Army Doctor During the East African Campaign of the First World War.

THE 9TH—THE KING'S (LIVERPOOL REGIMENT) IN THE GREAT WAR 1914 - 1918 by *Enos H. G. Roberts*—Like many large cities, Liverpool raised a number of battalions in the Great War. Notable among them were the Pals, the Liverpool Irish and Scottish, but this book concerns the wartime history of the 9th Battalion – The Kings.

THE GAMBARDIER by *Mark Severn*—The experiences of a battery of Heavy artillery on the Western Front during the First World War.

FROM MESSINES TO THIRD YPRES by *Thomas Floyd*—A personal account of the First World War on the Western front by a 2/5th Lancashire Fusilier.

THE IRISH GUARDS IN THE GREAT WAR - VOLUME 1 by *Rudyard Kipling*—Edited and Compiled from Their Diaries and Papers Volume 1 The First Battalion.

THE IRISH GUARDS IN THE GREAT WAR - VOLUME 2 by *Rudyard Kipling*—Edited and Compiled from Their Diaries and Papers Volume 2 The Second Battalion.

AVAILABLE ONLINE AT
www.leonaur.com
AND OTHER GOOD BOOK STORES

WW1-1

www.ingramcontent.com/pod-product-compliance
Lightning Source LLC
Chambersburg PA
CBHW030227170426
43201CB00006B/135